"Bishops teach in various ways, but few write catechism
clarity Bishop Donald Wuerl brings to this exposition
the work of a master catechist and a dedicated pastor. He finds a sureness of expression that can lead readers who reflect on his words to conversion of mind and heart."

—His Eminence Francis Cardinal George, OMI, Archbishop of Chicago

"Pastoral catechesis holds a privileged place in the priestly and episcopal ministry of Bishop Donald Wuerl. His ardent love for teaching the Faith undergirds a vast teaching experience which enriches his latest catechetical work, *The Catholic Way: Faith for Living Today*.

"Bishop Wuerl is extraordinarily gifted as a teacher. His ability to present the doctrine of the *Catechism of the Catholic Church* in clear and popular language is a splendid and timely contribution to our Church's mission of a new evangelization. *The Catholic Way: Faith for Living Today* will surely fulfill the Bishop's hope to 'stir up that flame of conversion that leads to Christ.' "

—Most Reverend Daniel Buechlein, OSB, Archbishop of Indianapolis, Chairman of the Bishops' Committee to Oversee the Use of the *Catechism of the Catholic Church*

"Bishop Wuerl does for Catholics today what Ambrose, Cyril, Chrysostom, and Augustine did for the ancient Church. As a bishop-theologian and a born teacher, he reveals the deepest mysteries with such clarity and realism that all can 'taste and see the goodness of the Lord.' "

—Scott Hahn, Ph.D., Professor of Scripture and Theology, Franciscan University of Steubenville, author of *The Lamb's Supper* and *Hail, Holy Queen*

"Bishop Donald W. Wuerl's interest in and commitment to the catechetical ministry is well known and appreciated. His previous catechism, *The Teaching of Christ: A Catholic Catechism for Adults*, was published a decade before the *Catechism of the Catholic Church*. What strikes me as unique and especially helpful in *The Catholic Way: Faith for Living Today* is the appealing style of the author.

"Written to introduce the reader to the *Catechism of the Catholic Church* with the hope that faith in Jesus will be renewed and strengthened, this local catechism is both comprehensive in the materials covered and precise in presentation. The reader will find the probing questions at the end of each chapter helpful for both individual and group reflection. In particular, I found the content, examples, and stories used in such sections as the Fourth Commandment and Medical and Moral Issues especially thought-provoking.

"As today's leaders in the Church's educational and catechetical ministries continue efforts to identify, prepare, and support future teachers and catechists, I believe that *The Catholic Way: Faith for Living Today* will prove to be an invaluable resource. Copies of this catechism will be on my gift list for the young adults in my family."

—Sister Lourdes Sheehan, RSM, Secretary for Education,
United States Catholic Conference

The Catholic Way

THE CATHOLIC WAY

Faith for Living Today

BISHOP DONALD W. WUERL

DOUBLEDAY
NEW YORK LONDON TORONTO SYDNEY AUCKLAND

PUBLISHED BY DOUBLEDAY
a division of Random House, Inc.
1540 Broadway, New York, New York 10036

DOUBLEDAY and the portrayal of an anchor with a dolphin are trademarks of Doubleday, a division of Random House, Inc.

Nihil Obstat:
Rev. Kris D. Stubna, S.T.D.
Imprimatur:
† Most Reverend William J. Winter, V.G., S.T.D.
Auxiliary Bishop and Vicar General
Diocese of Pittsburgh
November 3, 2000

Library of Congress Cataloging-in-Publication Data

Wuerl, Donald W.
The Catholic way: faith for living today / Donald W. Wuerl.
p. cm.
Includes bibliographical references.
1. Catholic Church—Catechisms—English. 2. Catholic Church—Doctrines. I. Title.
BX1961 .W84 2001
238' .2—dc21
2001028701

ISBN 0-385-50182-X

Printed in the United States of America
October 2001

FIRST EDITION

10 9 8 7 6 5 4 3 2 1

Book design by Casey Hampton

Contents

Preface

MOST OF THE MATERIAL in this volume is work I was privileged to do over the past seven years as a series of articles for *Columbia* magazine. Each article dealt with some particular aspect of the *Catechism of the Catholic Church*. A helpful source is the fourth edition of *The Teaching of Christ*, edited by Father Ronald Lawler, O.F.M.Cap., Thomas Comerford Lawler, and myself.

Putting together this book, *The Catholic Way*, has involved editing the *Columbia* articles and adding new material. But the goal is the same as in those earlier articles: to help unfold the richness of the Catholic faith, found so wonderfully summarized in the *Catechism of the Catholic Church*.

Part of the challenge is to present in a popular form the teaching contained in what Pope John Paul II called "a compendium of all Catholic doctrine regarding both faith and morals." He reminded us that the *Catechism of the Catholic Church* is not intended to replace all other catechisms; rather, "it is meant to encourage and assist in the writing of new local catechisms, which take into account various situations and cultures, while carefully preserving the unity of faith and fidelity to catholic doctrine" (*Fidei Depositum*).

My hope in preparing this book is that, both for myself and for those who read it, faith in Jesus will be renewed and strengthened. As disciples, we would once again stir up that flame of conversion that turns us to Christ and keeps us focused on him as the center of our lives.

Each chapter, while part of a far larger presentation, has the advantage of giving the reader a short section—built around one issue—to read as time allows. It also provides the reader the opportunity to pick a theme or particular subject for review. But this style of presentation necessarily carries with it a certain amount of repetition. All of the Church's rich teaching on faith and morals cannot be completely separated into neat subjects. Some overlap is helpful and even necessary.

In his apostolic exhortation *The Church in America,* Pope John Paul II reminded us that all conversion is a turning from what would lead us away from Christ and a turning back to him. The New Testament uses the word *metanoia,* which means a change in mentality. Today, we would probably be more comfortable speaking of a change in attitude or vision. In either case, the intention is the same—to change our way of thinking and acting so that our lives are centered on Christ.

In providing these reflections, I have found personally that the review of the teaching of the Church, the teaching of Christ, has continuously challenged me to penetrate more deeply the mystery of what it means to be a follower of Jesus—a person "turned to" Christ—in everything that we say and do.

At the same time, I recognize that not all the readers of this book are necessarily Catholics. One of the marks of this particular moment is the interest in the Catholic Church that many, Christian and non-Christian alike, have shown. If you are one who has come to this volume out of curiosity, I hope you find these reflections helpful. Perhaps you might wish to explore more fully any or all of the areas of the Catholic faith by turning directly to the *Catechism* itself.

This is the age of the new evangelization. We all know many people who have drifted away from the faith. Our task is to invite them back to the joy and completeness that is union with Christ. The more we know about our faith, the easier it is to share, and the more comfortable we feel about entering into discussion with others.

We are also called to look outward to the wider community and to be a voice of conscience in articulating the word of God and in continuing the ministry of Christ. The need for moral leadership and the obligation to be engaged actively in the formation of public policy are challenges and opportunities for all of us who have been called to be a leaven in society. The more we know of our faith, the more we are likely to cherish and share it. In making these reflections on the *Catechism of the Catholic Church,* I have been deeply impressed by how committed so many of the faithful are both to learning more about the faith and to living it in a way that realizes all the more God's kingdom in our lives.

One of the benefits that I found in working on this book was the need to go through every page of the *Catechism* very carefully. Each time I did,

I was impressed once again with the beauty of our faith and its richness. We are truly blessed as members of the Catholic Church to have a compendium of all the Church holds and teaches in matters of faith and morals—and to have it right at our fingertips. Knowing that the *Catechism* is not a collection of opinions, but an authentic presentation of the faith, makes the use of it all the more satisfying.

A number of people have assisted in the final preparation of this text, and for their work I am most grateful. Michael Aquilina, the editor, has worked diligently to attend to those editorial details that bring continuity and consistency to a series of articles written over many years. I am grateful as well to the Reverend Ronald Lengwin, who has carefully read each of the articles as they were prepared, and who, with Michael Aquilina, has provided the questions at the end of each chapter. A special thank-you to the Reverend Monsignor William Sullivan, who was kind enough to give up the greater part of his vacation to help proofread the text. Finally, I want to recognize the diligence of the Reverend Kris Stubna, who went through the text paragraph by paragraph to assure its conformity with the *Catechism of the Catholic Church.*

Some of the happiest moments of my life have been associated with teaching the faith—whether in a classroom setting, in an informal gathering, or from the pulpit in the form of a homily. This work found its beginnings in the same spirit. My overriding hope is that, whether I have been successful or not in presenting the content of the *Catechism of the Catholic Church,* the reader of this book will come away with some idea of the richness of the Catholic faith and a desire to know more about it. If that were true for just one person, then this effort over the past seven years would be well worth it.

Papal and Council Documents Cited in This Book

Ad Tuendam Fidem (To Defend the Faith), Apostolic Letter, Pope John Paul II, 1998

Apostolic Constitution on the Sacrament of Confirmation, Pope Paul VI, 1971

Apostolicam Actuositatem, Decree on the Apostolate of the Laity, Second Vatican Council, 1965

Benedictus Deus, Constitution, Pope Benedict XII, 1336

Christifideles Laici, Apostolic Exhortation, Pope John Paul II, 1988

Credo of the People of God, Solemn Profession of Faith, Pope Paul VI, 1968

Dei Filius, Dogmatic Constitution on the Catholic Faith, First Vatican Council, 1870

Dei Verbum, Dogmatic Constitution on Divine Revelation, Second Vatican Council, 1965

Dignitatis Humanae, Declaration on Religious Liberty, Second Vatican Council, 1965

Dives in Misericordia (Rich in Mercy), Encyclical Letter, Pope John Paul II, 1980

Divinum Illud Munus, Encyclical Letter, Pope Leo XIII, 1897

Doctrine of the Sacrament of Extreme Unction, Council of Trent, 1551

Evangelium Vitae (The Gospel of Life), Encyclical Letter, Pope John Paul II, 1995

Familiaris Consortio, Apostolic Exhortation, Pope John Paul II, 1981

Fidei Depositum (The Deposit of Faith), Apostolic Constitution, Pope John Paul II, 1997

Fides et Ratio (Faith and Reason), Encyclical Letter, Pope John Paul II, 1998

Gaudium et Spes, Pastoral Constitution on the Church in the Modern World, Second Vatican Council, 1965

Gravissimum Educationis, Declaration on Christian Education, Second Vatican Council, 1965

Ineffabilis Deus, Constitution, Pope Pius IX, 1854

Letter to Families, Pope John Paul II, 1994

Lumen Gentium, Dogmatic Constitution on the Church, Second Vatican Council, 1964

Munificentissimus Deus, Apostolic Constitution of Pius XII, 1950

Mystici Corporis, Encyclical Letter, Pope Pius XII, 1943

Presbyterorum Ordinis, Decree on the Ministry and Life of Priests, Second Vatican Council, 1965

Reconciliatio et Paenitentia (On Reconciliation and Penance), Apostolic Exhortation, Pope John Paul II, 1984

Sacrosanctum Concilium, Constitution on the Sacred Liturgy, Second Vatican Council, 1963

Unitatis Redintegratio, Decree on Ecumenism, Second Vatican Council, 1964

Veritatis Splendor (The Splendor of Truth), Encyclical Letter, Pope John Paul II, 1993

CHAPTER I

What Is a Catechism?

WHAT WILL YOU FIND when you open the *Catechism of the Catholic Church?*

Basically, you will find what Jesus Christ came to teach and what the Church, under the inspiration of the Holy Spirit over twenty centuries, has nurtured, applied, and articulated—the Catholic faith.

It is a wonderful gift to each one of us. The *Catechism* provides for every believer a summary of what we believe, of the faith that we so deeply cherish. In this little book you hold now, I hope we will deepen our understanding and appreciation of the richness and life-giving character of our Catholic faith as presented in the *Catechism of the Catholic Church.*

WHY WAS THE *CATECHISM* WRITTEN?

How did this catechism come about? Its roots go back deep into the Second Vatican Council, which took place from 1962 to 1965. From Pope John Paul II, we learned that "the principal task entrusted to the Council by Pope John XXIII was to guard and present better the precious deposit of Christian doctrine, in order to make it more accessible to the Christian faithful and to all people of good will" (*Fidei Depositum*).

Since its conclusion, the Second Vatican Council has continued to inspire the Church's life. Pope John Paul pointed out in 1985 how the council had been a "special grace" for him as a bishop and how as Pope the council was always "the fixed point of reference for all my pastoral activity" (Discourse of January 25, 1985).

But because some of the council documents have been interpreted in different ways, it became apparent that an authoritative compendium of the faith was not only desirable but necessary. In the middle 1970s, I spoke about these problems with Cardinal John Wright, who was then Prefect of the Vatican office responsible for—among other things—catechetics, the teaching of the faith. Out of that discussion came *The Teaching of Christ: A Catholic Catechism for Adults,* published in 1976 and subsequently revised three times. This catechism, a product of the collaboration and dedicated work of a large number of bishops, scholars, and catechists, was widely used almost immediately and was translated into more than a dozen languages. Yet there was still a need for a catechism for the whole Church.

At an extraordinary assembly of the Synod of Bishops in 1985, Cardinal Bernard Law, Archbishop of Boston, proposed that a new compendium of the faith be drawn up in the light of the teaching of the Second Vatican Council. This new catechism would function as a norm for all catechetical teaching. The idea was immediately and favorably received, and out of it came the decision of Pope John Paul II to create a worldwide commission of cardinals and bishops to produce a catechism for the whole Church—the *Catechism of the Catholic Church.*

WHAT IS THE *CATECHISM* FOR?

Essentially a catechism is a means to an end. God gives us the gift of faith, and the Church nurtures and sustains that faith through her teaching and sacramental ministry. A catechism is a tool for those involved in teaching the faith—and we all know how important it is to have the right tool. Whether we work in the yard, in the kitchen, or in the workshop, if we have the right tool the task is a lot easier.

Why is the *Catechism of the Catholic Church* the right tool for the task of teaching the faith today? First, it is complete. In this long yet somewhat concise book, we find a full survey of the whole body of Catholic teaching on faith and morals.

In an age that has come to think of the teaching of the Church as a cafeteria line where one picks and chooses what one wants to believe, the *Catechism* is a reminder that the whole meal is necessary for a well-balanced spiritual diet. The *Catechism* provides completeness.

It is also authentic. Its content is not someone's opinion about what the Church believes or should believe. It is the true teaching of the Catholic Church proclaimed with authority by those who are responsible for guarding the integrity of the faith. (In the next chapter, we'll talk more about what it means to teach with authority.) The *Catechism of the Catholic Church* represents the effort of Pope John Paul II together with the bishops to present a complete and authoritative proclamation of the faith of the Catholic Church today.

THE TEACHING OF JESUS

What does the *Catechism* rely on for its sources as it presents the faith? It turns to "the teaching of Sacred Scripture, the living tradition in the Church and the authentic magisterium as well as the spiritual heritage of the Fathers and the saints of the Church" (*Fidei Depositum* 3). The foundation on which the *Catechism* rests is the teaching of Jesus. That teaching is contained in the pages of Sacred Scripture and the living tradition of the Church, and it is articulated in the magisterium, the teaching office of the bishops. It is also found over centuries in the writings of the Fathers of the Church and its saints, who have lived out the faith in loving response to the will of God. All of these are source material for the faith presented in the new universal catechism.

HOW THE *CATECHISM* IS ORGANIZED

The *Catechism* is divided into four sections:

The first section deals with the creed or profession of faith. Here we find the revelation of Jesus that illumines and gives meaning to life.

The second section is devoted to the sacramental life of the Church, or, as it is called, the celebration of the Christian mystery. Here we consider how we express our faith through the sacramental presence of Christ.

The third part is devoted to how we live out in our daily lives the moral obligations of being a follower of Jesus Christ. How do we live in a way that pleases God? How do we become true followers of Jesus? This section unfolds the moral teaching of the Church and our vocation to live in the Holy Spirit.

The final section is devoted to prayer. Here the *Catechism* uses the petitions of the Our Father to guide us through an understanding of how we should pray and for what should we pray.

The *Catechism of the Catholic Church* is designed primarily for bishops, so that they will have an authentic source of teaching against which to gauge all catechetical efforts in their particular dioceses. However, this catechism is also for every believer. This present book, *The Catholic Way,* is meant to introduce you to the *Catechism*. Each short chapter explains one important idea in the *Catechism,* and at the end of each chapter are some questions to help you think about how the *Catechism* applies to your life. We start with the most fundamental ideas, of which the first is the most important question: Where does this *Catechism*'s authority come from?

CHAPTER 2

The Bishops: Teachers of the Faith

WE CALL THE *Catechism of the Catholic Church* "authoritative" or "authentic." What does that mean?

Both of these words have the same Latin root: *auctoritas.* They mean that the teaching is more than opinion—it has *authority.*

JESUS TAUGHT WITH AUTHORITY

In the New Testament, the followers of Jesus marveled that, unlike other teachers, he taught with *authority.* In Matthew's gospel, for example, we read: "Now when Jesus had finished saying these things, the crowds were astonished at his teaching, for he taught them as one having authority, and not as their scribes" (Matthew 7:28–29). Saint Mark recounts how Jesus "entered the synagogue and taught. They were astounded at his teaching, for he taught them as one having authority" (Mark 1:21–22).

Jesus had authority because of who he was. "I am the way, the truth, and the life," he proclaimed (John 14:6). The truth—the very reality of who Jesus is—is what he shares with us through the Church.

When Jesus was on trial, Pilate asked him, "Are you a king?" Jesus answered, "For this I was born. For this I came into the world to testify to the truth. Anyone who belongs to the truth listens to my voice" (John 18:37).

We call the truth that Jesus brings us *revelation.*

HOW REVELATION COMES TO US

In the early days of salvation history, God made himself known through the prophets. (See Chapter 5 for an explanation of what we mean by "salvation history.") God did not, however, communicate through them all that God wanted us to know. Finally, God spoke to us "by a Son, whom he appointed heir of all things, through whom he also created the world. He is the reflection of God's glory and the exact imprint of God's very being . . ." (Hebrews 1:1–3).

This explains why the teaching of Jesus is different from that of any other person. Christ, in his being, his deeds, and his words, is the perfect revelation of the Father. Jesus is God come into our midst to reveal to us the inner life and very word of God. Through him we have learned how we should live.

On our own, none of us could come to know the mind, heart, love, and identity of God because God is so far beyond us. But Jesus came to reveal truth—the truth about God and the truth about ourselves. As God's word among us, Jesus brings us a message from God that we could not otherwise have. Hence the teaching of Christ—his *revelation*—is spoken with full authority.

But how does the revelation of God in Jesus Christ continue to come to us?

It comes through the Church. God sent Jesus, and Jesus sent the apostles. And just as the word of God spread through the twelve apostles, so it must continue to be taught through today's apostles—the bishops. The Church continues to pass on the revelation of truth in the same way it has since the days of the apostles.

Because the teaching of the Church is rooted in the teaching of Christ that has come to us from the apostles, the Church is called "apostolic." That means it traces its origins to the apostles, and it still maintains continuity with them. It was Christ's will that his revelation should be preserved always for the salvation of all people. That was why he built his Church on Peter and the other apostles—the Catholic Church, which he protects by his own presence and the gift of the Spirit. It is through this teaching that God's revelation reaches us. Hence it is called *authentic* or *authoritative* teaching.

REVELATION CONTINUES IN THE TEACHING OF THE CHURCH

With the end of the apostolic age, the time of new public revelation came to a close. Since then, the task of the Church has been to hand on the word that had been entrusted to the apostles—the deposit of faith—to grow in it, to nurture its development, and to make it living and effective, a leaven to renew the earth.

We teach that revelation continues today, but only in the sense that the living God remains present to God's people, caring for them and providing the gifts of grace that enable them to recognize and love God and the good news of the gospel. But we affirm at the same time that Jesus proclaimed the full saving message and gave it to all who would continue after him. Now, as the Second Vatican Council teaches in the *Dogmatic Constitution on Divine Revelation,* "no new public revelation is to be expected before the glorious manifestation of our Lord Jesus Christ" (see 1 Timothy 6:14 and Titus 2:13) (*Dei Verbum* 4).

Theologians and scholars teach the word and help the Church to penetrate its full meaning. They are not *official* teachers in the way that bishops, the successors of the apostles, are; and theologians do not receive with the bishops that "sure gift of truth" (*Dei Verbum* 8) that apostolic witnesses of faith receive. But they are important companions of faith, for bishops look to scholars for appropriate assistance in understanding divine revelation.

Still other teachers are parents, whom the Second Vatican Council in its *Declaration on Christian Education* calls "the first and foremost educators of their children" (*Gravissimum Educationis* 6). Those who teach the faith in schools and in centers of catechetical learning are also very important teachers. They too do not rely on knowledge derived from human scholarship alone, from human philosophies and sciences: they rely on the teaching of Christ. They find a sure guide for their teaching in the voice of the pastors of the Church.

THE NEED FOR AN AUTHORITATIVE TEACHING

In the history of the Church there have always been people who have proclaimed their own interpretation of God's revelation. From time to time we hear people say "this is really what Jesus meant" and "that part of the teaching doesn't count, but this is the really important thing." People continue to make such claims today. They open the Bible, pick out a phrase, and conclude that their interpretation is authentic.

To avoid this confusion and the possibility of misunderstanding God's word, Jesus chose apostles and charged them and their successors with the responsibility of teaching the true faith, making sure that it is presented clearly and applying it to the problems and needs of the day.

Authentic Catholic faith is never partial or selective. It is always universal. We say "yes" to the whole mystery of the faith and to each of its elements because of our personal faith in God. We believe the truth that God reveals because we believe God, and we believe that God is still teaching in and through the Church. When Peter came to recognize that God was in Christ, he was prepared to believe any word of Christ, for it was clear to him that God is always to be believed. "You have the word of eternal life. We have come to believe and know that you are the holy one of God" (John 6:68–69).

While every Christian shares in the mission of spreading the truth and bearing witness to the gospel, the apostles, as we have noted, had the prime responsibility of guarding, proclaiming, and verifying the gospel message. For this reason the *Catechism of the Catholic Church* is directed primarily to the bishops, their successors, as an instrument to use in measuring the fidelity of all catechetical materials and as an authentic gauge with an authority rooted in the very revelation of Christ.

JESUS CHRIST STILL TEACHES WITH AUTHORITY

This brings us to the question of what means are available to us if we want to live the gospel and share the good news in a way that is faithful to the message of Jesus. It was precisely in the face of this concern that Pope John Paul II ordered the *Catechism of the Catholic Church* to be written so that everyone, bishops, priests, deacons, religious, catechists, teachers, and all the faithful would have a complete and authoritative presentation of the faith of the Church.

When we ask ourselves to whom should we turn to teach us about Catholic faith today, our answer ultimately is Jesus Christ! The revelation of Christ lives on in the Church today, which, through the bishops, continues the teaching mission of our Lord. The *Catechism of the Catholic Church* is a means by which the bishops in union with the Pope present the teaching of Christ with an authentic voice and with the authority of the Lord.

QUESTIONS TO THINK ABOUT:

1. When I have questions about the faith, where do I usually go for answers?
2. Who are the teachers in whom I have the most confidence? Where does their authority come from?
3. What are some of the qualities of a true teacher of the faith?

CHAPTER 3

To Give an Account of Our Faith

ONCE I WAS HELPING a couple prepare for their wedding. They had asked if I would officiate at it, and so I was instructing them about the sacrament of marriage. It was clear that the man was less than thrilled with the opportunity to review his faith. The young lady, however, was eagerly looking forward to the time to brush up on some aspects of her religious education. Finally, she said to him, "You're not paying attention."

He said, "Aw, I had all this crammed down my throat when I was in grade school."

She replied, "Well, not much of it stuck."

How right you are, I thought. This fine young man was convinced that he knew all he needed to know about faith. He was persuaded that he understood his religion because he had studied his catechism when he was in grade school. Thanks to the wonderful young woman who is now his wife, he came to see that there is a lot more to faith than a recollection of the responses we memorized as children.

"I KNOW MY RELIGION"

As soon as you say, "Let's talk about our faith," many people reply, "Oh, I know my religion. I know what the Church teaches." Yet the more we discuss it the more we find that some people who say they know their faith are really referring to knowledge they received in grade school or elementary CCD programs.

Why do we need to know more about our faith? There are two good and basic reasons to do this: one, so that we can live it more fully; and two, so that we can share it more effectively with others.

We need to know how to live our own faith first. Saint Paul said that as a child you do the things of a child, you are nourished as a child, you play with the toys of a child; but when you become an adult, you put those things aside and assume adult responsibilities (see 1 Corinthians 13:11). Now we have to attain an adult appreciation and understanding of what we believe.

The second part is equally important. We are called to share the faith. If all I have to fall back on are my childhood recollections of what we believe, how can I ever share with other people the fullness and richness of our faith so that it comes alive for them? How can I share the importance of my religion with them if I don't understand it and can't explain it myself?

In describing the immense value of the *Catechism of the Catholic Church,* Pope John Paul II pointed out that "it is offered to every individual who asks us to give an account of the hope that is in us (cf. 1 Peter 3:15) and who wants to know what the Catholic Church believes" (*Fidei Depositum* 3). The *Catechism* is meant to help us understand our faith better so that we in turn can help others accept the truth of our faith. The classical word for this effort is *apologetics*—the discipline that is concerned with the defense of or proof for Christianity. Apologetics does *not* mean "apologizing" for something wrong that we have said or done. It is a manner of clearly and reasonably explaining what we believe so that others will want to share the Catholic faith.

TRYING TO UNDERSTAND

Religious education is a lifelong process. First of all, it begins with the simple recognition that God's word, the revelation given to us in Jesus Christ, the truth presented to us in Christ, is utterly beyond us. It takes an act of humility to recognize this fact. The act of obeying and accepting the word of God is sometimes described as a "genuflection of the will": "I may not fully comprehend the mystery of what you are saying, God, but in humility, and recognizing my own limitation, I accept your word."

The next step is to try to understand. The task of understanding has been the work of the Church for two thousand years. What does it mean to say that Christ came among us, died, rose from the dead, and saved us? What does it mean to profess that we are justified, that we have been redeemed, that someday we will be united to Christ in glory? What does it mean to say that I am obliged now to apply the commandments and the beatitudes, the Sermon on the Mount, and the works of mercy to my daily life? Thus, the Church begins to unfold that revelation for us and to apply it to our daily lives.

REASON ENLIGHTENED BY FAITH

All of Christ's teaching, all that Jesus has revealed to us, has been under the inspiration of the Holy Spirit—the third person of the Trinity—who constantly leads and guides the Church. The teaching of Christ has also been applied to the problems of every age. Through the Church's teaching office, represented by the magisterium, the human condition and all the questions it poses have been confronted over and over again under the guidance of the Holy Spirit. The solutions that have been offered and that form the Christian moral code are the result of reason enlightened by faith—applying the truth of God's revelation, but always under the inspiration of the Holy Spirit.

It is one of the great gifts of Christ to his people that the Church can benefit from the fruit of two thousand years of examining the human condition under the guidance of the Holy Spirit as it offers a response to each situation. We can turn then both to the pages of Sacred Scripture and to the magisterial interpretation of those words in the living tradition of the Church to understand the teaching of Christ.

The Church has always taken this approach. Centuries ago, at the very beginning of the Christian era, Justin Martyr saw his task as explaining the revelation of Christ to the people of his age—the Roman world—through the words of their culture, the mind-set and frame of references they understood.

In effect, this first great apologist said to the Romans, "Let me tell you what Jesus is all about, but in your words, your language, your categories." He even wrote to the emperor to prove that what we believe is not only salvific but also logical. His first and second *Apology* and *Dialogue* and Aristides' *Apology* among others are examples of the effort to help people understand the truth about our faith in their own terms.

The task is the same for the apologists today—to translate the meaning of Christ and his revelation to our age in our categories, in our language, in our frame of reference, so that it can be truly understood and lived.

The *Catechism of the Catholic Church* is offered to us and to anyone who wants to share what we believe. With its help, we hope we will grasp more profoundly the teaching of Christ and be in a better position to share it with anyone who wants to know why we so much love our Catholic faith.

QUESTIONS TO THINK ABOUT:

1. When was the last time I really talked about my faith?
2. When I hear others disparaging the faith, do I keep silent, or do I offer to help them understand it better?
3. What help do I need to become a better "apologist"?

CHAPTER 4

The Human Capacity for God

GOD CALLS US AND we answer. God speaks to us and we reply. At its core, the profession of faith expressed in such words as "I believe" or "we believe" is a response to God. We refer to God's word to us as "revelation" and our response as "faith." The *Catechism of the Catholic Church* speaks about the human desire for God, the ways we come to know God, the knowledge of God according to the Church, and finally, how we can speak about God.

In the very act of creating us, God has written in our hearts a yearning for fullness and completeness that can only be found in him. "We know that if the earthly tent we live in is destroyed, we have a building from God, a house not made with hands, eternal in the heavens" (2 Corinthians 5:1). God willed that people should come to perfect fulfillment in eternal life—in union with him. In other words, we are created to be with God, and we will never be happy, whole, or complete until we attain full union with God.

But it was not God's will simply to create people who had already attained heaven's happiness; nor, on the other hand, was it his will to create people engaged in a life of endless struggle. God willed that we come to that perfect life through our own volition and cooperation. When God creates us, he gives us both the capacity and the desire to share in his knowledge and presence.

It is this yearning that accounts for the uneasiness, the sense of unfulfillment and dissatisfaction we have if we struggle through life without God. Money, self-satisfaction, power, or other finite realities can be a temporary substitute and provide us with limited happiness. But we know that all these things ultimately fail to bring true peace of mind and contentment of soul. It is for this reason that we say the beginning or seeds of our profession of faith can be found in the human longing for completion, fullness, and satisfaction—for God.

But if we are going to respond to God, we must recognize that it is he who calls us and he who speaks to us. How do we come to know God?

TWO WAYS TO KNOW GOD THROUGH REASON

The Church teaches that God, the beginning and end of all things, can be known with certainty from created things by the natural light of human reason: "For since the creation of the world the invisible things of him are perceived, being understood through the things which have been made" (Romans 1:20). It is the solemn teaching of the Church—reflecting the words of Sacred Scripture—that each of us has a natural ability to know our Maker. As the *Catechism of the Catholic Church* indicates, the ways of approaching God have two points of departure: the material world and the human person (see section 31 in the *Catechism*).

Knowing God through his creation

The first signs of the existence of God are visible to us in his creation. The beauty of creation and the wonder of the world in which we live are not only the subject of art and literature. A snail shell, a strand of DNA, a multitude of infinitely different snowflakes—these are also voices that speak to us of a creative power far beyond us, of a God who creates with great order and majesty.

Knowing God from the voice of conscience

At the same time, a reflection on the moral order of the universe can lead us to a natural knowledge of God. When we are aware that our human duties are just and truthful and temperate, we realize that this insistent call to goodness, which we hear in the voice of conscience, is, in fact, a manifestation of the presence of God within us. Sacred Scripture tells us, "When Gentiles, who do not possess the law, do instinctively what the law requires, these, though not having the law, are a law to themselves. They show that what the law requires is written on their hearts" (Romans 2:14–15).

Over the centuries, people of various nations and cultures have come to the knowledge of God by reflection on the physical world and the moral order he created. Philosophers and wise women and men of many nations have pointed out various paths by which people may come to know God, who is the source of all life. People have come to the realization that this world, which bears clear marks of its own transience and finitude, must be caused by One who is the Author of time and of all passing things. The *Catechism of the Catholic Church* reminds us of this truth. Through human reason, it is possible to know from the world in which we live that God exists.

KNOWING GOD THROUGH REVELATION

However, so that we do not have to rely on our own limited human experience alone, God manifests himself clearly through his own words to us, his revelation. Lest we be confused, God speaks to us directly. After all, even though we might know *that* God exists by natural human reason alone, we could never come to know *who* God is without his direct intervention. God is so far beyond us, so transcendent and holy, so eternal and infinite that our limited finite minds and hearts could never grasp the full truth of who God is. We need God's revelation to enlighten us about those things that exceed our understanding and about those religious and moral values that will guide us surely, directly, and quickly to him.

God reveals himself to us through the events of salvation history and through the words of the prophets. (See the next chapter for more about what we mean by "salvation history.") Most of all, he has spoken to us through his Son, Jesus Christ. To this voice of God—his revelation—we are called to respond in an act of faith that professes "I believe because you are God who can neither deceive nor be deceived."

Because God gives us this knowledge through revelation, we are able to speak about him. All human knowledge of God is limited, but we can understand him in relation to creatures and according to our limited human means of thinking and knowing. Hence, we are able to know him as a personal God who works through mighty deeds. We are also able to call God all-knowing, loving, and almighty, as well eternal, changeless, transcendent, and holy—the qualities that characterize his very identity.

God created us capable of responding to his word. That word comes to us in revelation, first in the Old Testament and then in the New Testament, and reaches its fullness in Jesus Christ. Echoes of that word are heard in creation and in our very human nature. All of this is done so that we might respond to God's loving call with a "yes" of faith—a faith that is firm in its conviction that it is God who speaks to us, and it is God to whom we reply.

QUESTIONS TO THINK ABOUT:

1. What things in God's creation do I find most wonderful?
2. When I hear the "insistent call to goodness," do I listen? Or do I try to put it out of my mind?
3. If God's revelation truly comes to us in the Old and New Testaments, have I gotten to know that revelation well enough? What could I do to get to know it better?

CHAPTER 5

The Revelation of God

GOD'S REVELATION IS THE beginning of our salvation. When we say "yes" to God—when we make an act of faith—it is in reply to his invitation. Only because God makes a completely free decision—a decision to speak to us—can we, with our limited and finite human knowledge, ever come to grasp anything about the nature of God and his plan to save us. The action by which God shares with us the mystery of himself and his plan for our salvation is what we call "revelation."

To explain what we mean by revelation, the *Catechism of the Catholic Church* turns to the Second Vatican Council and the *Dogmatic Constitution on Divine Revelation*. "It pleased God," says this significant document, "in his goodness and wisdom, to reveal himself and to make known the mystery of his will. His will was that men should have access to the Father, through Christ, the Word made flesh, in the Holy Spirit, and thus become sharers of the divine nature" (*Dei Verbum* 2).

We cannot come to know who God is by ourselves. God dwells in "unapproachable light" (see 1 Timothy 6:16), and we are ensnared by the burden of our sins and our own human limitations. But God wishes us to be raised up so that we might share his very life. God wants us to know him, and so God "in his goodness and wisdom, chose to reveal himself" (*Dei Verbum* 2).

GOD REVEALS HIMSELF IN HISTORY

One way God reveals himself is through his intervention in human history. We call these mighty acts of God "salvation history." The *Catechism of the Catholic Church* reminds us that God reveals himself in stages, beginning with creation itself. Again quoting the Second Vatican Council, the *Catechism* teaches us that "God, who creates and conserves all things by his Word, provides us with constant evidence of himself in created realities. Furthermore, wishing to open up the way to heavenly salvation, God manifested himself to our first parents from the very beginning" (see section 54 in the *Catechism*).

Even when our first parents sinned, the revelation was not terminated—as the *Roman Missal* teaches us in the Fourth Eucharistic Prayer. "Even when he disobeyed you and lost your friendship, you did not abandon him to the power of death. . . . Again and again you offered a covenant to man."

The Old Testament is the history of God speaking to us and offering over and over again a covenant with our ancestors in the faith. The patriarchs, whose stories are preserved in the Book of Genesis, received certain promises from God. We see the history of the nation of Israel as a fulfillment of these promises. Again, the exodus from Egypt was the mighty act by which God freed his people from slavery. It was a liberation and is seen as the fulfillment of God's promises to his people.

GOD REVEALS HIMSELF THROUGH MOSES AND THE PROPHETS

After God's people had escaped slavery in Egypt, they experienced a unique meeting with him. At Mount Sinai, God's people came to understand themselves as a community obliged by God's law and the teaching of Moses to live in a way that established and fulfilled the covenant with God. When the Israelites crossed over into Canaan, they secured a land for themselves in fulfillment of the covenant but they also understood that unless Israel was faithful to the covenant with God, the land, which was God's gift, would be taken away from them.

Through the prophets, God taught his people how to live. As the *Dogmatic Constitution on Divine Revelation* teaches, "With God himself speaking to them through the mouth of the prophets, Israel daily gained a deeper and clearer understanding of his ways" (*Dei Verbum* 14). The prophets were God's servants through whom God himself spoke. God called them and others soon recognized them as God's teachers. The words of the prophets were not always accepted, however, for they demanded personal faith and inner conversion and they insisted on faithfulness to all of God's law.

GOD REVEALS HIMSELF THROUGH HIS SON

Finally, God chose to speak to us most clearly in Jesus. He sent his own Son, Jesus Christ, the Eternal Word, who was in the beginning with God and who was God, to come among us. He took on flesh so that God's own Word could now speak to us in *our* words, and so that we might come to know directly and clearly within the limits of our finite human nature who God is and how much God loves us. The Letter to the Hebrews opens with the familiar words: "In many and various ways God spoke of old to our fathers by the prophets, but in these last days he has spoken to us by a Son" (Hebrews 1:1).

Jesus Christ, God's Son, the Word of God from all eternity, took on flesh and dwelt among us so that we might know the glory that is God. In his own words and deeds, he revealed to us a loving God whom he taught us to call "our Father." Jesus also told us that he came not to teach on his own but to reveal what he had received from the Father, so that we might all know the truth and in that truth find our salvation (see John 12:49).

With the coming of Jesus and his teaching, God's revelation is complete. Through the law and the prophets God prepared us to receive the fullness of his word to us. The Word was spoken in Jesus Christ. The deposit of the faith closed with the death of the last apostle. It is the firm teaching of the Church that there are no new public revelations by which we shall be saved. The *Catechism of the Catholic Church,* again quoting the Second Vatican Council, teaches us that "the Christian economy, since it is the new and definitive covenant, will never pass away and no new public revelation is to be expected before the glorious manifestation of our Lord Jesus Christ when he comes in glory to claim the living and the dead" (section 66).

OUR RESPONSE—FAITH

Our response to God's self-revelation is the act of faith. To have faith is to believe God bearing witness to himself. Such belief in God is not the final conclusion of a long philosophical argument. To believe is to recognize and accept that it is God himself who reveals himself to us. This recognition opens for us a whole new world of knowledge. As the prayer called the Act of Faith proclaims: "I believe all the truths which the holy Catholic Church teaches, because you have revealed them, who can neither deceive nor be deceived."

A HOUSE BUILT ON ROCK

The knowledge of God that grows out of faith is far more complete and reliable than any other knowledge we have. It is based not merely on the strength of human insight and interpretation, but on God himself. God gives to faith not only a rich content but also certainty on which we believers can build our lives. As Jesus himself taught, "Anyone then who hears these words and acts on them will be like a wise man who built his house on rock. The rain fell, the floods came, and the winds blew and beat on that house, but it did not fall, because it had been founded on rock" (Matthew 7:24–25).

The knowledge of God that has been given to us through Jesus Christ—who revealed the Father to us and who is himself "the fullness of all revelation"—is the beginning of our salvation. In Jesus the whole fullness of deity dwells bodily (see Colossians 2:9). In him "the kindness and generous love of God our savior appeared" (Titus 3:4).

We can never come to know God adequately without his revelation. This wondrous gift reaches its fullness in Jesus Christ. Through Christ, we come to know God, whose word we are to believe because he is God who can neither deceive nor be deceived. We come to know that God loves us so fully and completely that he offers us eternal life if we will only accept God's word and believe.

QUESTIONS TO THINK ABOUT:

1. Which Bible stories stick in my memory the most? Why do those particular stories stand out for me?
2. Which of Jesus' teachings stick in my memory the most? Again, why those particular teachings?
3. Do I know God well enough to call him "Father"?

CHAPTER 6

Passing On the Faith

HOW DOES THE TEACHING of Christ get from him to us? How can we claim that we truly know Jesus? God spoke through Jesus Christ, but we live twenty centuries after his resurrection and ascension.

The story of salvation was not simply for one generation. Jesus did not come just to save those who lived in his time and place and who had personally experienced his voice and saving power. We read in the First Letter to Timothy: "This is good and pleasing to God our savior, who wills everyone to be saved and to come to knowledge of the truth" (1 Timothy 2:3–4).

HOW THE STORY OF SALVATION COMES TO US

What brings that story down to our generation is the *apostolic tradition*. Through the apostolic tradition, the saving story of what Jesus said and did is passed on, under the inspiration of the Holy Spirit, in a way that guarantees that it is not forgotten, misunderstood, or lost from age to age and generation to generation.

The *Catechism of the Catholic Church* points out that this passing on of the faith takes place in two ways: orally and in writing. The gospel was transmitted orally "by the apostles who handed on, by the spoken word of their preaching, by the example they gave, by the institutions they established what they themselves had received—whether from the lips of Christ, from his way of life and his works, or whether they had learned it at the prompting of the Holy Spirit" (*Dei Verbum* 7).

We believe that revelation continues in a sense, because the living God remains present to his people. By his continuing care and his gifts of grace, God enables them to recognize and love him and the good news of the gospel. Jesus proclaimed the full saving message and gave it to his people for all ages through the apostles.

SUCCESSORS TO THE APOSTLES

Saint Peter and the other apostles were mortal, but the mission given them was to be carried out until the end of time (see Matthew 28:20). Thus, as the Second Vatican Council teaches, "For this reason the apostles took care to appoint successors in this hierarchically structured society" (*Lumen Gentium* 20). This apostolic succession is noted by the earliest Fathers of the Church who lived at the end of the apostolic age. Pope Saint Clement of Rome, writing around the year 96 A.D., says that the apostles themselves "laid down a rule once for all to this effect: when these men die, other approved men shall succeed to their sacred ministry" (Letter to the Corinthians).

From these first days of the Church, bishops appointed by or succeeding the apostles were recognized as shepherds who rightly ruled and guarded the Church in the name of Christ. Loyalty to Christ was visibly expressed by loyalty to the bishops. Saint Ignatius of Antioch, in a letter written in or about 106 A.D., praises the Church at Philadelphia in Asia as "a source of everlasting joy, especially when the members are at one with the bishop and his assistants, the presbyters and deacons, that have been appointed in accordance with the wish of Jesus Christ, and whom He has, by His own will, through the operation of His Holy Spirit, confirmed in loyalty" (Letter to the Philadelphians).

How then do we know what Jesus taught? We have received those truths from the apostles and their successors—through the apostolic tradition that brings us God's living word under the guidance, inspiration, and protection of God's Holy Spirit.

THE CANON OF SCRIPTURE

The *Catechism of the Catholic Church* also reminds us that the gospel is passed on in writing "by those apostles and other men associated with the apostles who, under the inspiration of the same Holy Spirit, committed the message of salvation to writing" (*Dei Verbum* 7). These writings are found in the New Testament.

What is the New Testament? The official or approved list of inspired writings is called the "canon," a Greek word used among the early Christians and meaning a measuring standard or rule. The canon of Scripture is divided into two main sections, called the "Old Testament" and the "New Testament," which contain the books written before and after the life of Jesus respectively. The word "testament" comes from the two testaments or covenants expressing the relationship between God and his people: the first one that was ratified at Sinai (the Mosaic covenant) and the second at the Last Supper (the new covenant).

ONE REVELATION, TWO MODES OF TRANSMISSION

While we speak of the gospel being passed on orally and in writing, there is one common source. Sacred Scripture and sacred tradition are closely related. Both flow from the same divine wellspring, and each of them makes present and fruitful in the Church the mystery of Christ who promised to remain with his own always till the end of all time (see *Dei Verbum* 9).

At issue here are not two revelations but two distinct modes of transmission of the one revelation of Jesus Christ. The apostles and the apostolic tradition pass on both the written word of the Scripture and the full teaching and experience of Jesus Christ that is found in the Church today, interpreted by the bishops who exercise the teaching office in the Church. The task of authentically interpreting the word of God, either in its written form or in its oral form, has been entrusted exclusively to this living teaching office. As both the *Catechism of the Catholic Church* and the Second Vatican Council point out, the Church's authority in this matter is exercised in Jesus' name (see section 85 of the *Catechism* and *Dei Verbum* 10). This means that the task of interpretation has been entrusted to the bishops in communion with the successor of Peter, the Bishop of Rome.

"Tradition" means "handing on," and the Church is responsible for passing on faithfully all that it has received from the Lord. Tradition also means that which is handed on. "Now that which was handed on by the apostles includes everything which contributes to holiness of life, and the increase of faith in the people of God; and so the Church, in her teaching, life, and worship, perpetuates and hands on to all generations all that she herself is, all that she believes" (*Dei Verbum* 8). Bishops and those who assist them in teaching the word of God are to pass on the saving message of Christ in its entirety.

There can also be in the Church human traditions, which may be of only temporary value—such as conventions of art, architecture, or devotion. It is only by Christ's gift of the Spirit, guarding the living teachers he sets over the Church, that the Church is able to distinguish that which is the enduring word of God from that which is only of passing worth.

THE MAGISTERIUM: SERVANTS OF THE WORD OF GOD

The *Catechism of the Catholic Church* goes on to tell us that it is the task of bishops or the magisterium to define the teaching of the Church, to nurture acceptance of the faith, and to increase understanding of the faith through contemplation, study, and prayerful reflection on what has been handed on to us.

Interpreting the word of God is a task of the magisterium or teaching office in the Church. This does not mean that the authentic teachers of the Church are above the word of God. They are servants of God's word. The bishops help the faithful to understand each element of God's word in the light of the whole message of salvation. They are faithful to God's word as taught and lived under the inspiration of the Holy Spirit and guarded by the assurance of truth that the Holy Spirit gives to the continuing apostolic office.

Tradition, Scripture, and the living magisterium, with the presence of the Spirit guiding the faithful to be open to the truth, are all gifts of God. The close union of these gifts cannot be forgotten. In accord with God's wise design, Sacred Scripture, tradition, and the magisterium of the Church are so linked that each in its own way—under the action of the Holy Spirit—contributes effectively to the salvation of souls (see section 95 of the *Catechism*).

QUESTIONS TO THINK ABOUT:

1. How well do I know the Scriptures? Have I made reading the Bible an important part of my daily life?
2. Has the Church taught things that I find hard to accept? What can I do to reach a better understanding of those teachings?
3. When the Pope or bishops issue a statement or write on some pertinent religious or moral issue, do I make an effort to read and reflect on what they say?

CHAPTER 7

Sacred Scripture

WHAT DO WE MEAN by "Sacred Scripture?" What exactly are the writings that make up the Bible?

The *Catechism of the Catholic Church* teaches us that "through all the words of Sacred Scripture, God speaks only one single Word, his one Utterance in whom he expresses himself completely" (see section 102 of the *Catechism*). Saint Augustine teaches us that "one and the same Word of God extends throughout Scripture, that it is one and the same Utterance that resounds in the mouths of all the sacred writers, since he who was in the beginning God with God has no need of separate syllables; for he is not subject to time" (*Commentary on the Psalms* 103, 4, 1).

WHAT WE BELIEVE ABOUT SCRIPTURE

Sacred Scripture or the Bible is a collection of writings composed over the course of many centuries. The Church recognizes these exceptional writings as God's message to us.

We believe:

- that God is the author of these sacred writings,
- that God inspired the human authors of the sacred books,
- that these inspired books teach the truth, and
- that if the Scriptures are to remain alive, Christ the Eternal Word of the Living God must open our minds to understand them through the Holy Spirit.

The Second Vatican Council's *Dogmatic Constitution on Divine Revelation* teaches us that "in the sacred books the Father who is in heaven comes lovingly to his children and talks with them. And such is the force and power of the word of God that it can serve the Church as her support and vigor, and the children of the Church as strength for their faith, food for the soul, and a pure and lasting fount of spiritual life. Scripture verifies in the most perfect way the words 'The word of God is living and effective' (Hebrews 4:12) and 'can build you up and to give you the inheritance among all who are consecrated' (Acts 20:32; cf. 1 Thessalonians 2:13)" (*Dei Verbum* 21).

Other groups besides Christians possess and revere collections of literature and religious writings, but the distinguishing characteristic of the Bible is its *divine inspiration*.

When we speak of the Scriptures as the inspired word of God, we mean that God is the author of the message that the human author communicates. Acting as the principal author, God inspired the human authors of the Scriptures to understand and freely write the truths revealed by God. The Catholic Church believes that God chose human authors who would use their own skills, abilities, words, and style to communicate God's message. So there is a great diversity in the writings of the Bible, and yet it all remains the word of God.

Though they all express God's word, the Scriptures are cast in a rich variety of literary forms from intricate and mystical psalm prayers to highly interpretive and often poetically formulated styles of religious historical narratives. Though they were common in the ancient Near East, these literary forms can at times be difficult for modern readers to understand. Yet because it is divine as well as human in origin, the Bible is able to use a wide variety of literary forms and yet remain free from any error regarding the truth that the divine author wished specifically to reveal.

THE OLD TESTAMENT AND THE NEW TESTAMENT

The Bible is composed of two major sections: the Old Testament and the New Testament.

There is no universally accepted sequence for the Old Testament canon, although the most frequent pattern places historical writings first. Within this class, the first five books of the Old Testament form a special set often called the Pentateuch, the Mosaic books, or the torah (meaning "the law"). The historic books are followed by the so-called wisdom or sapiential literature, and then the prophetic and exhortational writings.

A standardized order is more commonly found in the New Testament. It begins with four accounts of events and teachings in the life of Jesus that are called gospels. The word "gospel" means "good news," a term Christianity has applied from earliest times to its Founder's presence and deeds and their saving effects. All four canonical gospels present the "good news" in this basic sense. Differences in the gospel writers' ways of retelling the life of Christ—the words they use, the sequence of events, the details they include, and the like—reveal the different audiences for which the gospels were originally designed, as well as the theological emphasis of their human composers.

The fifth book of the New Testament canon is the Acts of the Apostles, in which we have a historical record of the first decades of the Church.

Next come the epistles, or letters of instruction and correction, written to the first Christian communities by their apostolic pastors. Varying in length from the sixteen chapters of the Letter to the Romans to the few sentences of the second and third letters of Saint John, they preserve a rich treasure of the joys and sorrows, the problems and glories of the first-century Church.

The last book of the New Testament, and therefore of the whole Bible, is the Book of Revelation or the Apocalypse. This is a highly symbolic depiction of the final triumph of Christ, the punishment of his adversaries, and the establishment of the righteous who share the divine glory in heaven.

The *Catechism of the Catholic Church* reminds us that there is a unity between the Old and New Testaments. Christians should read the Old Testament in the light of Christ crucified and risen—but we should also remember that "the Old Testament retains its own intrinsic value as Revelation reaffirmed by our Lord himself" (see section 129). The unity of the Old and New Testaments indicates the dynamic movement toward the fulfillment of God's divine plan. It demonstrates the very unity of God in God's revelation of himself to us.

BUT WHO CAN INTERPRET SCRIPTURE?

The interpretation of Sacred Scripture is one of the vexing questions of our age, and has been since the division of Western Christendom. Who can faithfully and authentically interpret the word of God and what God truly intended to teach us?

Certainly, history has demonstrated that if interpretation of Scripture is left to each individual's opinion, the message of the Bible is fragmented into a never-ending variety of conflicting and even contradictory opinions—all proclaimed as God's word and will.

On the other hand, it is evident that God's word was entrusted to the whole Body of Christ, the Church. Members of that body look to its visible head, the Pope, and to the bishops and their teaching office for an authentic rendering of God's word as understood and applied to today's world. Just as it has the exclusive ability to distinguish which writings constitute the Bible, so too the Church alone possesses the means to understand and interpret Scripture infallibly.

Interpreting the inspired word of God is a task of the magisterium or teaching office in the Church. The *Dogmatic Constitution on Divine Revelation* reminds us "the task of authentically interpreting the word of God, whether written or handed on, has been entrusted exclusively to the living magisterium of the Church, whose authority is exercised in the name of Jesus Christ" (*Dei Verbum* 10).

The Church urges us to read the Bible and to do so in the full context of the Church's centuries of reflecting on its meaning under the guidance of the Holy Spirit. Because God and God's self-revelation infinitely transcend and surpass us, God's help is an absolute necessity if we are to expand our horizons, so limited by sin, apathy, and human nature itself.

The study of the Bible by groups or individuals remains an occasion for God's continuous grace and enlightenment to those who avail themselves of its riches. This is why the Church so strongly urges that studying and praying from the Bible should be the lifelong project of every Christian. The Catholic, however, reads and studies the Scriptures always within the family of the Church. As the *Catechism of the Catholic Church* teaches us, since Sacred Scripture is inspired, it must always be read and interpreted in the light of the same Holy Spirit by whom it was written. We look to the family of the faith and the magisterium for correct interpretation of the words of Sacred Scripture, so that they do not remain a dead letter but rather "the living memorial of God's word" (111,113).

The Sacred Scriptures are a precious gift of God to his people and the priceless patrimony of the Church. They help us both to know and to praise the living God. Given the richness of God's revelation, is it any wonder that God has entrusted the Sacred Scriptures to the teaching office of his Church to protect, interpret, apply, and proclaim? We should rejoice and thank God for the wondrous gift of God's revelation to us in Sacred Scripture.

QUESTIONS TO THINK ABOUT:

1. Which parts of the Bible stand out most in my memory? Why did those passages make such an impression on me?
2. Are there any parts of the Bible that make me uncomfortable? Why?
3. If I have questions about the Scriptures, where do I usually go for answers? Am I looking for answers in the right place?

CHAPTER 8

The Creed and the Councils

WHEN WE SPEAK ABOUT the faith, we can refer to the *profession* of faith, the *deposit* of faith, or the *content* of faith. In this chapter, we will consider the *creed*—the profession of faith—as the statement of what we believe and accept as God's revelation. Before we discuss what the creed contains and how various creeds came to be, we need to reflect on why a creed or a profession of faith is so important.

THE CREED IS THE SUMMARY OF OUR FAITH

The Church has the responsibility to pass on the revelation of Jesus Christ. A creed is an expression or articulation of that saving word of God. We do not invent the faith. We do not form a Church by coming together and agreeing on what we believe. It is the other way around. The Church exists prior to you and me. The Church is God's gift to us. It is the Church or Body of Christ that proclaims salvation, God's word, Christ's teaching.

The creed is a summary of our faith. We come to the Church to learn and accept its teaching, God's revelation, so that we might be saved. For a Catholic, the Church is something to which we come precisely to find God and God's life-giving word. Because of that, the creed has vital importance.

Where do we find the faith of the Church? The *Catechism of the Catholic Church* tells us to look to the creed, the profession of faith, the "symbol" as it is called, the proclamation, the summary of the faith. Two of the most familiar of these creedal professions are the Apostles' Creed and the Nicene Creed.

THE APOSTLES' CREED

We are all familiar with the Apostles' Creed, which is considered the oldest summary of Christian faith. We recite it at the beginning of the rosary. In fact, for many people, the Apostles' Creed enters our prayer life precisely through the saying of the rosary. We are also familiar with the Nicene Creed, the profession of faith that we pray aloud together at Mass every Sunday. Let us examine these two professions of faith.

The Apostles' Creed takes its name from the fact that, as tradition testifies, it is a summary of the faith of the Church of Rome that traces its belief to the proclamation of Saint Peter and Saint Paul. The *Catechism of the Catholic Church* makes reference to the Apostles' Creed as the summary of the Petrine Creed, the ancient profession of faith of the Church at Rome that has its roots in the teaching of the apostle Saint Peter (see section 194 of the *Catechism*). Saint Ambrose points out that the Apostles' Creed is the best summary of what we believe because it is rooted in the faith of the apostle Peter, who was head of the Church.

THE NICENE CREED

Another profession of faith or creed with which we should be familiar is the Nicene Creed. The Nicene Creed is actually the work of two general ecumenical councils, the Council of Nicaea and the Council of Constantinople.

To understand the importance of these creeds, we need to answer two questions:

1. What is a council?
2. What is the council's role in relation to the formulation of professions of faith?

ECUMENICAL COUNCILS

At a time of great tension in the early Church, when some people were teaching doctrines opposed to the fundamental truths of Christianity, Church leaders gathered to discuss the matter. After Peter and others had spoken, there was agreement that the gentiles, the non-Jews, would not be bound to observe the whole law of Moses in the Old Testament. The announcement of this decision was made with great confidence: "It has seemed good to the Holy Spirit and to us to lay upon you no greater burden than these necessary things" (Acts 15:28). That is, they taught confidently that the Holy Spirit's guidance, which had been promised to the leaders of the Church, had in fact been given to them. When these leaders solemnly and publicly proclaimed that something was a part of the deposit of the true faith, it was with certitude. To them this conviction was clearly a joyful gift of God, a blessing freeing them from anxiety and doubt, to be able to be sure in this way of God's will and God's message.

Since the apostolic period, when major discords have arisen, the Church's bishops have gathered in ecumenical councils—councils that represent the whole Church. There have been twenty-one such councils in the course of the Church's history. The first was the Council of Nicaea in 325. The most recent was the Second Vatican Council from 1962 to 1965.

In the fourth century, there was some division in the Church over a true understanding of the Apostles' Creed. What does it mean to say that we believe in Jesus Christ and profess that he is the Son of God? In what sense is Jesus truly called the Son of God? Is this simply figurative language? Is this symbolic rhetoric? Is he only an adopted Son? How can he truly be the Son of God?

Because of such questions, the teachers of the Church, the bishops, successors of the apostles, gathered in the year 325 in the city of Nicaea and wrote a profession of faith. In effect, they said, "This is what the Church from the beginning has believed. This is what we have always understood. This is our faith." They proclaimed the symbol or profession of faith that we now call the Nicene Creed.

The discussion did not end. New questions arose and the exact meaning of the words of the Council of Nicaea were interpreted in a variety of ways. So the bishops gathered again in the year 381 in Constantinople and clarified the true faith of the Church. It is this profession of faith—issued by the Council of Constantinople and based on the creed of the Council of Nicaea—that we now recite at Mass on Sunday. This ancient creed is shared by the Eastern Church, the Western Church, the whole Church throughout the world.

The development of such creeds helps us understand the role of ecumenical councils in the Church. Since bishops are successors of the apostles and function in the Church today as the apostles did in the apostolic community, they have the responsibility to guarantee that the creed—the statement of what we believe—is passed on, understood, applied, and clarified so that each generation can answer correctly the question, "What does the Church teach as God's revelation? What is God's word to us?"

The most recent council, the Second Vatican Council, proclaimed seventeen constitutions, decrees, and declarations that address every aspect of the Church as we face the challenges of the modern world. These documents are all the fruit of the presence of the Holy Spirit, the Paraclete. They are written under the guidance of the Spirit, whom Jesus promised would be with us to preserve truth in the Church. The same is true of all documents of an ecumenical council, whether it is the creed from Nicaea or Constantinople, or a declaration from the Council of Trent, or a dogmatic constitution from the Second Vatican Council.

THE TEACHING OF THE COUNCILS

Faithful members of the Church have always been required to accept what the ecumenical councils teach as matters of faith. As the Second Vatican Council declared, the infallible teaching office of the bishops "is even more clearly verified when, gathered together in an ecumenical council, they are teachers and judges of faith and morals for the universal Church. Their definitions must then be adhered to with the submission of faith" (*Lumen Gentium* 25).

The *Catechism of the Catholic Church* reminds us that through the centuries many professions or symbols of faith have been articulated in response to the needs of different ages—from the Athanasian Creed to the *Credo of the People of God* of Paul VI (see section 192). Not everything proclaimed by an ecumenical council, however, is meant to be infallible teaching. Some conciliar statements are intended as pastoral documents or disciplinary legislation.

It is the firm belief of the Church that, when the bishops come together in an ecumenical council, the Spirit is present with them and formulates what will be taught in the name and with the authority of Jesus Christ. Hence, we look to the Church with great confidence in our search to know what we are to believe today as God's word. We look to the creeds and the councils that formulated creedal professions. We turn to their teaching to find a sure guide, a clear light, that focuses on Jesus Christ, knowing that he promised to be with us and to send the Spirit to enliven us and keep us in the truth.

QUESTIONS TO THINK ABOUT:

1. Can I recite the whole Apostles' Creed from memory? If not, which parts do I remember clearly? Why do those parts stand out for me?
2. Is there anything in the creeds that I find difficult to accept? Where would I look for help to understand it better?

CHAPTER 9

God the Creator of Heaven and Earth

WHERE DO I COME from? How did the universe come to be? Why am I here? How am I supposed to live? What will happen to me after death?

These are natural questions for human beings. They lead us to an awareness of the existence of God—whom revelation confirms as the God who created us and everything good that exists and who, therefore, gives meaning to life.

WE BELIEVE IN GOD

The first article of the Apostles' Creed states that we believe in God. It expresses our most fundamental belief. What does it mean, however, to say "I believe in God"?

First of all, it separates us from those who falsely conclude that all of creation including ourselves is somehow a result of chance or our own efforts and not of God's initiative. The creed as a profession of our faith unites us with those who recognize that there is a power and a reality far greater than ourselves to whom we are responsible. God is the name we give to this reality, this transcendent, all-powerful, spiritual, and personal force.

There is one God. That was the revelation of the Old Testament. It was confirmed by Jesus in the New Testament, and it is proclaimed by the Church in every age. God is a unity without division or multiplication. We profess our faith in one God. There is no other.

KNOWING *THAT* GOD IS AND KNOWING *WHO* GOD IS

If you walk into a dimly lit room, you will know if someone is there. But without enough light, you will not know who it is. That is our position in the midst of creation. We see God's wondrous work and ask ourselves, "Did I do all this? No! Did human beings bring all this into existence? No! Can human beings create life from nothing or bring back someone who is truly dead? No!" We know that there has to be something more to life on earth, but we do not know what it is and who is responsible for it.

If you turn on the light in that dimly lit room, you begin to see not only that there is someone in the room but also who it is. Revelation is the light that allows us to look at creation, ourselves, and the world and begin to see, through the light of God's word, not only *that* there is a God but also *who* God is.

In the Book of Exodus we find the story of Moses' encounter with God. The Lord calls Moses to lead his people out of Egypt into freedom and Moses asks in reply, " 'When I go to the Israelites and say to them, "The God of your fathers has sent me to you," if they ask me, "What is his name?" what am I to tell them?' God replied, 'I am who am.' Then he added, 'This is what you are to tell the Israelites: I AM sent me to you' " (Exodus 3:13–14).

God said, My name is I AM. In other words, I have no beginning, and I have no end. No one brings me into existence. I am.

This is the first great revelation of God to God's people. The creed sums it up in the simple statement, "We believe in God." God is, God exists. In that same article of the creed we recognize that the one and only God is also our Father and the Creator of heaven and earth.

JESUS COMPLETES THE REVELATION

The revelation of who God is came to completion only with the coming of Jesus. Not only is God the One who is, Jesus also tells us that God sent him and that he, as God's Son, came to invite us to call God our Father.

The mystery of Jesus could only begin to be grasped as his union with the Father was revealed. Jesus is not the Father; he was sent by the Father and honors the Father. They are different persons and have been together forever. "Do you not believe that I am in the Father and the Father is in me?" (John 14:10). "The Father and I are one" (John 10:30). They are not one person, for he says, "the Father and I"; but they are one in sharing the same nature, the same eternal love, wisdom, and power that created and sustains us and the world.

When we proclaim our faith in God our Father, we are at the same time proclaiming our belief that through the death and resurrection of Jesus we have become adopted children of God and hence empowered to call God Father.

GOD THE CREATOR

God also reveals himself to us as our Creator. To know his grandeur and to know our dignity as persons made in the image of God, we must begin to grasp God's creative power. "Thus says the Lord, the holy one of Israel . . . 'will you question me about my children or command me concerning the work of my hand? I made the earth, and created humankind upon it; it was my hands that stretched out the heavens and I commanded all their hosts' " (Isaiah 45:11–12). To know God is to know that he is "creator of heaven and earth."

In the opening of the Book of Genesis we read about the act of God that brings all things into existence—creation. This was the action of God that constituted everything that is, including us. God is not only the one who is but also the source of all things. God is our Creator, the Creator of everything.

In the first line of the Book of Genesis we read, "In the beginning, God created the heavens and the earth." Before there was anything, God, the one who is, created everything that is. "Let there be light," he said, and there was. Then he brought into being the planets, the sun, the moon, the plants, the animals, and finally in his own image and likeness—male and female he created us. All of this was the work of a loving God who said, "Let there be life and let that life be abundant and multiply and fill the earth."

When we say God made all things out of nothing, we mean that before God created there was no thing in existence. Only God has existed forever. There was a beginning to creation. Before creation there was no earth, no universe, no elements, not even time.

God needed nothing. Nothing he created was made so that he might benefit from it. There was nothing lacking in God that needed fulfillment. It is the clear teaching of the Church that out of God's immense love, without any urging external to himself, God freely choose to bring forth creation where there had been absolutely nothing but God. Creation is not difficult for God. "For he spoke and it came to be; he commanded and it stood firm" (Psalm 33:9).

In his generosity, God freely willed that what had not been should be, in order to taste the blessing of existence. Some creatures—human beings and angels—he made to share even in the glory of being persons, being free, and called to share the boundless riches of God's own life.

The sacred writer of the first creation account (see Genesis 1:1–2:4) portrays the work of creation as extending over a period of six "days," and says that on the seventh day God "rested from all the work that he had done in creation" (Genesis 2:3). This account is obviously not a technical report on the timing and mode of creation. As Saint Augustine noted centuries ago, the six "days" of creation could hardly have been solar days as we now know, for according to the account in Genesis, the sun was not made until the fourth "day." Rather, the structure and literary form of the creation narrative are there to help us grasp what God is teaching us about creation.

In presenting the creative activity of God in the way it does, Genesis also teaches us about the dignity of work and the sacredness of the sabbath rest. In the account of human origin, the dignity of human labor and our right to and need for times of contemplative quiet are established.

The first article of the creed calls us to belief in one God who creates all of life and who is our Father. Faith in this revealed word helps us answer the basic questions about the meaning of life: Who are we? Where did we come from? How are we to live? What is life all about?

QUESTIONS TO THINK ABOUT:

1. Why is the creation story important in our modern scientific world? What does it teach us about our relationship with God?
2. Knowing that I am God's creature, how do I treat the rest of creation? Do I respect God's other creatures as if I really believed that God created them out of love?

CHAPTER 10

The Attributes of God

AS GOD REVEALS HIMSELF to us in wonderful acts, we come to learn who God is. From these revealed words and deeds, we can attribute qualities to God that help us understand God's being. What are the characteristics or attributes of God?

THE LIVING GOD

The *Catechism of the Catholic Church* points out that the first and most obvious attribute of God is that he is the living God. Jesus teaches us that God is the God of the living. In a sense our own experience of life is a reflection, although a very dim one, of the reality of God's life.

But God is very different from us and everything we experience. We live, but we also die; we exist only because God created us. God not only exists and lives but he is also the source of all existence. Nothing exists without him. God is the author of all life and its final arbiter.

In times past people worshiped idols and inventions of their own imagination. None of them was living and true. Our God is the one true living God.

THE PERSONAL GOD

Another obvious attribute of God, who speaks to us, reveals his truth to us, and loves us, is that our God is a personal God. The saving God who, with forceful will and great mercy, led the Israelites out from slavery, gave them the precepts of life, overcame their foes, and brought them into a promised land—this God is not an irrational force or blind transcendent power but truly a person who sustains and governs all of life. Because God is a person, he can know us and care for us; and he does. God reveals that he is the beginning of all that is, including us. The world is not the product of some uncaring power or force. Mightier than all the forces of nature, the Lord who creates and gives life is a person who knows us and loves us.

Since God is the origin of all things and since all of creation reflects the mind of God, truth is also an attribute of God. As the *Catechism of the Catholic Church* teaches us, God's truth is his wisdom, which commands the whole created order and governs the world. God, who alone made heaven and earth, can alone impart true knowledge of every created thing in relation to himself (see section 216 of the *Catechism*). What this statement means is that the truthfulness of all reality is measured against God's will and word since it is both the will and word of God that create and bring reality into being. God's word is truth and all truth is measured against that word.

GOD THE FATHER

The most familiar title of God is "Father." Even in the earliest days of salvation history before God had revealed how all men and women belong to him and are called to become his children in his eternal Son, who became our brother, he made himself known as our Father. He can be infinitely trusted. He never fails us, "for you are our Father, were Abraham not to know us, nor Israel to acknowledge us, you, Lord, are our Father, our Redeemer you are named forever" (Isaiah 63:16). "It is the Lord, your God, who marches with you; he will never fail you or forsake you" (Deuteronomy 31:6).

The *Catechism of the Catholic Church* reminds us that God's love for Israel is compared to a Father's love for his son and that his love for his people is stronger than a mother's love for her children (see section 219). In John's gospel we read that "God so loved the world that he gave his only Son" (John 3:16).

Jesus came into the world precisely to share his Father's love and the knowledge that we are called to be adopted children of God. In this sense Jesus revealed that God is Father in an unheard-of way. He is Father not only by being Creator; he is eternally Father by his relationship to his only Son, who, likewise, is Son only in relation to his Father. "No one knows the Son except the Father, and no one knows the Father except the Son and anyone to whom the Son chooses to reveal him" (Matthew 11:27).

Jesus chose to reveal his sonship in order that we might know that we are also sons and daughters of God in so far as we are baptized into the life of Jesus, the only true, natural Son of God. It is because of our relationship to Jesus and his revelation to us that we can dare to pray "Our Father who art in heaven . . ."

GOD THE ALMIGHTY

God is also almighty. God's power and majesty are limitless. In the creeds of the Church we profess our belief in "God, the Father Almighty." The First Vatican Council speaks of the greatness of God. "There is one true and living God, Creator and Lord of heaven and earth, Almighty, eternal, immeasurable, incomprehensible, infinite in intellect and in will and in every perfection." (*Dogmatic Constitution on the Catholic Faith,* Chapter 1).

To say that God is almighty is to acknowledge that he can do all things. God is all-powerful, omnipotent. "For nothing will be impossible with God" (Luke 1:37). God never lacks the power to keep his promises. His will is never frustrated by those who oppose him. The God who can create out of nothing—and who can redeem sinful human beings, restoring to spiritual life that which was dead—is indeed all-powerful.

GOD THE UNCHANGING

In a restless and changing world, God reveals God's own unchanging nature. "Surely I, the Lord, do not change" (Malachi 3:6). God is both eternal and changeless, everlasting and faithful. In his very being, God is without change. Many elements in the changing world alter one another and depend on one another for their continued existence, but our all-powerful and merciful God is utterly independent and undergoes no alteration.

As the psalm proclaims: "Lord, you have been our dwelling place for all generations. Before the mountains were brought forth, or before you had formed the earth and the world, from everlasting to everlasting you are God . . . For a thousand years in your sight are like yesterday when it is passed or like a watch in the night" (Psalm 90:1–4).

While we may be swept along by the currents of time, God dwells in inaccessible light and in eternity to which every moment of time is always present. God watches over all things with unchanging love. His fidelity is forever trustworthy.

GOD IS EVERYWHERE

God is spirit. God does not have a physical body, nor is God restricted to any one place with the limitations imposed by matter. Sometimes we find it difficult to grasp the meaning of spiritual reality, to understand how something can be real without having spatial and temporal dimensions. Even Saint Augustine experienced difficulty in grasping the meaning of God's spirituality, but he rejoiced in proclaiming that God is truly a spirit.

As a spirit, God is present to all. "In him we live and move and have our being" (Acts 17:27–28). God is "omnipresent," which means present everywhere. As the psalmist proclaims, "Where can I hide from your spirit? From your presence, where can I flee? If I ascend to the heavens, you are there; if I lie down in Sheol, you are there too. If I fly with the wings of dawn and alight beyond the sea, even there your hand will guide me, your right hand hold me fast" (Psalm 139:7–10).

The Church's faith in the everpresence of God is a reminder of God's care, love, providence, and concern for each of us. But it is also a challenge that recalls that whatever is done in darkness shall be brought to light. God sees, knows, and will reveal all things.

GOD IS TRANSCENDENT

Because God is utterly beyond us and totally distinct from this world, we can speak of his transcendence and holiness. To proclaim that God is transcendent is to say that he is exalted far above the universe, which came into existence only at his bidding. Before the universe and its time, God is. His changeless and eternal reality is entirely distinct from the dependent reality of finite things. "The heavens and the highest heavens cannot contain you" (2 Chronicles 6:18). While traces of God are found in all of creation, all of life cannot begin to express the majesty of God.

Perhaps it is for this reason that great theologians of the Church such as Saint Augustine and Saint Thomas Aquinas have cautioned us that God is so far beyond us that, whatever we can say of God, much, much more remains unstated and unrevealed.

To reflect on the attributes of God is a humbling experience, because it reminds us how little God really needs us and yet how much God loves each of us. If fear of God is the beginning of wisdom, then recognition of God as eternal, unchanging omnipotence and awareness of God's everlasting love must be the beginning of our faith in God's word and our love of God.

QUESTIONS TO THINK ABOUT:

1. Do I really believe that "nothing will be impossible with God"? What limits does my understanding of time and space place on God's actions? Are those really limits for God or just for me?
2. How does it affect my life to know that the God of all creation loves me personally? How does it affect my prayer?
3. Do I try to flee from God? How?

CHAPTER 11

The Holy Trinity

WE TRACE THE CROSS on our body as we sign ourselves in the name of the Father and of the Son and of the Holy Spirit. The sign of the cross is the most familiar and concise summary of our Catholic faith.

We believe in three persons in one God. As the *Catechism of the Catholic Church* reminds us, we are baptized "in the *name* of the Father and of the Son and of the Holy Spirit." We do not say we are baptized in their *names,* because the Father, the Son, and the Holy Spirit together are one Holy Trinity. There is only one God (see section 233 of the *Catechism*).

THE TRINITY: AN INCOMPREHENSIBLE REALITY

The central doctrine of the Catholic faith is the mystery of the Holy Trinity. The Vatican General Catechetical Directory points out that "the history of salvation is identical with the history of the way and the plan by which God, true and one, the Father, the Son, and the Holy Spirit, reveals himself to men, and reconciles and unites with himself those turned away from sin" (n 47).

The Holy Trinity is in the strictest sense of the word a mystery of faith. It is one of those incomprehensible realities that the First Vatican Council in its *Dogmatic Constitution on the Catholic Faith* describes as "hidden in God which, unless divinely revealed, could not come to be known" (Chapter 4).

The fact that incomprehensible realities such as the Trinity can be grasped only by faith is in no way an affront to human reason. Divine mysteries are not contrary to human reason, nor are they incompatible with rational thought. Even in our relationship with other human persons, we must fall back upon faith—a form of human faith—to know the truth of their inmost lives and their love for us. When we speak of the inner life of God, it is a life so far beyond us that we can never completely and fully comprehend its true meaning. But, through faith, we can nonetheless be aware of the truth that God tells us about himself.

Centuries ago, Saint Thomas Aquinas pointed out that "It is impossible to believe explicitly in the mystery of Christ without faith in the Trinity, for the mystery of Christ includes that the Son of God took flesh, that he renewed the world through the grace of the Holy Spirit, and again, that he was conceived by the Holy Spirit" (*Summa Theologica* II—II, 2, 8). Obviously, we could not believe that Jesus is the Son of God and true God sent by the Father if we did not believe in the plurality of persons in one God. Neither would we be able to understand the meaning of eternal life, nor the grace that leads to it, without believing in the Trinity, for grace and eternal life are a sharing in the life of the most Holy Trinity.

The importance of the Trinity in Catholic teaching is evident from the beginning of the Church. When Christ sent the apostles forth to go and "make disciples of all nations" (Matthew 28:19), he instructed them to baptize in the name of the Trinity: "baptizing them in the name of the Father, and of the Son, and of the Holy Spirit" (Matthew 28:19). From the earliest centuries of the Church and in the most ancient professions of faith, we find a belief in the Trinity of the Father, the Son, and the Holy Spirit. The Quicumque Creed (more popularly known as the Athanasian Creed), which dates from the fourth century, declares, "Now the Catholic faith is this: that we worship one God in the Trinity, and the Trinity in unity . . . The Father is a distinct person, the Son is a distinct person, and the Holy Spirit is a distinct person, but the Father and the Son and the Holy Spirit have one divinity, equal glory and co-eternal majesty."

The preface for the Mass on Holy Trinity Sunday summarizes our belief in what God has told us about himself: "We joyfully proclaim our faith in the mysteries of your Godhead. You have revealed your glory as the glory also of your Son and of the Holy Spirit: three persons equal in majesty, undivided in splendor, yet one Lord, one God, ever to be adored in your everlasting glory" (Roman Missal).

The doctrine of the Trinity was not revealed with full clarity at the very beginning of God's revelation to us. Only gradually, step by step, did God make known to his people the mystery of his inner life. The word "trinity" does not appear in the New Testament; and the meaning of the words "person" and "nature," in the precise sense in which they are used to bear the mystery of God, had to be carefully refined in order that they might be properly understood.

Yet in truth what the New Testament teaches us is captured with clarity and reverence in the statements of the early councils of the Church that we use today—the Apostles' Creed, the Nicene Creed, the Athanasian Creed.

GOD THE FATHER AND GOD THE SON

The revelation of the Trinity begins when Jesus told us that he is God's Son. Jesus teaches us that God is not only the Creator of the universe but also the Father of the eternally begotten Son, who became one with us as the God-man Jesus Christ (see section 240). As Matthew's gospel teaches us: "No one knows the Son except the Father, and no one knows the Father except the Son and anyone to whom the Son wishes to reveal him" (Matthew 11:27).

Throughout history there have been countless claims of heaven touching earth. These pretensions reflect the longing of the human heart for the presence of God. Yet we know that the emptiness spoken about by the prophets and reflected upon by wise men finds its fullness and satisfaction only in Jesus Christ, God and man, our Brother and Savior. Jesus is God's Son and his revelation to us is that the great name of God is "Father."

GOD THE HOLY SPIRIT

In revealing God as Father and himself as God's Son, Jesus also made known to us the Holy Spirit. Before his death, Jesus announced the sending of the Paraclete or Advocate, the Holy Spirit. This is the Spirit of God who from the beginning was with God and who will now dwell as God with us after Jesus' death, resurrection, and ascension in glory. The Holy Spirit is thus revealed as another divine person with Jesus and the Father. The *Catechism of the Catholic Church* teaches that the Holy Spirit is sent to us "both by the Father in the name of the Son and by the Son in person, once he had returned to the Father" (see section 244). The coming of the Holy Spirit completes the revelation of the Trinity.

IMAGINING THE TRINITY

Holy writers, doctors and fathers of the Church, and great theologians have attempted to describe the Holy Trinity. Saint Hilary, Saint Ambrose, Saint Augustine, and Saint Thomas Aquinas, to name but some of the greatest teachers of the faith, have grappled with the challenge of explaining what it means to proclaim that God is one and three.

One of the most beautiful of these explanations is by Saint Thomas Aquinas, who throughout his *Summa Theologica* speaks of God as the Father who knows himself so fully and completely from all eternity that the image of himself is completely and fully equal to himself. The articulation of this divine likeness of God is the Eternal Word. This is the Eternal Word begotten from all eternity who "became flesh and made his dwelling place among us, and we saw his glory, the glory of the Father's only Son" (Jn 1:14).

God the Son, the Eternal Word, is equal to the Father and one with the Father in everything except being the Father. The Son so loves the Father that the love between the Father and the Son is from all eternity equal to the Father and Son and also one with them. The only difference is that this love, the Holy Spirit, is not the Father nor the Son, yet one with them as God.

Saint Patrick chose a more inexact but memorable image as a teaching tool—the shamrock with its three equal leaves, and yet all truly one plant.

Whatever explanation we choose to try to penetrate the mystery of the Holy Trinity, the essential elements remain the same: there is one God, and there are three persons in the one God or Trinity. The three divine persons do not share the one divinity among themselves, but each of them is God whole and entire. Yet each divine person is really distinct from one another. Hence we say that God has one divine nature and three divine persons.

In baptism we are called to share in the life of the Blessed Trinity as we are sealed in the name of the Father and the Son and the Holy Spirit in such a way that the one God in three persons actually comes to dwell within us. For this reason we need to remind ourselves that the Church's teaching on the Holy Trinity is not an abstract exercise in theology. It is a life-giving proclamation that we live in God and God in us to the extent that we live a life alive in God's grace. This truth we recall, affirm, and celebrate every time we sign ourselves in the name of the Father, and of the Son, and of the Holy Spirit. Amen.

QUESTIONS TO THINK ABOUT:

1. Is the doctrine of the Trinity a comfort or a stumbling block to me?
2. What images have helped me understand the doctrine of the Trinity?

CHAPTER 12

The Works of God's Hand

IN THE CREED WE profess our belief in God "the maker of heaven and earth, of all that is seen and unseen." The works of God's creation are heaven and earth and all that is in them. As the *Catechism of the Catholic Church* teaches, "heaven and earth" means all of creation (see section 326 of the *Catechism*).

There is a sense in which we can speak of three areas of God's majestic and creative action. A vision of creation promulgated by the Fourth Lateran Council in 1215 affirmed that God "from the beginning of time made at once out of nothing both orders of creatures, the spiritual and the corporal, that is, the angelic and the earthly, and then the human creature, who shares in both orders, being composed of spirit and body."

THE ANGELS

The first realm of God's creation is the spiritual order or noncorporal beings that Sacred Scripture calls angels. It is a truth of faith that God created a realm of spiritual beings who do not share the limitations of a physical body and yet exist as the result of God's all-powerful, loving act of creation. The *Catechism of the Catholic Church* tells us that "as purely spiritual creatures angels have intelligence and will: they are personal and immortal creatures, surpassing in perfection all visible creatures, as the splendor of their glory bears witness" (see section 330).

The liturgy speaks of countless hosts of angels that stand before God to do God's will. "They look upon your splendor and praise you night and day" (Roman Missal, Eucharistic Prayer 4). Almost every preface to each Eucharistic prayer has us unite with all the choirs of angels in heaven as we proclaim God's glory and join in the angelic hymn of praise.

The faith of the Church recognizes the words of Scripture about angels as far more than figurative speech about God's providential care. There are purely spiritual persons made by God who rejoice to know him and share his life. Though the number of angels is clearly large, Scripture gives us the names of only three: Raphael, Gabriel, and Michael. Jesus speaks of the angels and their care for us. "See that you do not despise one of these little ones, for I say to you that their angels in heaven always look upon the face of my heavenly Father" (Matthew 18:10).

God creates a wide range of physical reality—inert objects such as the very rock and dirt of the earth, through the vast array of flora and fauna that covers and colors our world, and the innumerable species of living things that crawl, swim, run, and walk this planet. We should not be surprised that he should also create an equally vast array of spiritual beings not inhibited by physical characteristics that mark and differentiate mineral, vegetable, and animal life. Nor should we be surprised that such splendid, intelligent, loving life would be used by God to communicate with us and that from time to time God would send angels as his messengers—as he did to Mary, to Joseph, and to his own Son in the Garden of Gethsemane. As the creed proclaims, we profess our faith in God who is the maker of all that is, "seen and unseen."

THE HUMAN BEING: GLORY OF GOD'S CREATION

We are far more familiar with the "seen" works of God's hand. God created the visible world in all its richness, diversity, and order. Scripture, as the *Catechism* teaches us, symbolically presents the action of the Creator as six days of work, with a "rest" on the seventh (section 337). All that exists is the result of the action of God. God did not need creation, but out of his immense love he brought forth the world in which we live. Not in order to increase or to acquire his own happiness, but in order to freely manifest his perfection, God created both spiritual and corporal creatures.

The glory of God's creation is the human being. As the first account of the creation of the world in the Book of Genesis reaches its climax, God is portrayed as creating man and woman as the crown of all that God has made. "Then God said: 'Let us make man in our image, after our likeness. Let them have dominion . . .' " (Genesis 1:26).

In what sense do we speak of human beings, a man and woman, as made in the image of God? It is not in the physical dimension of our life that we mirror him, because God has no body. We are made in the image and likeness of God because God has taken the goodness of his physical creation and breathed into it an immortal spiritual reality called the soul. Because of that principle of life, we, like God, are capable of knowing and loving. We can mirror the knowledge and love that lie at the very core of God's being; hence we are called images of God.

Each human person is composed of body and soul, not two distinct parts but two realities of a single living person. The soul is not alien to the body but is the living principle that causes the body to be the human reality it is. Likewise the flesh is not something extraneous that we should despise.

IT IS NOT GOOD FOR THE MAN TO BE ALONE

Just as God is three in one and enjoys the marvelous communion of the three divine persons, so too human beings are called to a life in community. "It is not good for the man to be alone" (Genesis 2:18). Male and female God created us. Man and woman were made for each other so that they would not be alone but form a community of mutual love and support.

The Genesis account of human beginnings, with much subsequent revelation, proclaims the divine origin and sacredness of human sexuality and its purposes, the divine institution of marriage, and the dignity and equality of men and women. Stressing the great unity of the human family, Genesis presents the image of Eve, the first woman, as being formed by God from the very flesh of Adam (Genesis 2:21–22). Sacred Scripture teaches that man and woman are equal and complementary. They complete each other, relieving the loneliness of the human condition. They must see each other as equals, so that in marriage they may become one. Even in these first acts of God's creation, there is an echo or faint mirroring of the very life of God.

Scripture tells us little about the condition of human beings in the beginning of creation. Genesis is not scientific anthropology, nor is it a record written as the events were actually occurring. Rather it is a reflection under the inspiration of the Holy Spirit on the true origins and purpose of human life. We learn that the first man and woman were not only created good but were also placed in a world of such surpassing harmony and peace that we describe it as paradise.

The inner harmony of the human person, the concord between man and woman, and finally the tranquil relationship between the first couple and all creation comprised that state we call "original justice" (see section

376). Scripture summarizes the teaching on creation by proclaiming that God looked on all he had made and saw that it was very good (Genesis 1:31).

THE DIGNITY OF LIFE

If we step back and look at the wondrous works of God's creation, what we find is simple yet awesome. In the beginning there was nothing. Out of love God freely brought into being everything that exists including the realms of angelic life and the whole physical world with its myriad forms of vegetable and animal life. At the pinnacle of this creative action, he made man and woman, composed of body and soul, called to build lives together that would flower into families and a community that would reflect the inner life of God.

Because all of creation and most particularly human life is a gift from God, we are obliged to respect and care for all of his creation. We must revere human life, and nurture and protect it, because man and woman are made in the image and likeness of God.

The Church has always proclaimed the dignity of each human person. Because we are images of our maker and are called through Christ to share in the personal life of the Trinity, each of us has a transcendent worth. In many ways, the Second Vatican Council addressed a special need of our age when it stressed again how human life must be honored and upheld, fostered and respected. Surely in our day, with so many threats to the dignity of human life, the words of the *Pastoral Constitution on the Church in the Modern World* are especially inspiring: "Through his bodily composition man gathers to himself the elements of the material world. Thus they reach their crown through him, and through him raise their voice in free praise of the Creator. For this reason man is not allowed to despise his bodily life" (14).

The teaching of the Second Vatican Council on actions "opposed to life itself" (*Gaudium et Spes* 27) is in the unwavering Christian tradition that insists that we must never attack the basic human value—human life—and that to do so is wrong. To uphold the dignity and value, the worth and sacredness of human life is to recognize and rejoice that every human being is wondrously made in the image and likeness of God.

QUESTIONS TO THINK ABOUT:

1. How are the angels in the Bible different from the angels presented in modern popular culture?

2. What responsibility do we have as the glory of God's creation? What does it mean that we "have dominion" over creation?
3. How do I personally uphold the dignity of human life? Do my ordinary dealings with people show them that I believe human life is sacred?

CHAPTER 13

The Fall from Grace

WHY IS IT SO difficult at times to be good and to do good? Why is it that even though we may have the best of intentions, we continually find ourselves doing what we know we should not do or failing to do the good we know we ought to do? There is a part of us that is determined to do good, but at the same time there is an element within us that continually turns away from the good we know we can be and do.

SOMETHING STRUGGLES AGAINST THE GOOD

Have you ever been in a situation where lanes of traffic come together, and as you try to merge someone cuts you off? Were you to meet the same person on the street, you would probably find a mild and caring neighbor, but other qualities emerge in traffic. We have all met people who, when the light turns from red to green, need to let you know—with their horns—that they saw it change half a second before you did. There is something within us that struggles against the other voice that urges us to be loving, kind, good, truthful, chaste, honest, and God-fearing.

In the seventh chapter of his beautiful letter to the Romans, Paul describes just this problem. "What I do, I do not understand. For I do not do what I want, but I do what I hate . . . I can will what is right but I cannot do it. For I do not do the good I want, but I do the evil I do not want. Now if I do what I do not want, it is no longer I who do it, but sin that dwells within me" (Romans 7:15–20).

Saint Paul's cry from the heart is probably something each of us has experienced. Why is it that we have the best of intentions, make New Year's resolutions, renew our aspirations, perhaps every day, and then come up against a situation that brings out the wrong response?

THE FALL

We can look for an explanation in the opening chapters of the Book of Genesis. Here this seemingly endless struggle between good and evil is described in the wonderful imagery of the serpent tempting Adam and Eve with the forbidden fruit.

God said, "You are free to eat from any of the trees of the garden except the tree of knowledge of good and bad. From that tree you shall not eat; the moment you eat from it you are surely doomed to die" (Genesis 2:16–17). The tempter, however, said, "You certainly will not die! No, God knows well that the moment you eat of it your eyes will be opened and you will be like gods who know what is good and what is bad" (Genesis 3:4–5). Adam and Eve ate the forbidden fruit. They chose their own desires over God's will and plan. The teaching, whatever the imagery, is very clear. Sin entered the world through the decision of a human being to choose self over God and God's plan.

At the same time the harmony of creation was also destroyed. If we continue to read the Book of Genesis, we see how Adam and Eve became aware of their sinful condition, were driven out of the garden, and were forced to live by the sweat of their brow. The beauty and harmony of God's creative plan was disrupted. This was not the way it was meant to be. Once sin entered into life and into our world, harmony with God, with each other, and with the world around us was shattered. We call this action original sin and its results the human condition.

ORIGINAL SIN

Each one of us is an heir to Adam and Eve. We are members of the human family. We trace our lineage back to this couple and their failure to respect God's law, will, and plan. The actions they took shattered God's created harmony not only for them but also for us. Their sin is reflected in us and who we are and is mirrored in our daily life. This explains why it is so difficult to do good, to do what we know we should do.

As the *Catechism of the Catholic Church* teaches, "the overwhelming misery that oppresses men and their inclination toward evil and death cannot be understood apart from their connection with Adam's sin and the fact that he has transmitted to us a sin with which we are all born afflicted, a sin which is the 'death of the soul' " (see section 403).

The *Catechism* goes on to teach us that original sin is not the same as a personal fault in each of Adam's descendants. Rather it is the loss of original holiness and justice that has wounded our human nature and inclines us to sin. Because each of us is born in this condition, we require baptism, which erases original sin and turns us back toward God by imparting the life of Christ's grace. It is because of original sin that the Church baptizes even infants who have not committed personal sin. Yet even after baptism the consequences of original sin remain in the form of a weakened human nature that is so readily inclined to evil.

The disharmony is rooted in the struggle of each one of us to lead a good life. But it is also reflected throughout the universe in which we live. We are constantly tempted to exploit, use, and manipulate others and the world in which we live in a way that is not in conformity with God's plan. This imbalance entered the world through original sin.

Saint Paul describes the consequences of original sin within us as a struggle between the old and new person. The old person is interested only in the selfish man or woman who dwells within each of us. The life of the new person, baptized and alive in God's grace, is directed outward to God, Christ, and our neighbors. This struggle deep within our human nature has continued from the days of Adam and Eve's sin. Our baptism washes away original sin but its effects still remain.

The *Catechism of the Catholic Church* reminds us that after the first, original sin the world was virtually "inundated by sin" (see section 401). Scripture and the Church's tradition continually recall the presence and "universality of sin in man's history."

WE CAN BE VICTORIOUS

Yet we are not lost. We are not left to our own devices. Paul reminds us that, just as in Adam sin was introduced into the world and, through sin, death and all the consequences of it, so too grace and new creation come to us in Christ. Just as death came through a human being, so too the resurrection of the dead came through a human being. As in Adam all people die, so too in Christ shall all be brought to life—a fullness of life, a new creation already beginning in us through grace (see 1 Corinthians 15).

This is the message we proclaim when we face the mystery of sin, the reality of original sin, and the problems of the human condition that lead us to personal sin. Just as Adam brought sin, disharmony, confusion, disruption, and struggle into our lives, so too now Christ, the new Adam, gives us grace, redemption, new life, and salvation. It is in Jesus Christ that we now find the roots and beginnings of the new creation. He came to restore what was out of balance, to bring harmony where it had been destroyed. Jesus came to give us the newness of life in grace that begins to restore our relationship with God, which will some day lead to full communion with God in glory. It is for this reason that we identify Christ as the new Adam. Grace is the beginning of a new creation for all of those baptized into Christ.

When we face daily frustrations and struggle to be good, we need to recall the teaching of the Church that we have the power to triumph over sin because we have Christ's grace within us. We have the capacity to be victorious, but we must face it every day with our Lord and Savior, the new Adam, Jesus Christ.

QUESTIONS TO THINK ABOUT:

1. Do I drive like a Christian?
2. What is my worst temptation? How do I overcome it? Or do I overcome it at all?
3. What would it mean for me to be victorious over sin? If I really had won the battle against sin, how would my life be different?

CHAPTER 14

Jesus Christ the Only Son of God

THE FAITH OF THE Catholic Church in Jesus Christ is summed up in the simple statement that he is God and man. Jesus, the son of Mary, is also the Son of God. In theological terms we call this reality the Incarnation. In liturgical and popular terms we speak of Christmas—Emmanuel—God with us.

The gospels speak with profound simplicity about the events surrounding the conception and birth of Jesus. While his coming is hardly what we could have expected for the advent of God's own Son, nonetheless the child born of Mary in Bethlehem was truly the Eternal Word made flesh.

MOTHER OF GOD

Only great faith could have accepted the announcement of the angel to Mary that she was to be the Mother of God. Only in faith was hope sustained in the utter poverty of Jesus' birth. The gospels go on to tell us that away from her home of Nazareth, at the royal city of Bethlehem, Mary "gave birth to her firstborn son" and "wrapped him in swaddling clothes and laid him in a manger, because there was no room for them in the inn" (Luke 2:7).

The two realities that stand out are the humanity of Jesus and his divinity. From his mother he received a complete human nature. At the same time, he was truly God, the Word made flesh who lived with us.

There was a sublime purpose to the way God's only Son came among us. Because he was to be our Savior, Jesus "had to become like his brothers in every way" (Hebrews 2:17). "He who is the 'image of the invisible God' (Colossians 1:15) is Himself the perfect man." He took on our human nature and became one with us. As the Second Vatican Council teaches in the *Pastoral Constitution on the Church in the Modern World,* Jesus "worked with human hands, he thought with a human mind, acted by human choice, and loved with a human heart. Born of the Virgin Mary, he has truly been made one of us, like us in everything except sin" (*Gaudium et Spes* 22).

THE DIVINE PLAN

It is important for us to remember that all of this was done according to divine plan. As the *Catechism of the Catholic Church* teaches, "The Word became flesh so that thus we might know God's love" (see section 458 of the *Catechism*). In the first letter of John we are reminded that "in this way the love of God was made revealed to us: God sent his only Son into the world so that we might have life through him" (1 John 4:9). In the gospel of Saint John more succinctly we are taught "for God so loved the world that he gave his only son, so that everyone who believes in him might not perish but might have eternal life" (John 3:16).

To understand what happened in the incarnation, we have to go all the way back to the beginning. In Genesis we read how God created us in friendship with himself so that we might enjoy life on this earth and someday be united in eternal happiness with God. All of this we ruined by sin.

Only God could restore the harmony between the created world and its loving Creator. Only the power of God could heal so great a wound. And yet God chose that the healing would involve the very creatures who rebelled. Thus in God's plan God would come among us, become one of us, and effect the healing in a way that combined both the power of God and the weakness of human nature.

Mary's role in all of this is essential, because God's Eternal Word would enter the world by taking on human nature through the very flesh and blood of Mary. It would be this human body fashioned from Mary that would suffer and die, rise from the dead, and thus win salvation for us. In order that this might happen, Jesus had to be truly man and truly God.

JESUS WAS TRULY A MAN

The solemn teaching of the Church has always confirmed the clear teaching of Scripture that Jesus is truly a man—one of us—a human being. He did not merely appear to be a man. He really became one of us. As John says in the majestic prologue to his gospel, "And the Word became flesh and made his dwelling among us" (John 1:14). He was, in the words of Saint Paul in his letter to the Galatians, "born of a woman" (Galatians 4:4). Jesus had not only a human body but also a human soul, a human mind, a human will, human emotions, and everything that makes us who we are as human beings. He experienced all the weakness and all the frailness of human flesh. He was like us in everything but sin.

For some this is a hard saying. Many find difficulty with the fact that God would come among us and endure the frailty of the human condition. As the *Catechism of the Catholic Church* reminds us, the first heresies denied not so much Christ's divinity as his true humanity. But from the beginning the Church has insisted on the true Incarnation: the Word became real flesh (see section 465).

Even before the Church was able to articulate it in clear and compelling philosophical language, she knew the revelation and what would happen to that truth if we did not teach that Jesus was truly human. If Christ was not truly one of us, then he did not participate in the human nature that died and rose. Hence the restoration of creation and certainly the restoration of our fallen human nature would not be accomplished.

JESUS IS TRULY GOD

On the other hand, there were those who found it impossible to admit that Jesus Christ could also be one with God. Already in the third century, the Church in a council at Antioch had to affirm that Jesus Christ is Son of God by nature and not by adoption. In 325, the first ecumenical council of Nicaea affirmed that the son of God is "begotten not made, of the same substance as the Father." That affirmation was necessary because Arius had claimed that the Son of God was not of the same substance as the Father (see section 465 of the *Catechism*).

This message lies at the heart of the good news of our faith. He who is almighty, the eternal Lord of all, whose unseen might and mercy sustain all things, in the words of Saint Augustine "stepped into the tide of the years" and in the words of Saint John "lived among us," in the visible humanity he had made his own.

Somehow we have to be able to explain how this is possible. How can it be that God, the almighty, transcendent, perfect, and eternal, can become united with frail, limited, and finite creation? This mystery requires of us both faith and an effort to explain in an intelligible manner the union of the divine and the human that allows us to attribute to one person,

Jesus Christ, that which is and belongs rightfully to both God the Creator and man the creature. Somehow we have to find effective ways to teach that Jesus is not the Father; he was sent by the Father and he honors the Father. At the same time he is one with the Father and yet truly one of us.

NATURE AND PERSON

To make that idea intelligible, the Church distinguishes between *nature* and *person*. In Jesus Christ the human nature, received through his mother Mary, and the divine nature, through union with his Father, are joined in the one person, Jesus Christ, who is thus God and man. Hence we can say that Jesus is human and Jesus is God, but Jesus is only one person, that "one and the same Christ, Lord, only-begotten Son, is to be acknowledged in two natures, without confusion, change, division, or separation," in the language of the Council of Chalcedon (see section 467 of the *Catechism*). We can also say that Jesus "is inseparably true God and true man. He is truly the Son of God who, without ceasing to be God and Lord, became a man and our brother" (see section 469).

With this mystery before us, we are able to attribute to Jesus Christ actions that are both divine and human. Because Jesus is one person who lives in two distinct natures, one can truly say of the Son of God whatever is true of him in either of his two natures. Thus it is possible to say, as we proclaim in the Good Friday liturgy, that he suffered and died in his human nature.

Somehow it is easier to celebrate all of this by paying homage to a child in a crib. Perhaps that is why Christmas has such a hold on the imagination and heart of Christian people. The mystery is bewildering, the explanation mind-boggling, and the reality overwhelming. Saint Francis of Assisi helped us visualize this great mystery by the simple act of placing a model of an infant in a manger at Christmas—a tradition we have developed, enjoyed, and celebrated all these centuries.

The liturgy speaks of our seeing and loving in Jesus a God we could not otherwise see. "In him we see our God made visible and so are caught up in love of the God we cannot see" (Christmas Preface). The God we see and love is truly manifest in the person of Jesus Christ, one of us, united with God in such a unique manner as to be "God with us."

The sublime truth that Jesus is one person, though he is both God and man, reveals how great is the generosity of God in the act of incarnation by which the Eternal Word humbled himself to become one of us.

QUESTIONS TO THINK ABOUT:

1. How would I have expected God's own son to come into the world? Why was God's way better than mine?
2. How does it affect the way I react to the story of the Passion when I recall that Jesus was truly human?
3. How does the Christmas story affect the way I think of the events of Jesus' adulthood?

CHAPTER 15

Christmas and the Incarnation

CHRISTMAS CELEBRATES THE MOST remarkable moment in human history. Two thousand years ago in Bethlehem of Judea, heaven and earth met. On the first Christmas Day, God came among us in the person of Jesus Christ, Emmanuel, God with us. Nothing is more exciting in the human experience than this fact, and no one has so changed history as has the infant son of Mary, who is also the Son of God.

Somehow this truth is overwhelmed by our very familiarity with it. We have grown up with Christmas, and perhaps, in the very closeness of it, we are less taken up with the power of its message. Christmas decorations, the tree, exchanging gifts, and enjoying Christmas celebrations are all good and happy events—but we should never let them distract us from the truth that is at the very heart of the Christmas season. A virgin named Mary, betrothed to a man named Joseph of the house of David, conceived and bore a son and gave him the name "Jesus." Great was his dignity, he was called "Son of the Most High," and he was to reign without end.

LOOKING BACK AND LOOKING FORWARD

In David's town of Bethlehem, Mary brought forth her child, who was also God's child, conceived of the Holy Spirit. Heaven and earth met in the person of Jesus Christ. No matter how familiar this story is to us, no matter how much we may take it for granted, the truth of it should still overwhelm us. God became one of us so that we might share in the very life of God. Jesus Christ became man so that we might know God, love God, and come to life everlasting with God.

Christmas, naturally, calls us to look back, to focus on Bethlehem and the birth of Jesus, and to celebrate this unique, historic moment. But the Church calls us also to look forward. The same creed that professes faith in Jesus Christ born of the Virgin Mary also proclaims that Christ will come again. This coming will take multiple forms. Ultimately, the second coming will herald the end of time as Jesus gathers his people and presents his kingdom to his Father. Sacramentally, the coming takes place in a regular and enduring manner, particularly when we celebrate the Eucharist.

In a very real and tangible manner, heaven touches earth in the presence of Jesus in the Eucharist. The Eucharistic presence of our Lord is not the only way in which he remains with us, but the wonder of the Eucharist is unique. It is not as though Jesus were present in a natural way but hidden beneath a thin layer of bread and wine. It is a supernatural mystery that the Lord who becomes fully present at Mass is the same Risen Savior who is seated at the right hand of the Father. Sacramentally present, Jesus Christ touches each of us who approaches the altar of the Lord.

WE ARE ALL LOOKING FOR GOD

If the meaning of Christmas can be obscured by our excitement in anticipation of the celebration and in all of the shopping and festivities that mark the season, then all the more can it be overwhelmed by the day-in and day-out proclamation of a secular and material gospel that knows no God, sees no manifestation of God with us, and does not experience God's loving care.

Interestingly enough, recent polls show that our fellow citizens are in the midst of a quest for spiritual meaning in their lives. While we see around us all kinds of new fads, New Age substitutes for religion, channeling, and other types of experiences, at the core is the atavistic human need for God. No amount of worldly goods, in whatever form we enjoy them, can ever satisfy this longing of the human heart. Perhaps it is best summed up by Jesus himself, who said that it is not by bread alone that we live.

THY KINGDOM COME

The *Catechism of the Catholic Church* reminds us that even after receiving the grace of our new life in Christ through baptism, we continue to experience human failure and the need for forgiveness. Christ's call to conversion continues to resound in our lives. "This second conversion is an uninterrupted task for the whole Church who 'clasping sinners to her bosom is at once holy and always in need of purification, and follows constantly the path of penance and renewal' " (see section 1428). The work of conversion is not just a human effort. It is the movement of a contrite heart drawn and moved by grace to respond to the merciful love of a gracious God who first loves us.

In the Christmas season, as we commemorate the Word made flesh among us, we can also reflect on our own personal spiritual renewal, recalling our pilgrimage of faith over the past years.

In the Lord's Prayer, we say "thy kingdom come." We are praying for the grace to manifest and make present more clearly the kingdom of God in our midst, as well as for the final coming of the kingdom in which we will be caught up in the glory of Christ and presented to his Father as the fruit of Jesus' death and resurrection. This is not theological speculation, but our firm anticipation of what is to come. At some point, the work that Jesus turned over to his Church to complete after his ascension into glory will reach a stage when the Lord as judge of the living and the dead shall return. He will claim what has been redeemed in his blood, reject that which is not made holy, and present to his Father his Church, his kingdom, the new creation for which he died and in anticipation of which he rose from the dead.

Each Christmas, as we remember and celebrate the story of Jesus' birth and the beginning of our redemption, may we do so with a fresh spirit of confidence in what we proclaim and a renewed spirit of solidarity, not only with our local diocesan church but also with the entire Body of Christ, the Church universal that also struggles with the challenge to be continually and constantly renewed in Jesus Christ.

May Christmas always be a time of confident faith, joy, and peace for us and our families—and a time when, in our own lives, heaven truly does meet earth.

QUESTIONS TO THINK ABOUT:

1. What is the true meaning of Christmas?
2. How does Jesus come to us today? What does it mean to say that Jesus will come again?
3. What does Jesus mean when he says that it is not by bread alone that we live?
4. What is meant by the Eucharistic presence of our Lord?
5. What am I doing to make manifest the kingdom of God right now?

CHAPTER 16

Mary, Mother of Jesus, Mother of God

WHY HAVE THE FOLLOWERS of Jesus always had such great love for his mother Mary? Why has there been such deep devotion for Mary, the mother of our Lord, from the very beginning of Christianity? Everywhere Christianity spread, there are signs of profound veneration of the mother of Jesus: chapels and churches bearing Mary's name, prayers in which Mary's name is invoked, and generations of children bearing the name Mary or some form of it.

The *Catechism of the Catholic Church* offers a clear answer: "Only faith can embrace the mysterious ways of God's almighty power. This faith glories in its weaknesses in order to draw to itself Christ's power. The Virgin Mary is the supreme model of this faith, for she believed that 'nothing will be impossible with God' " (see section 273 of the *Catechism*).

MARY'S FAITH IS OUR MODEL

Mary is the model of what our faith should be. Like us, Mary was a human being who had to struggle to hear and accept God's word and to grasp the mysterious ways in which God works. She did so with such consummate fidelity that she is forever the example of what we mean by faith—true, profound faith.

We cannot equal Mary in the wondrous mysteries in which she participated and in the privileges she received. But we can certainly emulate her faith. Mary said, in effect, "Although I do not always understand the unfolding of God's plan and God's providential order, nonetheless, if God calls I accept. If God challenges, I respond."

My faith and yours—the faith of all believers—is challenged to be the faith of Mary. As the *Catechism* says, she is the supreme model of what it means to believe.

The meaning of Mary's role in God's plan of salvation is summed up in Paul's letter to the Galatians: "But when the fullness of time came, God sent his Son, born of a woman, born under the law, to ransom those under the law so that we might receive adoption" (Galatians 4:4).

This explains why Mary has such an important role in the life of the Church. God sent his Son, the Eternal Word, into the world to take on flesh and become one of us for our salvation. It was through Mary that this happened. The incarnation required a human to cooperate with God's power and grace so that he who was conceived of Mary would be both divine and human. God told her, through Gabriel, that she was to be the Mother of God. When Mary said, "Let it be done to me according to your will" (Luke 1:38), through her faith she set in motion the divine plan that would lead to the restoration of all that was lost in the fall—and eventually to our salvation through the death and resurrection of her Son and our Lord Jesus Christ.

TITLES OF MARY

If we examine some of the titles of Mary, we discover that they are intimately connected with the fact that as the mother of Jesus she is also at the same time the Mother of God. These are her primary titles. She is the mother of Jesus. The Eternal Word took on flesh and became one of us through the cooperation of Mary, and thus she became the Mother of God.

"Theotokos" is a Greek title for Mary that the early Church selected to explain the mystery of how God is with us in Jesus Christ. As Jesus is truly God and truly man and Mary gave birth to him, she gave birth to the person who combines the human nature and the divine nature in one person. Hence the Church did not hesitate to call Mary the Theotokos or "the bearer of God."

Even before her son was born, Elizabeth called her "the mother of my Lord." As the *Catechism of the Catholic Church* teaches, "the One whom she conceived as man by the Holy Spirit, who truly became her son according to the flesh, was none other than the Father's eternal Son, the second person of the Holy Trinity. Hence the Church confesses that Mary is truly 'Mother of God' (*Theotokos*)" (see section 495).

It was God's providential design that his own Eternal Word would come among us, take on flesh, and be born as a human being. Through Mary, Jesus has a true human nature. Through the power of the Holy Spirit by which Mary conceived, Jesus has a true divine nature. The two natures are united in the fruit of Mary's womb, the person Jesus, who is God and man. Anything else we say about Mary will always refer back to the fact that she is the Mother of God.

THE IMMACULATE CONCEPTION

In anticipation that she was to bear the Son of God, Mary was preserved from her conception from any stain of original sin. We call this the Immaculate Conception. No taint of sin would touch her, so that she would be a fitting and worthy vessel of the incarnation.

The doctrine of the Immaculate Conception developed through many centuries, as its truth was better understood, and found expression in the Council of Trent as well as in the universal popular devotion of the faithful. In 1854, Pope Pius IX proclaimed in *Ineffabilis Deus* that "the Most Blessed Virgin Mary was, from the first moment of her conception, by a singular grace and privilege of Almighty God and by virtue of the merits of Jesus Christ, Savior of the Human Race, preserved immune from all stain of original sin."

The *Catechism of the Catholic Church* (in section 492) goes on to remind us, quoting the Second Vatican Council, that " 'the splendor of an entire unique holiness' by which Mary is 'enriched from the first instant of her conception' comes wholly from Christ: she is 'redeemed in a more exalted fashion, by reasons of the merit of her Son' " (*Lumen Gentium* 53, 56).

THE PERPETUAL VIRGINITY OF MARY

When it came time for Mary to give birth, she remained a virgin before, during, and after the birth of Jesus—a privilege granted to her to manifest that this was a unique moment in human history, the birth of Jesus who is God's Son as well as Mary's. The Church proclaims that Mary remained a virgin from the time of Jesus' conception on through his birth and afterward. As the *Catechism of the Catholic Church* points out, "the deepening of faith in the virginal motherhood led the Church to confess Mary's real and perpetual virginity even in the act of giving birth to the Son of God made man" (see section 499).

THE ASSUMPTION OF MARY

Since Mary was freed from original sin and its consequences, death could not claim Mary in the same manner that it takes each of us. It is the teaching and faith of the Church that Mary was assumed bodily into heaven when her earthly days were complete. Quoting from the Apostolic Constitution of Pius XII, *Munificentissimus Deus,* the *Catechism of the Catholic Church* teaches us that "the Immaculate Virgin, preserved free from all stain of original sin, when the course of her earthly life was finished, was taken up body and soul into heavenly glory, and exalted by the Lord as Queen over all things, so that she might be the more fully conformed to her Son, the Lord of lords and conqueror of sin and death" (see section 966). The Church speaks of Mary's "falling asleep" when it came time for her earthly life to end. She was assumed into heaven, so that—unlike the rest of the faithful, who must wait until the last judgment—Mary, body and soul, has already entered into heavenly glory.

MARY, MOTHER OF THE CHURCH

There is yet another title of Mary that relates her to each of us in a particular and personal manner. Mary is also our mother—she is Mother of the Church and therefore of each believer. The Second Vatican Council speaks of Mary as "clearly 'the mother of the members of Christ' . . . since she has by her charity joined in bringing about the birth of believers in the Church, who are members of its head" (*Lumen Gentium* 53). Pope Paul VI is quoted in the *Catechism of the Catholic Church* forcefully and clearly teaching that "Mary, mother of Christ" is "Mother of the Church" (see section 963).

THE ROSARY

When we turn to Mary as the mother of Jesus, the Mother of God, and our mother, we do so in prayer. One of the most enduring and beautiful devotions to Mary is the rosary.

The rosary is a manner of praying that both commemorates and meditates on the mysteries of the life of Jesus. It begins with the annunciation by the angel to Mary that she was to be the Mother of God, and continues through the other joyful mysteries, the sorrowful mysteries of Jesus' passion and death, and finally the glorious mysteries of our Lord's resurrection, his ascension, and Mary's final triumph as a sign of our own pending victory over death. (For a list of the mysteries of the rosary, see Chapter 47.)

By using the words of Scripture, the rosary challenges us to meditate on all of the mysteries of Mary's relationship to Jesus our Savior. For this reason, devotion to Mary and particularly the recitation of the rosary are an integral part of the prayer life of the Church. If we intend to put our faith into practice, the rosary is certainly a powerful instrument to help us accomplish that goal.

Why do we have such devotion to Mary? The *Catechism of the Catholic Church* reveals all the elements that explain our enduring and profound veneration of the mother of Jesus. We find our answer both in who Mary was, the mother of Jesus and the Mother of God, and in who she continues to be—our mother and model of faith. That answer prompts us to ask her to pray for us both now and at the hour of our death. We pray to Mary confident that she is "full of grace" and "blessed among women," and that her son and our Savior, Jesus, is "the fruit of her womb."

QUESTIONS TO THINK ABOUT:

1. What does God challenge me to do? Do I respond with Mary's faith?
2. How do I show my devotion to Mary? In what way is her faith my model?

CHAPTER 17

The Public Life of Jesus

THE EARLIEST RECORDED CHRISTIAN preaching stressed our Lord's death and resurrection. Examples of this apostolic teaching appear in Saint Luke's history of the Church's early years, the Acts of the Apostles, and also in the pastoral letters that we find in the New Testament. As the *Catechism of the Catholic Church* reminds us, the creed speaks only about the mysteries of the Incarnation (Christ's conception and birth) and the great paschal mystery (our Lord's passion, crucifixion, death, burial, descent into hell, resurrection, and ascension into heaven—see section 512 of the *Catechism*).

Interestingly enough, the great professions of faith do not mention the public life of Jesus—the rest of his life. Both the preaching of the faith and its articulation in the creed were intended to set before us the wonderful action of God by which we were saved through the death and resurrection of Jesus Christ. The creed is not intended to be an account of the life of Christ. But the faithful longed to know and preserve more details about Jesus and his life than those summed up in the creed.

THE GOSPELS: THE HONEST TRUTH ABOUT JESUS

To satisfy this desire, the four gospels were written. The core of each of the gospels is, of course, the account of the passion, death, and resurrection of Christ. In two cases, Matthew and Luke, the gospels begin with an account of the birth of Jesus. The rest of the four gospels is the effort of the writers—Matthew, Mark, Luke, and John—to proclaim Jesus as the

Messiah. To do that, they not only related his saving death and resurrection but also filled in the rest of the picture with details from the life, ministry, and teaching of Jesus in the three years that we call his public life.

Scripture scholars speak of three periods in the tradition or passing on of the story of Jesus: his own teaching and life here on earth; the subsequent testimony and teaching of the apostles and the early Church; and the eventual commission of the oral tradition to writing in the composition of the four gospels. As the Second Vatican Council's document on divine revelation confirms, the evangelists "told us the honest truth about Jesus" (*Dei Verbum* 19). In fact, Saint Luke tells us that care was taken to search out the testimony of those "who from the beginning were eyewitnesses and ministers of the word" so that the reader or hearer of the gospel might know "the truth concerning the things of which you have been informed" (Luke 1:2,4). The gospels tell us, not myths or stories about Jesus, but real events from his life and teaching that were cherished and passed on by his disciples and followers.

THE BAPTISM OF JESUS

Jesus' public life begins with his baptism by John in the Jordan. The Baptizer recognized and greeted Jesus with the title of the classical sacrificial figure from the Old Testament, "Lamb of God" (John 1:29; compare Isaiah 53:7). Later, as Jesus rose out of the water after being baptized, this acknowledgment was confirmed by an extraordinary vision. The Spirit of God was seen in the form of a dove over Jesus' head, and a voice was heard from the heavens proclaiming, "This is my beloved Son, with whom I am well pleased" (Matthew 3:17).

As the *Catechism of the Catholic Church* teaches us, the baptism of Jesus is on his part the acceptance and inauguration of his mission as God's suffering servant. He allows himself to be counted among sinners and is already proclaimed the Lamb of God who will take away the sins of the world (see section 536).

THE TEMPTATION OF JESUS

Closely following on his baptism come Jesus' temptations. The gospels speak of a period of retreat when Jesus went off into the desert where he remained for forty days, at the end of which he was tempted by the devil. The *Catechism* reminds us that Jesus' temptations reveal the way in which the Son of God is to be Lord, Messiah (see section 540). God's plan and

Jesus' fulfillment of that plan will be very different from the way proposed by Satan and expected by those who want an earthly Messiah, a temporal kingdom, and the fleeting power and riches of this world.

SIGNS AND MIRACLES

From the time of his baptism and temptation until his entrance into Jerusalem on what has come to be called Palm Sunday, Jesus filled his days teaching and working great signs or miracles that called attention to the kingdom that he proclaimed.

The first of Jesus' miracles was worked at Cana, a small village not far from where Jesus was raised. While he was attending a wedding reception with his disciples and his mother, the wine ran out. At Mary's request, Jesus changed ordinary water, six large stone jars of it, into wine (see John 2:1–11). It was the first of many signs. Jesus would continue to show his divine power over the elements of nature, sickness, and the frailty of the human body as well as possession by demons.

The purpose of Jesus' miracles was to draw people's attention to his message. To give credence to his proclamation, Jesus healed the sick, raised the dead, drove out evil spirits, calmed storms, and worked a host of other wonders. The gospels abound with stories of the blind seeing, the lame walking, and bread and fish multiplied to feed thousands. Interspersed through all of this ministry is the teaching of Jesus that the kingdom of God is at hand.

THE TEACHING OF JESUS

The public life of Jesus is filled with his teaching. He began in the synagogue at Nazareth when he read one of the messianic prophecies, rolled up the scroll, handed it back to the attendant, sat down, and announced that the prophecy was being fulfilled in him (see Luke 4:16–22). The kingdom, the manifestation of God's love, justice, truth, and salvation in our world were already present in Jesus. His preaching ministry was devoted to helping his followers see the truth of his revelation, the reality of his proclamation, and the presence of God's kingdom already coming to be in our world.

In John's gospel it is recorded that "never before has anyone spoken like this one" (John 7:46). Remember that Jesus taught with an authority rooted in his identity (see Chapter 2 of this book). He was able to speak with authority because of who he was. Jesus was "God with us,"

Emmanuel, and so he taught not as the Scribes and Pharisees did but rather as one having authority. He spoke with calm and compelling authority, and people recognized it. Scriptures tell us that they marveled at his words.

To help them and us grasp the mystery of God's kingdom breaking into our world, Jesus chose to speak in parables. At the same time as he worked the miracles to confirm the truth of what he had to say, Jesus used parables to help us grasp the meaning of what he revealed. The parables speak of ordinary things the agricultural people of the Holy Land knew well: sowing and harvesting crops, baking bread, lending and losing money, patching clothes, and so on.

Jesus used these simple examples to teach important lessons or to show the paradoxical nature of commonplace events in a way that captures the interest of readers down to our own day. The value of these stories, however, lies not simply in their style but in the fact that Jesus uses them to communicate the mystery of divine revelation. Jesus' preaching reveals the kingdom of God, the reign that God intends to exercise among his people. The parables illustrate that kingdom in ways we can understand.

Matthew's gospel, in particular, is rich in the collection of parables Jesus used to describe the kingdom of God. Here we learn, as the *Catechism of the Catholic Church* points out, that everyone is called to enter the kingdom (see section 543 of the *Catechism*). The kingdom belongs to the poor and the lowly, which means those who have accepted it with humble hearts (section 544). We find that Jesus invites sinners to the table of the kingdom (section 545). We also learn that Jesus was laying the foundation for the Church, which is the enduring presence of that kingdom (section 551).

PETER: FIRST AMONG THE TWELVE

From the beginning of his public ministry, Jesus chose certain men, twelve in number, to be with him and to share in his mission. He empowered the Twelve to participate in his authority and sent them out to preach the kingdom of God and to heal.

The *Catechism* underlines what the gospels have already highlighted—that Simon Peter holds the first place in the college of the twelve, and that to him Jesus entrusted a unique mission. It is on Peter that Jesus builds his Church, and it is to Peter that Christ consigns the keys to the kingdom of heaven. Almost as a culmination of his entire public ministry of preaching and working miracles, Jesus confronts Peter and asks him, "Who do you say that I am?" Peter responds as each of us seeks to respond each day with a lively and rich faith: "You are the Messiah, the Son of the Living God" (Matthew 16:15–16).

A look at his public life reveals for us Jesus' ministry of proclaiming the kingdom of God, his miracles to confirm the truth of his teaching, and the faith that he called forth from those who would accept his words. Each of us who follows in the footsteps of those first disciples is called to the same response—an act of faith.

Today, when we read the life of Jesus in the New Testament, we are not interested solely in history. We are disciples seeking in the actions and words of Jesus the reason for our faith in God's word, the motivation for our hope in the coming of the kingdom, and the strength to love as Jesus did with an intensity that manifests and actually brings into existence the kingdom of God in our midst.

QUESTIONS TO THINK ABOUT:

1. Which details in the gospel accounts of Jesus' life are clearest in my memory? Why did those details stand out for me?
2. Do earthly influence and power tempt me? Am I prepared with an answer to those temptations?
3. Would I be found among the poor and lowly who Jesus said would inherit the kingdom?

CHAPTER 18

The Cross and Our Redemption

NOT LONG AGO, WHEN I began the liturgy with the rite of blessing and the sprinkling of holy water, I heard a young child comment, "He splashed water on me!" His mother blessed herself with the sign of the cross and bent down to help him do the same. It was only with her quiet and caring assistance that he came to understand that something more significant was happening than just being "splashed" with water.

So it is with all the sacred events of our redemption. The Church, a holy mother, carefully relates what has happened and explains the theological significance of the event to us.

UNDERSTANDING JESUS' DEATH

In one of the most familiar and cherished forms of the Way of the Cross, we find this invitation to prayer: "We adore you, O Christ, and we praise you." To which the people reply, "Because by your holy cross you have redeemed the world." In this brief invitatory and response, Saint Alphonsus Liguori captures the essence of the article of the creed that proclaims Jesus Christ "suffered under Pontius Pilate, was crucified, died and was buried."

There is much more to this statement of faith than the simple recognition that Christ died. If by his cross Christ had not redeemed us, his death would have had little meaning. With the eyes of faith, the apostles and all the believers after them gaze on the cross and see much more than just the instrument on which Jesus hung until he died.

The fact of Jesus' death is the core of the historical account and personal witness found in Matthew, Mark, Luke, and John and referred to in other parts of the New Testament. Jesus was arrested, tried, sentenced, executed by crucifixion, and was buried.

The gospel accounts are not news reports like the ones we see in newspapers or on television. The historical fact of Jesus' death must be understood through the eyes of faith. The passion narratives report an actual event, but with the primary purpose of providing its theological significance and meaning. In other words, the death of Jesus is a theological reality that can be interpreted only with eyes of faith.

THE NEW ADAM

Toward the end of Mark's gospel, as Jesus takes his last breath, the eyes of the Roman centurion are opened and he recognizes the meaning of what is happening. "Truly this man was the Son of God!" (Mark 15:39). Later, in explaining more profoundly the theological significance of Jesus' death, Saint Paul points out that "just as through one transgression condemnation came upon all, so through one righteous act acquittal and life came to all" (Romans 5:18).

In explaining the meaning of Jesus' death, Paul develops the image of the new Adam, contrasting our fall from grace through the actions of the first Adam and our restoration to God's favor through the obedience of Jesus Christ, the second Adam. Jesus was sent into this world as a perfect redeemer. Though he is God, he is also truly man, our brother. As the new Adam (see 1 Corinthians 15:45) and head of the mystical body (see Ephesians 1:22), Christ has profound solidarity with all of us. He makes his disciples one with himself, as a vine is one with its branches (see John 15:15). Since we are united with him, his saving acts are our salvation.

Jesus' saving actions are the work of a person who is both God and man. They have, therefore, superabundant value. The man Jesus Christ, who is God's true Son, is the only one who could offer the Father a fitting atonement for sin. It is here that we see the immensity of God's saving mercy. Not only does God save us, but he brings about salvation in a generous way, in a manner that honors the humanity he saves. In Christ, God allows a human being to bring gifts worthy of salvation. Saint Paul puts it this way: "For if by that one person's transgression the many died, how much more did the grace of God and the gracious gift of the one person Jesus Christ overflow for many" (Romans 5:15).

THE PERFECT SACRIFICIAL LAMB

The *Catechism of the Catholic Church* speaks of Christ's cross and resurrection as the *paschal mystery.* To understand the full meaning of Christ's death, we must turn to the Passover sacrifice of the old law.

On the eve of the liberation of the chosen people from slavery under the pharaohs, the Lord spoke to Moses and Aaron: "Tell the whole community of Israel: On the tenth of this month every one of your families must procure for itself a lamb, one apiece or each household. . . . The lamb must be a year-old male and without blemish. . . . You shall keep it until the fourteenth day of this month, and then, with the whole assembly of Israel present, it shall be slaughtered during the evening twilight. They shall take some of its blood and apply it to the two doorposts and the lintel of every house in which they partake of the lamb. That same night they shall eat its roasted flesh with unleavened bread and bitter herbs" (Exodus 12:3, 5–8).

The Passover meal was integrally connected with the circumstances of the salvation—the liberation—of Israel. The symbols of nourishment procured for each household and eaten in haste while prepared for flight captured in ritual what God was about to effect in history. The whole series of saving events was ritually preserved in the annual repetition of the Passover meal in what was called a "memorial feast."

At the Last Supper the Lord instituted a new memorial sacrifice. The true "Lamb of God" (John 1:29) was about to be slain. By his cross and resurrection he was to free not just one nation from bondage, but all humanity from the more bitter slavery of sin. He was about to create a new people of God by the rich gift of his Spirit. There was to be a new law of love, a new closeness to God, a new promised land. All was to be new when God fulfilled the promises of the centuries in the paschal mysteries.

Jesus became the new Passover, the unique and final sacrifice by which God's plan of salvation was accomplished (see section 571 of the *Catechism*). In God's holy plan it was determined that the Word of God, made flesh in Jesus Christ, would be the expiatory sacrifice that would take away the sins of the world. In fact, we continue at the celebration of every Eucharist, in the holy sacrifice of the Mass, to proclaim before we receive the body and blood of Christ in communion: "This is the Lamb of God who takes away the sins of the world."

Jesus, as a man, recognized the command from his Father. "This command I have received from my Father" (John 10:18). Jesus freely accepted what his Father's will required. "This is why the Father loves me, because I lay down my life in order to take it up again . . . I lay it down on my own" (John 10:17–18). With free and obedient love, Jesus gave himself to his Father's will in his passion and death (Luke 22:42).

WE ARE ALL RESPONSIBLE FOR CHRIST'S PASSION

The *Catechism of the Catholic Church* reminds us that all of us by our own personal sins were in some way responsible for Christ's passion. In her teaching and in the witness of her saints, the Church has never forgotten that "sinners were the authors and ministers of all of the sufferings that the Divine Redeemer endured" (*Roman Catechism* I, 5–11). The Church does not hesitate to attribute to Christians a share in the responsibility for the passion and death of Christ. Through our sins, which he took on himself, and by his holy cross, Jesus redeemed the world.

It is also the Church's firm conviction and teaching that Jesus died for our sins in accordance with the Scriptures. The Sacred Scriptures foretold this divine plan of salvation. In the prophet Isaiah, we read of the Suffering Servant, who "through his suffering . . . shall justify many, and their guilt he shall bear" (Isaiah 53). Referring to a confession of faith that he himself "received," Saint Paul reminds us that "Christ died for our sins in accordance with the scriptures" (1 Corinthians 15:3).

The Catholic faith firmly believes and teaches that Jesus truly saved us by deeds performed in his human nature, by his obedient love, and by his patient endurance, as well as by offering his life as "a ransom for many" (Matthew 20:28). It was in his humanity that Jesus took on our sin and by dying atoned for it. The tragic consequences of Adam's sin could have no other remedy than the merit of the one mediator, our Lord Jesus Christ, who reconciled us to God in his own blood. As the Church has consistently taught, it is Jesus who merited for us justification by his most holy passion on the wood of the cross and made satisfaction for us to God the Father. The *Catechism of the Catholic Church* confirms that Christ's death is "both the paschal sacrifice that accomplishes the definitive redemption of men . . . and the sacrifice of the new covenant, which restores man to communion with God" (see section 613).

THE CROSS POINTS TOWARD THE RESURRECTION

The sufferings of Jesus and the glory of his resurrection are inseparably joined in the paschal mystery. The preface for Easter proclaims, "By dying he destroyed our death and by rising he restored us to life." The Father saved us not only by delivering up his son for us but also by raising him from the dead (see 1 Peter 1:3–5). It is for this reason that we say the cross of Christ points toward and is fulfilled in the resurrection. The paschal mystery includes both the death and the resurrection, both the expiation and the glorification, both the dying and the rising to new life.

When we reflect on the article of the creed that proclaims that Jesus was crucified, died, and was buried, we find ourselves joining Saint Paul, Saint Alphonsus Liguori, and so many others. With them we proclaim, "We adore you O Christ and we praise you, because by your holy cross you have redeemed the world."

QUESTIONS TO THINK ABOUT:

1. Am I as ready as the Roman centurion to recognize that Jesus is truly the Son of God?
2. How often have I crucified Jesus? In what ways are my sins responsible for his death?

CHAPTER 19

The Resurrection

"THIS IS THE NIGHT when Jesus Christ broke the chains of death and rose triumphant from the grave."

The Church begins the celebration of Easter with that proclamation (*Exsultet*). At the beginning of the Easter Vigil liturgy, after having witnessed the death and burial of Jesus on Good Friday, suddenly with unsurpassed joy the Church proclaims that Christ is risen, Christ is truly risen as he said.

With simple but firm conviction the creed affirms, "On the third day he rose again." The resurrection is the central mystery of our faith. It is an utterly astounding truth, because we have no point of reference against which to measure a rising to new life like Jesus' resurrection.

THE RESURRECTION IS A REAL EVENT

The one reality of which we are universally aware in human existence is death. Death offers no appeal or reprieve. There is an arrogance to its finality—no one comes back from the grave. This human experience is the reason why we fear death and stand in awe of it. It has a totality about it unlike anything we experience in life.

The story of Jesus should have concluded when he was placed in the tomb. The entrance was closed and life was ended. Yet for the apostles and for us it was only the beginning. The life, teaching, ministry, and promises of Jesus are all verified and authenticated in his resurrection. His kingdom is real and is unfolding in our very world through the power of his rising from the dead.

The Scriptures give witness to the resurrection as a real event. The apostolic Church, looking to both the empty tomb and the witnesses who saw Jesus alive after his death on the cross, affirms the teaching of the apostles (see section 639 of the *Catechism*).

THE LIVING TRADITION OF THE RESURRECTION

Already in just one generation after the resurrection of Jesus, Saint Paul could write to the Corinthians that he was passing on to them "what I also received: that Christ died for our sins in accordance with the scriptures; that he was buried; that he was raised on the third day in accordance with the scriptures . . ." (1 Corinthians 15:3–4). Paul is calling the attention of the Church to the living tradition passed on from those who saw the risen Lord. He is speaking of an established, verifiable tradition within the lifetime of people who could vouch for what they had seen and what they had preached. We are dealing with a real person, and there is continuity between the person who was taken down from the cross, wrapped in the shroud, and placed in the tomb and the one who is now risen from the dead and who appeared to numerous people.

Paul continues by pointing to the number of witnesses. The Risen Lord "appeared to Kephas, then to the Twelve. After that, he appeared to more than five hundred brothers at once, most of whom are still living, though some have fallen asleep. After that he appeared to James, then to all the apostles. Last of all, as to one born abnormally, he appeared to me" (1 Corinthians 15:5–8). Paul is reminding us that there is an unbroken line, and not a very long one at that, from those who could bear witness to the Lord's resurrection because they had seen him alive and Paul's own day. He is speaking of living, verifiable people in the community who can say, I know Jesus; I am his disciple; I was with him when he died. I have seen him after his resurrection. Jesus is alive!

THE WITNESS OF THE EMPTY TOMB

In addition to the witnesses there is the fact of the empty tomb. Jesus was placed in the tomb after his death. The tomb was sealed. Then some women came back on the morning of the first day of the week so that they could complete the work that they were not able to do because of the Passover. They wanted to prepare the body properly for its burial. They found an empty tomb.

Even in the New Testament, we hear about attempts by people who would rather explain away the resurrection than accept it. "You are to say, 'His disciples came by night and stole him while we were asleep' " (Matthew 28:13). It makes no sense that those men who were sent to guard the tomb would not have tried to stop the apostles from taking Jesus' body away. Clearly the fact of the empty tomb loomed very large in the minds of the apostles and disciples—the ancient Church. This truth makes its way into the creed. Why? Because it is a permanent and fixed memorial that confirms what the witnesses proclaim: Jesus has come back from the grave.

THE PHYSICAL REALITY OF THE RISEN CHRIST

All the scriptural accounts witness to the continuity of the life of Jesus before and after his resurrection. All insist that the Risen Jesus is truly the same Lord who had died. The physical reality of his presence is stressed. The disciples not only see the Risen Christ with their eyes but they are urged to touch his solid flesh and to know that he is bodily among them (Luke 24:39). When doubts arise, the Risen Jesus asks for food, so that by eating he might convince his followers of the tangible reality of the resurrection (Luke 24:41–43). Thomas is invited to examine the wounds to see that the very body that was crucified is now present (John 20:27). It was not a vision they saw. It was Jesus himself.

The apostles could see and touch the Risen Lord. Scripture reports a number of occasions on which he was seen by those who had not yet come to believe. The disciples on the road to Emmaus, for example, saw and spoke with him before they recognized him and believed. Mary Magdalene saw him at the tomb and mistook him for a gardener. But to believe in the Lord's resurrection today requires grace and faith. Even though Jesus is risen in his body, it still requires God's grace and an act of faith to believe that he is risen from the dead and that his resurrection is our new life.

BECAUSE JESUS ROSE, WE WILL RISE

As John Paul II reaffirmed in his encyclical letter *Dives in Misericordia:* "The fact that Christ 'was raised from the dead' (1 Corinthians 15:4) constitutes the final sign of the messianic mission, a sign that perfects the entire revelation of merciful love in a world that is subject to evil. At the same time it constitutes the sign that foretells 'a new heaven and a new earth' (Revelation 21:1), when God 'will wipe away every tear from their eyes and there will be no more death, or mourning, no crying or pain, for the former things have passed away' (Revelation 21:4)" (8).

The ultimate glory of the resurrection is that we too shall share in the new life, the eternal life that Jesus won by conquering death. As the *Catechism of the Catholic Church* teaches (see section 655), Christ's resurrection foretells our own. "For just as in Adam all die, so too in Christ shall all be brought to life" (1 Corinthians 15:20–22).

Jesus not only rose from the dead, but he promised that we would also share in his resurrection. Easter is not so much a time of historical reflection as it is one of rejoicing in our own hope of resurrection. While it is true that we look to the past and see in Christ's risen life new and eternal existence, we do so to confirm our own faith that some day we too shall rise from the dead.

In fact, Jesus described his whole mission as one of giving new life. "I came so that they might have life and have it more abundantly" (John 10:10). What Jesus offers is a life richer than any we could ever otherwise have, a life so radically new that we must be born again to receive it, a life that participates in his own resurrection in a glorified and eternal body.

This new life can fulfill our deepest yearnings. It has the power to make what is good in human life far better and richer. It takes our broken lives and heals them. It invites us to share in God's life so that we can actually be not just creatures of a loving God, but his friends. The good news of Jesus is proclaimed to the world by those who have already tasted the new life—his risen life—which he has given us through the Holy Spirit. Easter takes on an aura of celebration and an evangelical dimension as we recognize that we are called to share in the wonder of new life.

Death no longer has dominion over us. The Church sings at the Easter Vigil, "This is the night when Jesus Christ broke the chains of death." Those bonds also held us. Every time we proclaim our faith in Jesus, who on the third day rose again, we announce our own conviction that we too shall rise from the dead, break the bonds of death, and destroy the ultimate dominion of the grave.

QUESTIONS TO THINK ABOUT:

1. How do I know that Jesus really rose from the dead? Why do I accept that truth?
2. At Easter we celebrate Jesus' resurrection. What does this mean for me?
3. Have I attended and participated in an Easter Vigil to share in the richness of this particular liturgical commemoration? Should I plan to do so?

CHAPTER 20

Jesus' Return in Glory

"CHRIST HAS DIED, CHRIST is risen, Christ will come again."

When we proclaim that refrain at the eucharistic liturgy, we announce the firm conviction of the Church that Jesus will return—his second coming—this time to claim the new creation, his kingdom, and to judge the living and the dead.

Because of our personal concern for what happens to us after death, we tend to concentrate on our particular judgment and individual fate. This is understandable, since eternal life is in the balance when we face the Lord as our judge. But because of this legitimate preoccupation, we may fail to accentuate the article of the creed that reminds us Jesus will return in glory some unknown day in the future to bring an end to the world as we know it and claim those who form his new creation.

WE KNOW THAT JESUS WILL RETURN

The Catholic faith has always looked forward with confident hope to the final coming of Christ in glory. The early Christians' *marana tha,* Aramaic for "our Lord come" (1 Corinthians 16:22, Revelation 22:20), was an expression of their eager desire to witness the final triumph of Christ's saving work. The Lord was present to his people in many ways, but they awaited the definitive coming that would crown the effort to build his kingdom, end all sorrow and pain, and bring his people to the fulfillment of all their hopes and dreams.

In the Lord's Prayer we say "thy kingdom come." We are praying for the grace to manifest and make present more clearly the kingdom of God in our midst, but we are also praying for the final coming of the kingdom, in which we will be caught up in the glory of Christ and presented to his Father as the fruit of Jesus' death and resurrection.

This is not theological speculation. It is our firm anticipation of what is to come. At some point, the work that Jesus turned over to his Church to complete after his ascension into glory will reach a stage when the Lord will return. As judge of the living and the dead, he will claim what has been redeemed in his blood, reject that which is not made holy, and present to his Father his Church, his kingdom, the new creation for which he died and in anticipation of which he rose from the dead.

Jesus himself promised that he will come in glory as Lord and judge (Matthew 16:27; 26:64). At his ascension, when he ceased to be visibly present to his disciples, the promise was renewed: "This Jesus who has been taken up from you into heaven will return in the same way as you have seen him go into heaven" (Acts 1:11). Expectation of his coming shines through the New Testament and in the creed. The Church ever professes its faith in his promise: "he will come again in glory to judge the living and the dead."

The awaited coming of Christ in glory is called the *parousia.* Literally the word means "presence" or "arrival." The ceremonial entry of a king or triumphant conqueror into a city was called a parousia. The coming of Jesus, his parousia, in which he will be universally recognized as Lord of all, will be very joyful and triumphant. On that day those who have believed in him and served him will be vindicated; his glorification will be the beginning of the "life of the world to come."

THE FINAL TRIAL

The *Catechism of the Catholic Church* reminds us, however, that before Christ's second coming "the Church must pass through a final trial that will shake the faith of many believers" (see section 675). As the Church makes its pilgrim way through the centuries, it will always face persecution. In one form or another there will always be attacks on the Church—as there were on Christ. His new body, the Church made up of members united in him as head, will endure persecution, suffering, treachery, and abandonment. But it will endure, grow, and continue its ministry by bearing witness to the truth of everything Jesus taught.

The Church will enter the glory of the kingdom only through what the *Catechism* describes as the "final Passover," when she will follow her Lord in his death and his resurrection. The kingdom will be fulfilled then, not by a historic triumph of the Church through "a progressive ascendancy," but only by "God's victory over the final unleashing of evil, which will cause his bride to come down from heaven" (see section 677). God's triumph will take the form of the last judgment after the final cosmic upheaval that brings the universe as we know it to an end.

THE LAST JUDGMENT

On the wall behind the altar in the Vatican's Sistine Chapel, Michelangelo painted his version of the last judgment. Christ stands as the awesome central figure in the fresco. In much the same way that Saint Matthew's gospel depicts this final rendering of justice, we see that those who have been found worthy are already in heaven. Those who are sentenced to separation from Christ for all eternity are in various stages of despair. "When the Son of Man comes in his glory . . . all the nations will be assembled before him. And he will separate them one from another, as a shepherd separates the sheep from the goats. . . . Then the king will say to those on his right, 'Come, you who are blessed by my Father, inherit the kingdom prepared for you from the foundation of the world' " (Matthew 25:31–34).

Jesus is Lord. To him has been given the right to pass definitive judgment on the works and hearts of every person, since they belong to him as their redeemer. As the *Catechism of the Catholic Church* teaches, Jesus' death on the cross gave him the authority to judge us all (see section 679).

The Church makes a distinction between the particular judgment and the general judgment. At death, each of us will be judged according to our deeds. We will be found worthy of eternal life or will be counted among the damned. At the end of time, when Christ returns in glory, there will be a general judgment that brings an end to all of creation. The old order will pass away and a new creation—life in Christ—will be established. Particular judgments will be confirmed and God's glory will be affirmed.

The general judgment will not be simply a collective summary of all the particular and individual judgments of men and women after their deaths. The last judgment will be far more than a judicial passing of sentence upon the good and the evil. Through his judgment, God will establish the heavenly community, the final stage of his kingdom. In judging he will bring all to completion. As the *Catechism of the Catholic Church* succinctly states: "On judgment day at the end of the world, Christ will come in glory to achieve the definitive triumph of good over evil which, like the wheat and the tares, have grown up together in the course of history" (see section 681).

Only then shall we cease to be pilgrims and strangers. We shall know that we have come to the land where we are fully at home. Our period of exile will be ended when we have come to the life to which our whole heart can give itself in gladness. We shall begin to know and love one another fully in the light of God. We shall remember and understand all the experiences and trials of this life without regret, infinitely grateful that God has enabled us to serve him freely and has crowned his first gifts with the second life that exceeds all our longing and expectation.

AN INVITATION TO LIFE IN CHRIST

To this life, which we now understand so poorly, Christ earnestly invites us. To eternal life with him, the ultimate judge calls us. Now, in time, he challenges us through the promptings of the Holy Spirit and the voice of his bride, the Church. "The Spirit and the bride say, 'Come.' Let the hearer say, 'Come.' Let the one who thirsts come forward, and the one who wants it receive the gift of life-giving water" (Revelation 22:17).

On both the first Sunday of Advent at the beginning of the Church's liturgical year and at its conclusion on the Feast of Christ the King, the Church presents readings that recall the final coming of Christ—as if to say in the strongest possible way that the first coming of Christ, his birth at Bethlehem and his life with us, was to prepare us for his second coming. Then he shall return not as child, not as one of us, not as a crucified victim, but as the King of Glory who will call his good and faithful servants into his everlasting kingdom.

QUESTIONS TO THINK ABOUT:

1. When I think of Jesus' return, does it fill me with hope or with fear?
2. How do I respond to the invitation to life in Christ? Am I ready to say yes? Or am I still too much tied to this world?
3. What does it mean for me when I pray the petition in the Our Father, "Thy kingdom come"?

CHAPTER 21

The Holy Spirit

GOD SO LOVED US that he sent his only Son, Jesus, who also out of love died to save us. Jesus continues that work of salvation through the presence of God's Holy Spirit with us today. It is the mission of the Spirit to fill us with God's presence, so that we can be elevated in grace and truly become adopted children of our heavenly Father.

In Saint John's gospel Jesus told his disciples "I have much more to tell you, but you cannot bear it now. When he comes, however, being the Spirit of truth, he will guide you in all truth. He will not speak on his own, but he will speak only what he hears and he will announce to you the things to come" (John 16:12–13). Our understanding of the Holy Spirit begins with Jesus' explicit declaration that when his work was finished he would return to his Father in glory and that they would send the Holy Spirit to continue the work of salvation.

TOUCHED BY THE HOLY SPIRIT

In his First Letter to the Corinthians, Saint Paul teaches that "no one can say, 'Jesus is Lord,' except by the Holy Spirit" (1 Corinthians 12:3). In writing to the Galatians he tells us that God has sent the Spirit of his Son into our hearts crying "Abba, Father!" (Galatians 4:6). The *Catechism of the Catholic Church* reminds us that the knowledge of faith that allows us to call Jesus Lord, and to call God our Father, is possible only in the Holy Spirit. If we are to be in touch with Christ, we must first have been "touched" by the Holy Spirit (see section 683 of the *Catechism*).

The creed professes, "We believe in the Holy Spirit, the Lord, the giver of life, who proceeds from the Father and the Son." The Holy Spirit is a person of the Blessed Trinity, truly and eternally God. He is the Paraclete, the counselor that Christ promised the apostles would be given "to be with you forever" (John 14:16). In the Letter to the Romans we read that "the love of God has been poured into our hearts through the Holy Spirit that has been given to us" (Romans 5:5).

Catholics believe that God dwells with us most intimately by the gift of the Holy Spirit. The Spirit is sent by the eternal Father and by Jesus to give us light, comfort, and strength, and to stir up within us a newness of life. At the same time, the Holy Spirit seals our friendship with God and unites us with one another by the divine love that the Spirit pours into our hearts. When we profess our faith in God's Spirit, we do so aware that we are touching the mystery of the Holy Trinity. There is one God, but three divine persons—all equal, all eternal, each truly God.

THE GRADUAL REVELATION OF THE HOLY SPIRIT

The Holy Spirit is not simply a name given to the movement of grace within us. The Spirit is God. He is a distinct person of the Blessed Trinity. The *Catechism of the Catholic Church* states that the one whom the Father has sent into our hearts, the Spirit of his Son, is truly God. "Consubstantial with the Father and the Son, the Spirit is inseparable from them, in both the inner life of the Trinity and his gift of love for the world" (see section 689).

Centuries of salvation history show a gradual revelation of the Holy Spirit. In the Old Testament, we see a growing awareness and understanding of the working of God's Spirit in this world. The prophets taught that God was present in the world by his Spirit, and that in messianic days the life and joy given by the gift of God's Spirit would be abundant.

But the mystery of the Trinity, one God in three divine persons, was not yet revealed to the chosen people of God. Not until the time of the New Testament, the days of the paschal mystery and in the joys of Pentecost, was the Holy Spirit revealed as a distinct, divine person.

THE POWER OF THE SPIRIT AT PENTECOST

While Jesus spoke, particularly in his farewell discourse, of the Holy Spirit, and while it was clear that the apostles grasped something of the distinctive quality of the Spirit, the full impact of the Holy Spirit on the apostles and the Church was not felt until Pentecost. Even after the resurrection, the apostles remained timid, frightened, and unsure of themselves and the message that they were to proclaim. All that changed with Pentecost.

The Acts of the Apostles described how "When the time for Pentecost was fulfilled, they were all in one place together. And suddenly there came from the sky a noise like a strong driving wind, and it filled the entire house in which they were. Then there appeared to them tongues as of fire, which parted and came to rest on each one of them. And they were all filled with the Holy Spirit and began to speak in different tongues, as the Spirit enabled them to proclaim" (Acts 2:1–4). What is so striking is the change in each of the apostles after the outpouring of the Spirit. Timid, fearful, unsure, frightened men become bold, confident, assured witnesses of all that Jesus had taught them.

This is the power of the Spirit at work. Poured out into the heart of each believer in baptism and confirmation, the Spirit comes to make us a new creation. What is purely natural, tied to this earth and limited to the confines of the flesh, gives way to a new fullness and richness that can only be described as a new life, the life of God welling up within us. If it is nurtured and cared for, that new life will know no end.

THE HOLY SPIRIT IS THE SOUL OF THE CHURCH

Just as an individual comes alive through the outpouring of the Holy Spirit, so does the whole Church, the Body of Christ. As we are its members and Christ is the head, it is the Holy Spirit who is the "soul of the Church," as Pope Leo XIII said in his encyclical letter *Divinum Illud Munus,* quoting from Saint Augustine. In the words of Pope Pius XII in *Mystici Corporis,* it is the Holy Spirit "who, with his heavenly breath of life, is to be considered the principle of every vital and truly saving action in all parts of the body. It is he who, though he is personally present in all the members and is divinely active in them, yet also works in the lower members through the ministry of the higher ones."

The Church lives the life of the Spirit, and in the gifts of the Spirit the Church is able to continue the saving work of Christ—proclaiming the gospel, forgiving sins, healing what is broken, redeeming what struggles for salvation. Through the Church, individual members of the Body of Christ are made one with Christ in the Holy Spirit. Hence the Church is referred to as the very temple of God, the dwelling place of the Holy Spirit.

Baptism is conferred by water and the Holy Spirit. In confirmation the Christian is strengthened by the power of the Holy Spirit. When the sacrament of penance is administered, the very form of absolution notes the role of the Holy Spirit in the forgiveness of sins. The formula for the anointing of the sick calls down the grace of the Holy Spirit. The Eucharistic prayers of the Mass invoke the sanctifying power of the Holy Spirit so that the bread and wine might become the body and blood of Christ.

It is clear that the Holy Spirit, the presence of God in our world today, is found in his richest and fullest form in the Church, the Body of Christ, made alive by the power of the third person of the Trinity. As Saint Paul says in his First Letter to the Corinthians, "Do you not know that you are the temple of God, and that the Spirit of God dwells in you?" (1 Corinthians 3:16).

All the generous gifts by which God calls us to holiness are attributed to the Holy Spirit, the "sanctifier." The expression "gifts of the Holy Spirit" is also used in a particular sense to refer to a special set of endowments that are most conducive to growth in the life of grace. These gifts of the Spirit are traditionally listed as wisdom, understanding, counsel, fortitude, knowledge, piety, and fear of the Lord. It is from the prophet Isaiah that we learn the names of these gifts (Isaiah 11:2–3). For those receptive to God's presence, there is an experience of what are known as the Fruits of the Holy Spirit: Love, Joy, Patience, Kindness, Generosity, Faithfulness, Gentleness, Faith, Modesty, Self-Control, and Chastity (see Galatians 5:22–23).

THE AGE OF THE SPIRIT

Some spiritual writers and theologians call this the age of the Spirit. They refer to the fact that from the ascension of Christ into glory until his return to judge the living and the dead, the mission of building his kingdom and manifesting his saving love has been entrusted to his Church. It is the Spirit that gives life and power to the Church—a new life that allows us to call God Father, and a power that enables us to transform this world into the very presence of God's kingdom. When we call upon the Holy Spirit, we are in fact recognizing that power—a power that will be with each member of the Church, and the Church itself, as we make our way through this life to everlasting life with God in heaven.

QUESTIONS TO THINK ABOUT:

1. How do I know if I have been touched by the Holy Spirit?
2. Do I act as though I were God's temple, with God's Spirit dwelling within me? Do I manifest the fruits of the Holy Spirit? Would people who know me think of me that way?

CHAPTER 22

The Mystery and the Images of the Church

WE PROFESS OUR FAITH in the one, holy, catholic, and apostolic Church. What does it mean to say we believe in the Church?

As we answer this question, we come face to face with the mystery of Christ's presence in the Church.

THE CHURCH IS THE BODY OF CHRIST

The *Catechism of the Catholic Church* begins its discussion on the Church's origin, foundation, and mission by reminding us that the Church begins with God's plan for salvation, a plan that unfolded gradually in history (see section 758 in the *Catechism*).

The Father so loved us that he sent his Son to redeem us. Jesus so loved us that he died and rose again for our salvation. To continue the work of salvation, he selected apostles upon whom he would build his Church, his new body, which would have as its responsibility the task of carrying out and completing the work that he began.

The Church, then, shares in the very life of the risen Lord. Its members, those baptized into the Church, form a body with Christ as its head. It is through this Church that women and men are saved by coming to know Jesus Christ and through him united in grace to the Father through the outpouring of the Holy Spirit.

THE CHURCH IS THE PEOPLE OF GOD

The Second Vatican Council chose in a particular way to speak of the Church as the "people of God" (*Lumen Gentium* 9–17). The Church is not an abstraction. It is certainly not merely a group of officials in important positions, nor is it a group of individuals who determine what they will believe and how the Church will be constituted. The new Body of Christ is made up of all the members of the family of faith who are blessed with the gifts of the Spirit and are united as one body around the apostles and their successors—with Christ as its head.

The Pope, laymen and laywomen, bishops, religious, priests, and deacons, all gathered together in Christ, are the Church. We are the "people of God." Though each person has some specific call, a particular mission with its own responsibilities and functions, still all, together in Christ, make up a single, united people. All receive the same Spirit in baptism, all are nourished with the one Eucharist, all share the same hope of our calling. The fundamental equality in the new dignity of children of God is the basic note of the people of God.

The Church—the Body of Christ, the people of God—is structured, visible, and identifiable. The Lord Jesus endowed his community with a structure that will remain until the kingdom is fully achieved. He willfully chose the Twelve, with Peter as their head, as the foundation stones of "the new Jerusalem" (see Matthew 19:28). The apostles and the other disciples share in Christ's mission and his power precisely to lead and serve his new body, so that together through works of faith and love the kingdom of God may become manifest in our world.

THE CHURCH AND THE KINGDOM OF GOD

The Church and the kingdom of God are not precisely synonymous. The Church is a realization on earth of God's kingdom, whose final fulfillment is in eternity. The gospels tell us that Jesus "went around all Galilee . . . proclaiming the gospel of the kingdom" (Matthew 4:23). He taught a reality that was a real part of the messianic hopes of the Jewish people, which centered on the glorious kingdom that the messiah would establish. Yet when Christ spoke of the kingdom of God, he was careful to free the idea of the "kingdom" from the nationalistic hopes of the people among whom he lived. To accomplish this, he often emphasized the heavenly aspect of the kingdom and its interior religious character.

Aware of the intimate bond between the kingdom of God on earth and the Church, we need to look at what Jesus taught about his kingdom.

Like the reign of God, the kingdom is spiritual and will be perfected in the last days. It is not a political kingdom: "My kingdom does not belong to this world" (John 18:36). Yet Christ's kingdom is rooted in this world. Christ shows it to us as something visible, a community called together by him, of which he is the Good Shepherd, the true and lasting head.

The Church instituted by Christ and alive through the power of the Holy Spirit is both visible and spiritual. The *Catechism of the Catholic Church* quotes the Second Vatican Council: "The one mediator, Christ, established and ever sustains here on earth his holy Church, the community of faith, hope and charity as a visible organization through which he communicates truth and grace to all men" (*Lumen Gentium* 8). This one visible Church is at the same time a "society structured with hierarchical organs and the mystical body of Christ; the visible society and the spiritual community; the earthly Church and the Church endowed with heavenly riches" (*Lumen Gentium* 8).

IMAGES OF THE CHURCH

The New Testament is replete with many images that help us grasp the profound nature of the Church.

One of the most beautiful images used by Saint Paul to portray the nature of the Church and its relation to Christ is that of a bride whom Christ deeply loves. So much does he love the Church that he "handed himself over for her" (Ephesians 5:25). Through his gifts, sacraments, and saving words, he cares for her and makes her holy "cleansing her by the bath of water with the word" (Ephesians 5:26). His love makes her a resplendent bride, "the Church in splendor, without spot or wrinkle or any such thing . . . holy and without blemish" (Ephesians 5:27).

One of the most ancient images of the Church, and one of the best known, is our "holy mother Church." The Church is called mother because, in virtue of Christ's love, she gives birth to many children. All the faithful are born of her: "by her preaching and by baptism she brings forth to a new and immortal life children who are conceived of the Holy Spirit and born of God" (*Lumen Gentium* 64).

Because Christ continues to nurture our life through the Church, we should honor her as both mother and teacher. By the grace of God, we are enlightened by the Spirit to recognize the Church as Christ's faithful bride, with whom he is inseparably united and in whom he cares for his people. Therefore we owe unfailing loyalty to her. As Saint Cyprian expressed it so clearly centuries ago: "You cannot have God for your father if you have not the Church for your mother" (*On the Unity of the Catholic Church* 6).

Perhaps the most powerful image of the Church is that of the Body of Christ. As the *Catechism of the Catholic Church* teaches us, "The comparison of the Church with the body casts light on the intimate bond between Christ and his Church. Not only is she gathered around him; she is united in him, in his body" (789). The Body of Christ is one. Christ is head of the body. The faithful are the members of the living body alive in the Holy Spirit.

THE ONE, HOLY, CATHOLIC, AND APOSTOLIC CHURCH

Probably no article of the creed today is as much misunderstood as our profession of faith in the one, holy, catholic, and apostolic Church. All around us we see clusters of people who claim to be the Church. People speak of being born again in Christ, of finding Christ, of living in Christ—and yet some would fashion their own teaching, step aside from the two-thousand-year-old continuity of Christ's living Church, minimize the sacramental life available to us in the Church, and reject the apostolic leadership of the Church as if it were not a part of Christ's will.

The true Church, the one Church founded by Christ, is not of our making, nor can it and its teaching be interpreted by us according to a majority vote. The Church of Christ, the Body of Christ in the world today, is the visible, structured, hierarchical manifestation of the Risen Lord at work to complete the task assigned him by the Father—to bring all women and men together into one family, anointed in one Holy Spirit, made holy through the presence of Christ in the Eucharist. The faith of this body is to be translated into works of love that will transform the world and make it here and now the manifestation and realization of the kingdom of God. We have not yet arrived, but the beginnings of that kingdom, the presence of God's Spirit, the saving power of the sacraments, are found in our world and are at work in our lives in that Church that we profess in the creed to be the object of our faith.

QUESTIONS TO THINK ABOUT:

1. How close does my own parish come to treating all the children of God as fundamentally equal? What can I do to help us come closer to that ideal?
2. Why did Jesus establish a Church?
3. How would I respond to the statement that it really doesn't matter if you belong to the Catholic Church or go to Mass as long as you have faith in Jesus?

CHAPTER 23

The Marks of the Church

RECOGNITION IS EVERYTHING, WE are told. Each year, corporations all over this land spend hundreds of millions of dollars on brand-name recognition—television or radio commercials, billboards, magazine advertisements, celebrity endorsements, or direct mailing to millions of households. Sometimes the name becomes so familiar that it becomes generic. We ask for Kleenex, Coke, and Jell-O as if they were the only facial tissue, cola soft drink, or gelatin dessert on the market.

Politicians, too, believe that recognition is everything. At election time, candidates do all they can to get their name in the public eye.

Recognition is also important to Christ's Church. How are we to identify the one true Church founded by Jesus Christ as his body and the way to our salvation?

IDENTIFYING THE TRUE CHURCH

In ancient professions of faith, the Catholic Church identifies itself as "one, holy, catholic, and apostolic." These words, found in the Nicene Creed and used at Sunday Mass, refer to what are traditionally known as the "marks" of the Church—that is, traits that make it possible for a person to recognize the true Church.

In section 811 of the *Catechism of the Catholic Church,* we find this citation from the *Dogmatic Constitution on the Church* of the Second Vatican Council: "This is the sole Church of Christ, which in the Creed we profess to be one, holy, catholic, and apostolic" (*Lumen Gentium* 8).

As the Holy See teaches, these four characteristics, inseparably linked with each other, indicate essential features of the Church and her mission on earth. In an 1864 letter from the Holy See to the bishops of England, we find that "each of these marks is so linked to the others that it cannot be separated from them." Each quality, which we call "a mark," is so joined with the others that all of them form one coherent and interrelated idea of what Christ's Church must be. Those qualities must be present, verifiable, and interrelated in such a way that each sign or mark supports the others. The purpose of these identifying marks, which grow out of the very nature of the Church, is to help strengthen the faith of the believer and at the same time attract the unbeliever to investigate the Church more fully. When we look to them for a "trademark" to identify the true Church, we expect to find all the qualities of unity, holiness, universality, and rootedness in the apostles.

HUMAN IMPERFECTION

Each of these signs also has a human dimension. Side by side with these wondrous qualities that the Church possesses through its identity with Christ, there exist human imperfections. In fact, the effectiveness of the signs is sometimes compromised by the scandals that arise from the sinfulness of the human members of the Church, both clergy and laity. Each sign has a paradoxical aspect.

The Church is one, and yet we find divisions among the faithful—and even more marked divisions among a wide range of communities of people who designate themselves as followers of Christ and members of "denominations." We attest to the universality of the Church, and yet we find some members of the Church placing their allegiance to their ethnic origins over the call to oneness. These and other examples give us pause. Yet we must remember that the qualities of the Church called "marks," while diminished in the human membership of the Church, are nonetheless real, enduring, and identifying signs that grow out of the divine quality of Christ's Church.

THE ONE CHURCH

When the *Catechism of the Catholic Church* addresses the "sacred mystery of the Church's unity," it states quite clearly that the Church is one because of her source, the unity of God (see section 813). The *Catechism* goes on to remind us that the Church is one because of her founder, Jesus Christ, who is the Word made flesh and who came among us to restore the unity of all in one people and one body. The Church is also one because of her soul. Here the catechism quotes the Second Vatican Council in teaching us, "It is the Holy Spirit, dwelling in those who believe and pervading and ruling over the entire Church, who brings about that wonderful communion of the faithful and joins them together so intimately in Christ that he is the principle of the Church's unity" (*Unitatis Redintegratio* 2.2).

The Church is also one in the faith that its members believe and profess. It has an essential unity of worship. All are united to the one saving sacrifice of Christ in the Eucharist, and eat of the one sacred bread that unites all in Christ. The faithful members of the Church all receive the same sacraments. There is also a unity in our communion with the Church throughout the world. The "local Churches" or dioceses, each under its own bishop, are united in communion with and in a common allegiance to the Pope, who is a sign and servant of the unity of the Church. The unity we speak of is a living reality springing spontaneously from the gift of Christ's grace.

THE HOLY CHURCH

It is the grace of Christ that also makes the Church holy. First and foremost, this holiness exists in its founder, Jesus Christ. From him and from his Holy Spirit comes all true holiness. Because of Christ's presence, the doctrine the Church teaches is holy; it remains unalterably his teaching that brings us to salvation. The Church's worship is holy. The sacraments it administers to the members of the Church throughout the whole world make it possible for every believer to live a truly Christian life conformed to Jesus Christ.

It is to this holiness that the Church invites all of us. In this holiness rooted in the presence of the Holy Spirit and manifested in the sacramental life of the Church, particularly the Eucharist, the Church continues in spite of the many sins of its members.

We see all around us the fruits of holiness in the lives of truly faithful followers of Christ, even in an imperfect world marred with failure, compromise, and sin. Our own era is not without its testimony to the holiness found in the lives of so many faithful women and men. While we cannot easily identify the hidden crosses that many people carry or the silent sorrows they bear, their persistent fortitude and courage rooted in their faith in God's loving care sustains them and us in ways not always visible as works of the Church. All of us are aware that there are modern martyrs for the faith. The holiness of Christ's Church continues to be evident.

Wherever the Catholic faith is lived sincerely, Jesus brings forth healthy fruit that only a good tree can bear.

THE CATHOLIC CHURCH

According to the *Catechism of the Catholic Church,* the word "catholic" means "universal," in the sense of "according to the totality" or "in keeping with the whole" (see section 830). The catechism notes that the Church is catholic both because of Christ's presence in her and because she has been sent to proclaim his gospel to all the people of the world (see sections 830–31). The Catholic or universal Church makes its home throughout the entire world, with the successor of Peter as its head.

THE APOSTOLIC CHURCH

Finally, we speak of the Church as apostolic because it is founded on the faith of the apostles. The Church today is in living continuity with the Church of the apostolic age. Christ founded his Church on the apostles, and they in turn appointed successors. The Church is apostolic because it continues to be governed by such successors, who pass on the faith "that comes from the Apostles" (see the First Eucharistic Canon).

The *Catechism of the Catholic Church* succinctly summarizes the Church's teaching. The Church is built "on a lasting foundation: 'the twelve apostles of the Lamb' (Revelation 21:14). She is indestructible . . . She is upheld infallibly in the truth: Christ governs her through Peter and the other apostles, who are present in their successors, the Pope and the college of bishops" (section 869).

Even though the Church is a spiritual communion, a divine reality, a mystical body, it nonetheless is identifiable in the world through the marks or signs that distinguish it and point to it as Christ's one true Church.

EAST AND WEST

The one Church of Christ is found throughout the entire world. Each diocese, or as it is technically called "particular" church, is an expression of the one, holy, catholic, and apostolic Church. Particular churches attempt to live the faith in their own culture using local languages and traditions.

The Eastern Churches are those whose origins are found in that part of the world that was once the Eastern Roman Empire. The churches of the East have their own distinctive traditions evident in their liturgy, theology, and law. The Western Church finds its focus in Rome, and is sometimes referred to as the Latin Church. All of the individual particular churches, Eastern or Western, in communion with the Apostolic See, Rome, are part of the Catholic Church.

QUESTIONS TO THINK ABOUT:

1. How does my own human imperfection obscure the marks of the Church—unity, holiness, universality, and rootedness in the apostles? What could I do to let those marks show through me?
2. What divisions mar or cloud the unity of the Church in my own parish and diocese? What can I do to make those issues less divisive?
3. Do I really think of the Church as "catholic"—that is, universal? Do I sometimes value my particular parish more than the universal Church?

CHAPTER 24

Who Speaks for the Church?

WHO SPEAKS FOR THE Catholic Church? People frequently send me articles or letters that raise this fundamental question. It calls for an answer that reflects the Church's understanding of what the Church is and how it functions.

A HIGHER AUTHORITY?

One article that I received, with a number of attachments, challenged some very basic liturgical practices that resulted from the liturgical reform following the Second Vatican Council. With supporting declarations from a purported "seer," the author of the article denounced all priests and bishops around the world who distribute communion in the hand. The person who wrote me made it very clear that the "seer" who spoke from allegedly personal revelations had denounced such a practice and that her authority superseded that of bishops including the Pope.

In the same mail was a letter from a person who challenged the Church's doctrine on the indissolubility of the marriage bond, the teaching that sexual relations should be reserved for marriage, and a number of other Catholic beliefs. He cited a theologian who taught him at a Catholic university as his authority for rejecting the teaching of what he called the "institutional" Church. The basic thrust of his argument was that he was free to disagree with the teaching of the Church if he felt he had sufficiently good reason to do so.

These two positions represent currents in the Church today that cause us to ask, "Who speaks for the Church?" In both instances, an appeal has been made to a higher authority. In the first case the higher authority is direct communication with God, a revelation through Mary, or an appeal to the writers' own interpretation of tradition—which they insist overrides present papal and conciliar magisterium. In the second case, the appeal is to personal knowledge that, supposedly, is sufficient to form conscience and override the direct and explicit teaching of the Church. The result for both is the same: the claim to have authority to speak for the Church in a way that sets aside the role and place of the Pope and the bishops.

CHRIST IS THE SOURCE OF THE CHURCH'S AUTHORITY

Against both of these interpretations of the nature of the Church and in response to the question of who speaks for the Church, the *Catechism of the Catholic Church* devotes a large section entitled "The Hierarchical Constitution of the Church" (section 874). It tells us that Christ himself is the source of the Church's authority.

Jesus established the Church on the apostles and gave to Peter a unique and enduring authority. The Pope is the visible source of the Church's unity (section 882), and the individual bishops are the foundations of unity in their own dioceses (section 886). Following the traditional teaching of the Church, the *Catechism* lists the duties of the bishops as teaching, sanctifying, and governing. In each of these areas, the bishop in the local church or diocese, together with the Pope for the whole universal Church, speaks for the Church.

Why? The answer is found in Jesus' guarantee that the Church would not be led astray. As the *Catechism* teaches: "In order to preserve the Church in the purity of faith handed on by the apostles, Christ who is the Truth willed to confer on her a share in his own infallibility" (see section 889). Christ chose men as apostles whom he would anoint in the Holy Spirit and guide as they taught and led his Church. They in turn chose successors through the laying on of hands and the imparting of the Spirit to continue this work. It is the Spirit, poured out in the sacrament of holy orders, who is the ultimate source of the bishops' fidelity to the truth.

THE BISHOPS ARE THE TEACHERS

The responsibility of the bishops is to teach in the name of Christ. This authority extends to applying the gospel to our own day. Theologians may speculate and attempt to understand more deeply the revelation of our

Lord, but theological opinion can never be placed on an equal footing with the authoritative teaching of those to whom Christ has entrusted the care of his flock. Theological examination, questioning, interpretation, and testing the limits of Catholic teaching have their academic purpose, but a theologian or even a school of theological thought cannot presume to cross the line from theological speculation to pastoral guidance of the faithful. The pastors of the Church, the Pope and bishops, have been explicitly charged to guide the faithful in the way of salvation. In a confrontation between theological speculation and authoritative Church teaching, it is the latter that is the sure norm that guides us along Christ's way to eternal life.

A HARD SAYING

On one occasion when Jesus was teaching, he spoke of how he intended to give his own Body and Blood for "the life of the world." Some, who found this teaching difficult, disputed it and walked away. As Saint John tells us: "Many of his disciples, when they heard it, said, 'this is a hard saying; who can listen to it?' " (John 6:60). But Jesus did not change his teaching because some of the disciples disagreed. In fact, the gospel says Jesus repeated it. He did not amend it. He affirmed that he intended to give us his own Body and Blood for our salvation.

Tragically, the same narrative recounts: "After this many of his disciples drew back and no longer went about with him" (John 6:66).

Still, our Lord did not back down. He is the way, the truth, and the life. We come to him for enlightenment, grace, and redemption. It is God's plan that Jesus reveals. We do not set the rules. We are not the ones who fashion the way in which we are saved, redeemed, and granted a share in the glory of God's kingdom—God does.

When confronted with dissent, Jesus said to the twelve, "Will you also go away?" Simon Peter answered him, "Lord, to whom shall we go? You have the words of eternal life; and we have believed, and have come to know, that you are the Holy One of God" (John 6:67–69).

LEAVING THE CHURCH IS LEAVING CHRIST

As the Church has always taught and has again reaffirmed in the *Catechism of the Catholic Church,* the bishops are the successors of the apostles. They have the God-given task of teaching in the name of Christ, sanctifying by the power of Christ, and governing with the authority of Christ (see sections 888–96). Given Christ's identification with his Church, which is his

Body, it is an illusion to think that one can walk away from the Church and not in some way step aside from Christ.

Recently I read a newspaper account about a man who defiantly announced that he had ceased going to church or attending Mass because his former parish church was closed as a result of diocesan reorganization. The paper reported this man's assertion that he had not been to Mass in over two years. The news account went on to say that the same man claimed the only church he belonged to is the building now closed.

I feel a deep pain for anyone who walks away from the Eucharist, whatever their anger or disagreement. I have an equally profound concern for those who mistake one building for the saving, grace-filled reality that is the Catholic Church, the Body of Christ, the beginnings of God's kingdom in our world. The Catholic Church is a far greater reality than any edifice built by human hands.

THE BISHOPS: STEWARDS OF THE LITURGY

The bishops also have responsibility for the liturgy, the worship of the Church. Citing the Second Vatican Council the *Catechism of the Catholic Church* reminds us "that the bishop is 'the steward of the grace of the supreme priesthood' " (*Lumen Gentium* 26; see section 893 of the *Catechism*). The current liturgical norms approved by the Holy See and the bishops of the United States for the Church in this country are binding on all the faithful. To invoke a private revelation or a personal preference to set aside liturgical norms is to vest oneself with an authority one cannot possibly have.

There is today, as there has always been, a temptation to treat the Church as if it were incidental to salvation. This theory places the individual's personal feelings and preferences at the center. Yet Christ founded his Church to be the gift to lead us to eternal life. We walk away from that gift at our own peril. We do not get back at the Lord, the Church, the Pope, the bishops, or our pastors if we, for whatever reason, step aside from the sacramental life of grace or from the Church itself. But we can do irreparable harm to ourselves.

Perhaps the *Catechism of the Catholic Church* has devoted such a large section to the function of bishops because the acceptance of the authority of Christ exercised by bishops throughout the world is a "hard saying" today. Nevertheless, it is clear that it is the bishops with the assistance of the Holy Spirit who have the responsibility for the guidance of the whole Church and particularly for the local church entrusted to their individual care.

QUESTIONS TO THINK ABOUT:

1. Have I ever thought of leaving the Church? What held me back?
2. Do I treat the teachings of the Church as though they had the full authority of Christ behind them?
3. Which teachings of the Church do I find most difficult to accept? Where would I go for help in understanding them?

CHAPTER 25

The Church's Teaching Office

HOW OFTEN DO WE hear people outside and sometimes even inside the Church say, "Why should I follow the teaching of the Pope and the bishops when I have my conscience to guide me?" The question may also take the form of "How can the Church bind me in conscience?" The answers to these questions are found in the *Catechism of the Catholic Church,* where it deals with such words as magisterium, infallibility, and authority. In order to answer the question of why we should follow the teaching of the Church, we need to look at each of these words.

MAGISTERIUM

Magisterium is a Latin word that is best translated into English as "teaching office." It refers to the bishop's responsibility as teacher for the Church.

In a commentary on the *Catechism of the Catholic Church, The Teaching of Christ* in its fourth edition points out (pages 181–82) that "Only God can make known to us the truths we most need to know, the mysteries hidden in God, the purposes and plans of Him who is the source and final goal of all that is real. God stirred up people of His own choosing to speak in His name (cf. Rom. 10:14–15), and in His providence He made it possible for hearers to recognize that these chosen ones, called prophets, did speak for Him . . . God's Son continues to speak to us through those He chooses to send in His name (cf. Jn. 15:16). They must not be self-appointed; they must be called in His name (cf. Jer. 23:13–28)."

Christ did not leave us as orphans. Once he returned to his Father in glory, he called those he had chosen and anointed in the Holy Spirit to continue to teach everything that he had made known to them and to proclaim it even to the ends of the earth. As Christ gathered a people that was to be his Church, so the apostles were to continue the mission of bringing all men and women into this one family. By Jesus' will, the apostles would speak in his name and with his authority when they taught on matters of faith and morals.

AUTHORITY, IN CHRIST'S NAME

When you think about it, it is only logical. How else would Christ's words, their meaning and their application, be passed on generation after generation, century after century, once he was no longer with us in the flesh? There would have to be those who could articulate his will with the assurance that they were guided by his Holy Spirit.

Christ committed to the apostles the task of preaching his word in his name—that is, with his authority. He assured them of the assistance of the Spirit, who would guard them in all truth in speaking (see John 14:16, 26). He commanded them to teach his word to all nations, binding the hearers to believing their words as the words of God and he promised to be with them in their preaching until the end of time (see Matthew 28:20).

The Church, however, does not hand on doctrine in a static way. It teaches and believes a living faith. While there is a deposit of faith—a core of teaching that the Church and specifically the bishops are charged to preserve and maintain—there is also the obligation, under the guidance of the Holy Spirit and with prayer and study, to arrive at a greater understanding of the divine word. In their postresurrection faith, Mary and the apostles may well have grasped the mystery of Jesus far more richly than we, though not in the technically articulated ways to which centuries of reflection on the faith led, because for the whole community of faith—the Church—there has been a growing understanding of the revealed word.

Development of doctrine does not mean the abandonment of doctrine or the substitution of new dogmas for old; the Church will never deny what it has firmly believed. The First Vatican Council taught "that meaning of the sacred dogmas which has once been declared by holy mother Church must always be retained." Genuine development of doctrine always proceeds along consistent lines with full continuity to the apostolic tradition of the Church.

THE ORDINARY MAGISTERIUM

Theologians and scholars help the Church to grow in the full understanding and appreciation of truth. To be sure, they are not official teachers, as bishops are, and theologians do not as such receive with the bishops that "sure gift of truth" (*Dei Verbum* 8), which the apostolic witnesses of faith receive. But they are important helpers of the bishops, for they are a resource providing the Church with appropriate assistance in understanding divine revelation.

When bishops teach, they normally teach in a very direct, pastoral way. They preach the gospel. They see to the catechetical instruction of the faithful in their care. They watch over the forms of prayer and worship in which the faith is lived and exercised. They also teach in their instructions and pastoral letters in accord with the revelation that has been entrusted to them in their pastoral office. This is called the Church's *ordinary magisterium*.

We sometimes see the term "universal and ordinary magisterium" of the Church. This technical term means a teaching that is universally held "everywhere, at all times and by all people in the Church" and taught as the ordinary teaching of the Church. This teaching is presumed to be infallible, and does not require any other activity on the part of the bishops to assume that the faithful hold that teaching in a definitive manner.

EXTRAORDINARY TEACHING

But every once in a while in the life of the Church something that has been taught as true is challenged. It then becomes imperative for the Church to exercise its *extraordinary magisterium*—to speak out clearly and to define in an extraordinary way that a particular teaching is to be held by anyone who claims to be Catholic. The exercise of the extraordinary magisterium is a rare event. When the Church declared in the Council of Trent that in the Eucharist we find the presence of Jesus' Body and Blood, soul and divinity, that was an extraordinary act of the magisterium to address an apostolic teaching in the Church that was being challenged in the Reformation. Closer to our own time, the 1950 definition of Mary's assumption provides us another example of the exercise of an extraordinary magisterium.

INFALLIBILITY

The gift that empowers the Pope and bishops to proclaim the truth unhesitantly and with full confidence that what they teach is true is called *infallibility.* Christ gave the shepherds of his people the gift of infallibility in matters of faith and morals (see sections 889 and 890 of the *Catechism*).

The gift of infallibility is a gift for the whole Church. The Pope and bishops teach infallibly—that is, with the assurance of the Holy Spirit that what they teach is true, when they proclaim a teaching as something to be definitively held. The Church may teach infallibly any element in the whole deposit of divine revelation that Christ has entrusted to his Church. Theologians generally point out that infallibility extends also to other truths not actually contained in revelation but intimately associated with God's divine revelation.

There is also an infallibility in believing. The unerring faith of the Church is a gift of the Holy Spirit, who dwells in all of the faithful. This gift enlightens the eyes of faith, so that they may recognize and obediently acknowledge the word that God causes to be spoken definitively in his Church as the word of God, certain and entirely reliable. The two aspects of infallibility, that of believing and that of teaching, are intimately related.

AUTHORITY

As a rule of thumb we can measure our obligation to respond to the teaching of the Church by recognizing that what the Church teaches in her ordinary proclamation of the faith obliges us to full assent of intellect and will. When it is clearly noted that any specific teaching is proclaimed as held by the whole Church at all times as a part of her ordinary teaching, then it is assumed that all the faithful must hold that teaching in a definitive way. All such teaching is infallibly taught. The category of extraordinary magisterium is also an example of infallible teaching, but this time by an explicit statement on the part of the hierarchy because an article of the faith has been contested.

When we talk of magisterium, infallibility, and teaching with authority we do so as a way of clarifying what every faithful member of the Church knows intuitively—that when the Church speaks in matters of faith and morals it speaks with the authority of Christ and it speaks for our good.

QUESTIONS TO THINK ABOUT:

1. Which activities of the magisterium are most visible to me? How do they affect the way I live my life? Do I take the teaching of the Church seriously?
2. Do I make an effort to read documents issued by the Pope, the United States Conference of Catholic Bishops, or my own bishop—or do I rely just on media reports?

CHAPTER 26

Called to the Service of God

WHEN WE THINK OF the Church, one image of it is a great family of men and women united with Christ and with each other in baptism. Saint Paul uses other images. He speaks of the Church as the Body of Christ with our Lord as the head and we as the members. Paul develops the teaching on the mystical body in a number of his epistles. Writing to the faithful at Corinth, he says: "Now you are Christ's body, and individually parts of it" (1 Corinthians 12:27).

ONE BODY, DIFFERENT MEMBERS

In baptism Christ gave each of us the gift of the Holy Spirit. It is this Holy Spirit, the soul of the Catholic Church, that binds us together in a unity that overcomes every kind of division. "For in one Spirit we are all baptized into one body, whether Jews or Greeks, slaves or free persons . . ." (1 Corinthians 12:13).

Just as in the natural body, the eyes, ears, and feet have diverse functions, so there are diverse roles for the members of the Church. In the Body of Christ, some are apostles, some are teachers, some are administrators, and some have other roles (see 1 Corinthians 12:28–31). All, however, are called to the greatest gifts and duties, to the glory of believing, hoping, loving. This diversity of roles does not harm, but serves the unity of the body. God arranged the organs of the body, each one of them, as he chose. If all were a single organ, where would the body be? As it is, there are many parts, but one body (1 Corinthians 12:18–20).

The Eucharist in its own unique way nurtures the unity of Christ's Body. "The bread that we break, is it not a participation in the body of Christ? Because the loaf of bread is one, we, though many, are one body, for we all partake of the one loaf" (1 Corinthians 10:16–17). Thus it is precisely through our union with Christ that we become members of one another in the Church (cf. Romans 12:5). So united, the members are to love one another as themselves, even to love one another as though loving Christ. "If one part suffers, all the parts suffer with it; if one part is honored, all the parts share its joy" (1 Corinthians 12:26).

CHRIST THE HEAD

Christ is the head of his body. "He is the head of the body, the Church" (Colossians 1:18). To live as a Christian is to grow in Christ, to be more closely identified with him, to have his rich life penetrate us more and more and to be our very life. When we understand that the Church is the Body of Christ, we will learn to love the Church more earnestly and see in it more clearly the reflection of Christ.

Out of the body of believers, all one in baptism, Christ calls those who will serve him as servants of the body. In a special sacrament that differentiates those who are called to minister to the whole body, certain men are set apart by sacred ordination. They are called to the unique work of Christ in building up, sustaining, and leading his body on earth—the Church.

THE HIERARCHY OF THE CHURCH

On the sacramental level, the basic structure of the Church is determined by two sacraments: baptism, which makes a person a member of the Church, and holy orders, which constitutes a person as a sacred minister at the service of the Church.

By ordination, the sacrament of holy orders, a man is configured to Christ in a unique and special way that allows him to exercise the authority of Christ, to speak in his name, and actually, in certain instances, to function in the person of Christ.

The hierarchy of the Church from earliest times is clearly seen as the ministerial priesthood, which in its fullness is the order of bishops. The presbyter or priest is a loyal coworker with the bishop to extend the ministry of orders throughout the Church. Deacons are ordained to the ministerial service that focuses on doing those works in the Church that free the priest for his distinctly apostolic activity.

We recognize in the bishop powers unique to that order. Only a bishop can ordain. He is also the ordinary minister of confirmation. Within his diocese the bishop is the chief shepherd, liturgist, and teacher.

All the bishops form a college in the same way that the apostles formed an apostolic college. At the head of this college of bishops is the Pope, the successor to Peter, with the prerogatives and responsibilities of Peter. Thus we speak of the Bishop of Rome as the visible head of the Church on earth. Bishops throughout the world pledge to him reverence and obedience, just as priests in an individual diocese pledge reverence and obedience to their bishop. The Church is constituted in this way so that the hundreds of millions of faithful will be served in a way that not only reflects but makes present the loving, caring, pastoral ministry of Christ himself.

Priests, most regularly encountered in parish ministry, are responsible for the spiritual and pastoral care of the people entrusted to them, the celebration of the Eucharist, the administration of the sacraments, the preaching of the word, and the direction of the ordinary business of the parish.

RELIGIOUS COMMUNITIES

Christ taught the rich young man in the gospel that every one is obliged to love God and his neighbor in the faithful observance of the commandments (see Luke 18:18–25). But those in whom God's grace stirs a hunger for a more demanding life are called to share with Christ a willingness to give up much that the world offers so that they might cling to God in a richer freedom.

Christ's invitation to many to close discipleship endures in the Church in a special way in the religious life. Those who enter religious life bind themselves, as the Second Vatican Council teaches, "either by vows or by other sacred bonds which are like vows in their purpose" (*Lumen Gentium* 44) to an observance of the evangelical counsels of perfection—that is, the gospel counsels of chastity, poverty, and obedience.

A decision to follow Christ closely through the observance of his evangelical counsels involves cutting away many perfectly laudable objectives which one might otherwise pursue: sexual and domestic fulfillment in marriage, ownership of property, the development of other abilities. Yet giving up these things can be counted as nothing by those who long to cling to Christ immediately with a full and freer heart—to share that emptying of self with Christ that is proclaimed in the letter to the Philippians (see Philippians 2:1–11; compare 1 Corinthians 7:32–35).

As the *Catechism of the Catholic Church* points out, quoting directly from the Second Vatican Council's *Dogmatic Constitution on the Church,* "The state of life which is constituted by the profession of the evangelical counsels, while not entering into the hierarchal structure of the Church, belongs undeniably to her life and holiness" (see section 914). The evangelical counsels are lived out in a range of callings, including the eremitic life, the commitment as a consecrated virgin, religious life within a community that is distinguished by "its liturgical character, public profession of the evangelical counsels, fraternal life led in common, and witness given to the union of Christ with the Church" (925). At the same time, secular institutes and societies of apostolic life exist so that their presence might act as a leaven in the world even in those societies whose members do not take religious vows.

All of these forms of response to a call from God share a common desire: to build up the Church through the exercise of a unique gift from God, and at the same time to bear public witness to the coming of the kingdom that will bring about the full glory and completion of the Church.

QUESTIONS TO THINK ABOUT:

1. How would I feel if my son decided to become a priest? If my daughter decided to join a religious community?
2. How does Christ call me? If I am not called to be ordained, what is my place in the Body of Christ?

CHAPTER 27

The Role of the Laity

THE SECOND VATICAN COUNCIL met from 1962 to 1965, and during that time the Church in the United States—like the Church throughout the world—saw more priestly vocations and more membership in religious communities than at any other time in the Church's recent history. Seminaries were filled. Religious communities of women and men rejoiced in ever-increasing numbers of candidates, novices, and postulants. Throughout the Church in North America there was the highest ratio of priests to Catholics that we had ever experienced.

In the last session of the Second Vatican Council, 1965, the fathers of that ecumenical synod approved among other documents the *Decree on the Apostolate of the Laity* (*Apostolicam Actuositatem*). It reminded the whole Church that lay Christians—like the clergy and those in consecrated life—are entrusted by God with the apostolate by virtue of their baptism and confirmation. They have the right and duty, individually or grouped in associations, to work so that the message of salvation may be known and accepted by all people throughout the world.

Sometimes we hear that the increasing emphasis on the role of the laity in the life of the Church today is the result of a shortage of priests and religious. But both the *Decree on the Apostolate of the Laity* and its timing say otherwise. At a time when vocations were at their highest point, the Church called the laity to assume their responsibility, bestowed on them in baptism and confirmation, to spread the gospel of Jesus Christ. Especially, the laity are called to transform the temporal order, which is their particular domain.

WHO ARE THE LAITY?

The *Catechism of the Catholic Church* defines laity as "all the faithful except those in Holy Orders and those"—such as monks and nuns, sisters and brothers—"who belong to a religious state approved by the Church" (see section 897). The text goes on to explain that the faithful "who by Baptism are incorporated into Christ and integrated into the People of God, are made sharers in their particular way in the priestly, prophetic, and kingly office of Christ, and have their own part to play in the mission of the whole Christian people in the Church and in the world" (section 897).

Both the identity and the work of the laity are clearly defined. By far, the majority membership in the Church is the vast array of women and men baptized into Christ and confirmed in the gifts of the Spirit. The Second Vatican Council defines the work of the laity as to "take on the renewal of the temporal order as their own specific obligation" (*Apostolicam Actuositatem* 7).

THE RENEWAL OF THE TEMPORAL ORDER

When something happens in the community, or when laws are enacted challenging some of our most cherished convictions, bishops and priests will often hear from some people, "Why doesn't the Church do something about this?" While it is true that clergy are called to proclaim the gospel, it is equally true that lay women and lay men are challenged to apply the gospel to the situation and circumstances of our time. It is not enough to presume that the hierarchy will address serious social and moral problems in our society. Everyone has to be involved and take an active role. We sometimes hear politicians say that, while they may hear from bishops and priests on specific issues, they do not hear much from significant portions of the Catholic laity.

The principle of lay involvement holds for other areas as well. The voice of Catholic physicians needs to be heard in the area of medicine. Catholic lawyers need to speak out on the ethics involved in the law. Catholic parents need to be involved in education issues. The list goes on. This is what the Second Vatican Council meant when it said that the laity are responsible for the "renewal of the temporal order."

To attend to the temporal order is to care for the goods of life and of the family, for culture and business, for the arts and professions, for political and social institutions. The *Pastoral Constitution on the Church in the Modern World* teaches that "this . . . order requires constant improvement.

It must be founded on truth, built on justice and animated by love" (*Gaudium et Spes* 26). Lay people have responsibility for the temporal order because it requires all the knowledge, the skills, the talents, and insights they acquire and exercise in their varied secular skills. The temporal order must be renewed with reverence by those who respect its own "stability, truth, goodness, proper laws, and order" (*Gaudium et Spes* 36), while bringing it into conformity with the higher principles of Christian life (*Apostolicam Actuositatem* 7).

THE VOCATION COMES WITH BAPTISM

In his postsynodal apostolic exhortation, *Christifideles Laici,* Pope John Paul II wrote that "the voice of the Lord resounds in the depths of each of Christ's followers, who through faith and the sacraments of Christian initiation is made like to Jesus Christ, is incorporated into a living membership in the Church, and has an active part in her mission of salvation" (*Christifideles Laici* 3).

Baptism gives each believer an apostolic vocation. "Go, therefore, and make disciples of all nations, baptizing them . . . teaching them to observe all that I have commanded you" (Matthew 28:19–20). Spreading the kingdom of God everywhere for the glory of God the Father is not a job for the clergy alone, but is carried on by the Church through all its members.

The task of proclaiming and spreading the faith is not always easy. Living in an age of aggressive secularism we may be tempted at times to view it as an impossible task. But the Lord never promised it would be easy. He warned us that not everyone would have ears to hear the good news. On the other hand, the need for God is still as widely felt in the world today as it ever was. In fact, the new idealism that we find among so many of our young people provides an opportunity to make present to them the person of Jesus and his gospel of love and salvation.

A BLUEPRINT FOR GOD'S KINGDOM IN OUR WORLD

We have yet to accomplish the goal so clearly articulated at the close of the Second Vatican Council. But we are more closely approaching it. The vision of the Church that the council, the Pope, and the *Catechism of the Catholic Church* present is of one body working in unity, harmony, and peace, guided by the Spirit under the leadership of the bishops and priests, and gifted with the blessing of consecrated life. But the monumental task of establishing the new creation that is God's kingdom manifest in our world—the extraordinary mission of bringing all things to Christ and making of this temporal order a truly blessed expression of God's love, truth, and justice—falls to lay women and lay men. They are empowered to transform every aspect of life, so that permeated with God's grace it will truly correspond to God's kingdom in our midst.

This is not a dream. It is a blueprint. Imagine a world in which the professions—law, medicine, education, the sciences, culture, art, building, commerce, industry, and the daily lives of those involved in the trades—are all permeated with the Christian values of truth, justice, and above all love. This vision is God's kingdom coming to be in our world through the conscientious, dedicated, and Spirit-driven work of each baptized lay woman and lay man who takes seriously the call of the Church to restore all things in Christ.

QUESTIONS TO THINK ABOUT:

1. What have I done to better reflect Christ's gospel in the area where I work? What could I be doing in my own family, in my job, or in my school?
2. What special experience do I have that I could use in my own lay apostolate?
3. Have I ever expressed my views, especially on moral or ethical issues, to those who represent me in the political order?

CHAPTER 28

The Role and Mission of the Pope

WHO IS THE POPE?

There is both a theological answer and a historical answer. The historical answer is simply the name of the current Pope. The theological answer is that he is Peter.

THE POPE AS PETER

The Pope is the successor to Peter as Bishop of Rome and Vicar of Christ. The *Catechism of the Catholic Church* teaches that Peter's successor as "pastor of the entire Church has full, supreme, and universal power over the whole Church" (see section 882). The *Catechism* continues quoting the Second Vatican Council's *Dogmatic Constitution on the Church* in pointing out that the Pope "is the perpetual and visible source and foundation of the unity both of the bishops and of the whole company of the faith" (*Lumen Gentium* 23; see section 882 of the *Catechism*).

As a part of God's plan, Christ constituted the twelve apostles as a permanent group. At the head of them he placed Peter, chosen from among them. Just as by the Lord's institution Saint Peter and the rest of the apostles constitute a single apostolic college, so in like fashion the Roman Pontiff, who is Peter's successor, and the bishops, who are the successors of the apostles, share a relationship with each other and are united with each other. The Pope is to the college of bishops what Peter was to the apostolic college. Together, the Pope and bishops are to the Church what Peter and the apostles were to the apostolic Church.

In the pages of the New Testament we read in a number of gospel accounts the names of the twelve. Peter is always at the head of this group and functions as their leader. In Matthew's gospel we read how Jesus appointed Peter to be the "rock" on which he would build his Church. It was to Peter that he gave authority over his Church; it was Peter he selected as shepherd of his whole flock. The *Catechism* teaches us: "The Lord made Simon alone, whom he called Peter, the 'rock' of his Church" (see section 881). The text goes on to quote from the Second Vatican Council that "the office of binding and loosing which was given to Peter was also a sign to the college of apostles united to its head" (*Lumen Gentium* 22). This pastoral office of Peter and the other apostles belongs to the Church's very foundation and, as the *Catechism* reminds us, is continued by the bishops under the primacy of the Pope.

The Pope is the person chosen to walk in the footsteps of Peter. In his election as Bishop of Rome, he assumes the responsibility as universal pastor for the Church and takes on the awesome authority of the Vicar of Christ to preside over the whole Church, to oversee its activities, and to build up the Church in faith and love.

In its treatment of the role of the Pope, the *Catechism of the Catholic Church* always speaks of the Bishop of Rome in the context of the episcopal college, with the Holy Father as head—as if to emphasize both the collegial nature of governance in the Church and the special leadership role of the head of that college, the Roman Pontiff.

THE POPE AS TEACHER

The responsibility of the Pope is to build up the unity of the Church, to teach, to lead, and to sanctify God's people. Exercising his supreme teaching office, the Pope also, with great regularity, writes to the whole Church in the form of encyclical letters, apostolic exhortations, and other messages. These are a rich source of teaching. Each message is directed to a specific issue, concern, or problem that the Church must face.

Pope John Paul II used another forceful teaching mechanism, called postsynodal apostolic exhortations. These are letters that summarize the work of a synod of bishops. A synod is a gathering of bishops representative of the episcopate around the world. Pope John Paul II regularly convened these so that he could hear from his brother bishops their thoughts on matters affecting the life of the Church.

Of all the publications in John Paul's pontificate, perhaps the most ambitious in its scope is the *Catechism of the Catholic Church*. As you know by now, it is an extraordinarily thorough, complete, and authoritative summary of our Catholic faith.

In all of these efforts the Pope was exercising his teaching office—one of the major responsibilities of the Vicar of Christ. Another manifestation of his responsibility is the selection of bishops in communion with the Apostolic See—a task that continually renews the episcopal college and permits the Holy Father an opportunity to exercise his ministry of unity.

THE POPE'S SANCTIFYING OFFICE

Finally, as we consider some of the responsibilities that regularly face the Vicar of Christ, we recognize the exercise of his sanctifying office. The *Catechism of the Catholic Church* tells us that "the bishop is 'the steward of the grace of the supreme priesthood,' especially in the Eucharist which he offers personally or whose offering he assures through the priests, his co-workers . . . The bishop and priests sanctify the Church by their prayer and work, by their ministry of the word and of the sacraments" (section 893). As Bishop of Rome, and bishop of the universal Church, our Holy Father is regularly at his task of sanctifying the Church through the celebration of the sacraments, most particularly the Eucharist, in Rome and in all of those lands he regularly visits.

So we return to the initial question, "Who is the Pope?" Having reviewed the text of the *Catechism of the Catholic Church,* we are once more renewed in our awareness that the answer to that question will always be twofold. The Pope today is the current Vicar of Christ, the Bishop of Rome, and he is at the same time Peter.

QUESTIONS TO THINK ABOUT:

1. Which teachings of the current Pope do I remember best? Why do I remember those particular teachings?
2. Have I ever had difficulty accepting the Pope's teachings? Where could I go for help in understanding them better?
3. How could I help other Catholic Christians understand the importance of the Pope's role as teacher?

CHAPTER 29

The Communion of Saints

HOW OFTEN WE SEEK the presence of the saints! Particularly in times of need, large or small, we pray to Mary and the saints to intercede for us. Saint Therese, Saint Anthony, Saint Jude, Saint Elizabeth Ann Seton all have their devotees. The Church provides us each year in the liturgical calendar with a reminder of these heroic women and men, virtuous and undaunted, who have gone before us, giving an example of what it means to follow Christ. We feel comfortable invoking their names and asking their intercession because we are all members of the same family. They have achieved the goal to which we are still working.

THE CHURCH IS THE ASSEMBLY OF SAINTS

The creed professes our faith in "the communion of saints." The *Catechism of the Catholic Church* reminds us that in a certain sense this article is a further explanation of what it means to profess our faith in the "holy catholic Church." " 'What is the Church if not the assembly of all the saints?' The communion of saints is the Church" (see section 946 of the *Catechism*).

Just as eternal life begins in baptism, so our fellowship with the saints in heaven begins by our membership in the Church on earth. It is the same family bound together by one bond—the Holy Spirit—which finds its beginning here on earth and its culmination in glory. When we profess our faith in the communion of saints, we are really addressing the essence of the word communion: community.

Our explanation of communion takes us back to the opening of the Acts of the Apostles, when the Spirit is poured out upon all of those who hear the proclamation of Peter and accept Jesus as Lord. "Therefore let the whole house of Israel know for certain that God has made him both Lord and Messiah, this Jesus whom you crucified" (Acts 2:36).

When they heard this the crowd was deeply touched and asked Peter and the other apostles, " 'What are we to do, my brothers?' Peter said to them, 'Repent and be baptized, every one of you, in the name of Jesus Christ . . . and you will receive the gift of the Holy Spirit' " (Acts 2:37).

The account goes on to tell us the fruit of their baptism: "They devoted themselves to the teaching of the apostles and to the communal life, to the breaking of the bread and to the prayers" (Acts 2:42). These first followers of Jesus who received the gift of faith and the outpouring of the Holy Spirit became a community of believers—just as we do through our baptism—and joined in their new life as a Church by the celebration of the Eucharist and their attentiveness to the word of God. They became in a profoundly spiritual and equally real sense one with Christ in this new communion in the Holy Spirit.

In the one Spirit in which we are baptized, we take on a new life that transcends any bonds, blood or ethnic, that tie us to this world. We become brothers and sisters through the power of the Holy Spirit that makes us adopted children of God.

THE CHURCH IS ONE FAMILY

It is for this reason that the Church calls us to recognize our spiritual unity and prays incessantly for the peace and unity of all the members of the Church, so that we might become what we have the power to be—one family embracing all people of all colors, ethnic backgrounds, and national origins, united in the truth that is Jesus Christ and in the gift of his Holy Spirit.

We are still a long way from that full communion. But the Church is its beginning, and we should be prepared to see in what the Church teaches, in her sacramental life and in her challenge to unity, the far deeper reality that will develop and mature into a universal oneness before God if we allow it.

The growth of the Christian community parallels the gradual growth of our own spiritual life. While in baptism we receive the seeds of eternal life, we can only see that life flower into everlasting life if we nurture and strengthen it through prayer, the sacraments, and our good works that manifest the love of God within us. So too the communion that we speak of is struggling to come to be. Every word or deed that encourages fellowship and community in fact builds up the communion of saints. The *Catechism of the Catholic Church* lists a number of spiritual goods that manifest and build up the unity of the Church. It speaks of a communion in the faith, a communion of the sacraments, a communion of charisms, and a communion in charity (see sections 949–53).

OUR COMMUNITY TRANSCENDS DEATH

Our bonds of community are not broken in death. The death of an individual must be understood in terms of the communion of saints. For the Church is not only the family of those living in faith here on earth; it is also an eternal communion of persons made blessed in the Holy Spirit. Such a family reaches into eternity, embracing also those who are being purified to enter the blessed vision and all who are already rejoicing in beholding God's glory.

The entrance into eternal life of those we love has not ended their relevance to us. In a sense, by their passing on to glory we are somehow brought nearer to God. The *Catechism of the Catholic Church* teaches that "the union of the wayfarers with the brethren who sleep in the peace of Christ is in no way interrupted, but on the contrary, according to the constant faith of the Church, this union is reinforced by an exchange of spiritual goods" (*Lumen Gentium* 49; see section 955 of the *Catechism*).

Here the *Catechism* speaks of the three stages of the Church. Directly quoting from the Second Vatican Council, it reminds us, "When the Lord comes in glory, and all his angels with him, death will be no more and all things will be subject to him. But at the present time some of his disciples are pilgrims on earth. Others have died and are being purified, while still others are in glory, contemplating 'in full light, God himself triune and one, exactly as he is' " (*Lumen Gentium* 49; see section 954 of the *Catechism*).

Our faith in the communion of saints is a belief that the bonds that hold us together as a spiritual family in the Church endure after death. They keep us one with those who are being purified of their transgressions as well as with those who are already with God in heaven. There is more that unites us than separates us. What keeps us apart is the termination of this natural life and the passage of some through the doors of death into the life yet to come. But what binds us together are the threads of the new life begun in baptism, nurtured in the Eucharist, strengthened on our pilgrim way by the sacraments, purified of any stain or mark after death, and flowering into eternal fullness in the life that sees God as he is, face to face.

WHY WE PRAY FOR THE DEAD AND TO THE SAINTS

It is because of this belief that the Church, in the full consciousness of this communion of the whole mystical body of Jesus Christ, has honored with great respect the memory of the dead. Because it is "a holy and pious thought" to pray for the dead "that they may be freed from this sin" (2 Maccabees 12:45), the Church offers her prayers for them. A significant part of this long-standing tradition is the practice of having a Mass celebrated for the repose of the soul of a beloved deceased person. In this holy remembrance, we both pray for the dead and affirm our solidarity with them in Christ through the Eucharist.

We cannot reflect on the communion of saints without also being reminded of our obligation to each other in the Church. We are called to build up this visible community of God's people. At the same time, we recall our obligation to pray for those who have gone before us marked with the sign of faith and who await the fullness of union with God. Finally, our study of the communion of saints reminds us of the fruitfulness of praying to those who, like us, were members of the Church in its pilgrim journey. Through perseverance, faith, and love they have now arrived at full communion with God and stand before the throne of justice prepared to intercede for us.

Is it any wonder, then, that we pray to those holy men and women who have gone before us, and for whom the battle is over and the triumph secure? First among these is Mary, the Virgin Mother of God and our mother, who with particular care responds to our needs and hears our cries for help. In addition, each of us who has been baptized carries the name of a personal patron with whom we are well advised to build up bonds of friendship that allow us to call upon him or her in our own particular needs.

Our faith in the communion of saints is nothing less than our belief in the enduring power of God's promise, the life-giving gift of the Holy Spirit, and the unity we all share. We are all in some way already one with each other through the grace of God's life within us—whether we are still struggling in this temporal order, enduring purgation in anticipation of heaven, or already enjoying the glory of the vision of God.

QUESTIONS TO THINK ABOUT:

1. Do I have any favorite saints to whom I frequently address my prayers? What about those saints makes me feel especially close to them?
2. How do I include the faithful departed in my prayers?
3. Do I feel close to my patron saint? How much do I know about him or her?
4. Do I make a practice of having Mass offered for the faithful departed?

CHAPTER 30

The Forgiveness of Sins

IN A VERY GRAPHIC way, the stations of the cross depict the power of sin. Jesus accepted the cross and took on our sins. Spiritual tradition tells us that Jesus fell three times under the weight of the cross and got up each time to continue his sorrowful way to Calvary, the crucifixion, and our redemption.

Each of us bears the weight of crosses we fashion with our own sins, and without God's grace we would never be able to get back up after each fall. Only the grace of God's forgiveness extends the helping hand that lifts us from our failure, fault, and sin, and allows us to continue our journey to God.

WE ALL FAIL

In baptism all sin is wiped away. The saving waters of baptism remove original sin, with which we are born, and any personal sin we might have committed. But it is a sad fact that we do not "live happily ever after." Only in fiction or fairy tales does that happen. The human condition is marred by countless personal failings that challenge even our best intentions. But we are not left to our own failure.

The Church professes a belief in "the forgiveness of sins." Not only did Jesus die to wash away all sin, and not only in his public life did he forgive sin, but after his resurrection Jesus also extended to his Church the power to apply the redemption won on the cross and the authority to forgive sin.

THE POWER OF THE KEYS

In addressing this article of the creed, the *Catechism of the Catholic Church* points out that our faith in the forgiveness of sins is tied in with faith in the Holy Spirit, the Church, and the communion of saints. "It was when he gave the Holy Spirit to his apostles that the risen Christ conferred on them his own divine power to forgive sins: 'Receive the Holy Spirit. If you forgive the sins of any, they are forgiven; if you retain the sins of any, they are retained' " (section 976).

This power to forgive sins is often referred to as the "power of the keys." Saint Augustine pointed out that the Church "has received the keys of the kingdom of heaven so that, in her, sins may be forgiven through Christ's blood and the Holy Spirit's action. In this Church, the soul dead through sin comes back to life in order to live with Christ, whose grace has saved us" (Sermon 214).

Where do we find this forgiveness? Who can blot out sin and wipe away our failure? In the sacrament of penance we meet Christ in his Church ready to absolve and restore us to new life. The graces of Christ are conferred in the sacraments by means of visible signs—signs that are acts of worship, symbols of the grace conferred, and the recognizable gestures through which the Lord confers his gifts. Forgiveness of sins and the restoration of baptismal graces are also attached to an outward sign. In the sacrament of reconciliation, the sinner comes before Christ in his Church in the person of the priest who hears the sins, imposes a penance, and absolves the sinner in the name and power of Christ.

THE SACRAMENT OF RECONCILIATION

The sacrament of penance is an unusual tribunal. We, the guilty party, the penitent, accuse ourselves and approach the Lord in sorrow, admitting guilt before his representative. The priest, who is Christ's minister in penance, listens to the confession in the name of the Lord to discover in the penitent the openness, sorrow, and will to conversion that are the conditions for forgiveness. It is for Christ that the priest hears the confession of guilt; the words spoken to him are therefore guarded by the most solemn obligation of complete confidentiality. It is in the name of Christ that the priest pronounces the Savior's mercy: "I absolve you from your sins in the name of the Father, and of the Son, and of the Holy Spirit."

As the *Catechism of the Catholic Church* reminds us: "Sin is before all else an offense against God, a rupture of communion with him. At the same time it damages the communion with the Church. For this reason conversion entails both God's forgiveness and reconciliation with the Church, which are expressed and accomplished liturgically by the sacrament of Penance and Reconciliation" (section 1440). Here we find the elements of a true confession: contrition, confession of sins, absolution, and satisfaction.

What leads us to the sacrament of reconciliation is a sense of sorrow for what we have done. The motivation may be out of love of God or even fear of the consequences of having offended God. Whatever the motive, contrition is the beginning of forgiveness of sin. The sinner must come to God by way of repentance.

From the beginning of the gospel, penance is preached as the preparation and condition for entering the kingdom of God. John the Baptist appeared "proclaiming a baptism of repentance for the forgiveness of sins" (Mark 1:4). This repentance signifies a complete change of mind and heart, a way of thinking and living; it is a turning around, a turning away from sin and a turning toward God. In it we find ourselves again at the heart of the paschal mystery, dying in order to live. "For we who live are constantly being given up to death for the sake of Jesus, so that the life of Jesus may be manifested in our mortal flesh" (2 Corinthians 4:11).

TRUE SORROW FOR SIN

There can be no forgiveness of sin if we do not have sorrow at least to the extent that we regret it, resolve not to repeat it, and turn back to God. Our sorrow for what we have done must lead us to the sacrament of penance. As Pope John Paul II teaches in the postsynodal apostolic exhortation *Reconciliatio et Paenitentia,* a worthy reception of the sacrament is "the ordinary way of obtaining forgiveness and the remission of sins committed after baptism. . . . It would be foolish as well as presumptuous . . . to claim to receive forgiveness while doing without the sacrament which was instituted by Christ precisely for forgiveness" (*Reconciliatio et Paenitentia* 31).

True sorrow for sin implies a firm resolve not to fall back into it. While we cannot be certain that our human frailty will not betray us again, our present resolve must be honest and realistic. We must want to change, to be faithful to the Lord, to take steps to make faithfulness possible. Christ's forgiveness always calls for such a commitment. "Go and from now on do not sin any more" (John 8:11).

The *Catechism of the Catholic Church* teaches us that "confession to a priest is an essential part of the sacrament of Penance" (see section 1456). There is a comforting simplicity to confession. With sincere contrition, we need simply to open our hearts to the priest, recount our failings, and ask for forgiveness. What follows is one of those moments in the life of the Church when the awesome power of Jesus Christ is most clearly and directly felt. In the name of the Church and Jesus Christ, the priest absolves the penitent from sin. At the heart of confession is the momentous action of absolution that only a priest can grant by invoking the authority of the Church and acting in the person of Jesus Christ.

To complete the process, a penance is imposed on the penitent. We must make satisfaction for our sin. Not that we are capable of truly satisfying God for the evil we have done, but nonetheless we must undertake some action or prayer that will express our desire to make amends for what we have done wrong.

The penance given in earlier days was often rather severe. Today the penance is usually the recitation of specified prayers. In the rite of penance we are reminded that "The kind and extent of the satisfaction should be suited to the personal condition of each penitent so that each one may restore the order which he disturbed and through the corresponding remedy be cured of the sickness from which he suffered. Therefore, it is necessary that the act of penance really be a remedy for sin and a help to renewal of life" (Introduction).

In the simple actions of contrition, confession, absolution, and satisfaction, we are restored to a whole new life. It remains one of the great marvels of God's love that God would make forgiveness so accessible and so readily available to each of us. For that reason we have an obligation to admit our sins, approach the sacrament of penance, and restore ourselves to friendship with God and communion with God's holy Church.

QUESTIONS TO THINK ABOUT:

1. How do I fail most often? Have I prayed for help in avoiding those sins?
2. Am I thoroughly honest when I confess my sins? Am I honest even with myself?
3. Do I make regular use of the sacrament of reconciliation?

CHAPTER 31

The Resurrection of the Body

EACH OF US WILL enjoy our own Easter day. On the first resurrection morning, Christ broke the chains of death and rose from the tomb to a life that would have no end. In the same way, we, followers of Jesus and believers in his word, look forward to a personal resurrection of the body. This is not a casual hope or unfounded expectation, but rather a firm conviction essentially tied to our faith in the Risen Lord.

WE WILL RISE BECAUSE JESUS ROSE

The *Catechism of the Catholic Church* tells us that "the Christian creed . . . culminates in the proclamation of the resurrection of the body on the last day and in life everlasting" (see section 988). It goes on to proclaim that we "firmly believe, and hence we hope that, just as Christ is truly risen from the dead and lives forever, so after death the righteous will live forever with the Risen Christ and he will raise them up on the last day" (section 989).

Faith in our resurrection is inseparable from faith in Jesus' resurrection. He is the new Adam. He rose not for his own sake, but as our head, as the pattern of our rising and as the life-giving source of our new life. Saint Paul teaches: "If the Spirit of the one who raised Jesus from the dead dwells in you, the one who raised Christ Jesus from the dead will give life to your mortal bodies also, through his Spirit that dwells in you" (Romans 8:11).

Catholic teaching on what it is to be a human person, and on the power of Christ's resurrection, calls for faith in our bodily resurrection.

All of us, both those who are saved and those who have rejected salvation, will rise again with our own bodies. Those who have died will no longer be dead. The Church firmly believes and steadfastly teaches that on the day of judgment all will appear before the tribunal of Christ with their own bodies to give an account of their deeds.

The Second Vatican Council's *Dogmatic Constitution on the Church* reminds us "before we reign with Christ in glory we must all appear 'before the judgment seat of Christ so that each one may receive good or evil, according to what he has done in the body' (2 Corinthians 5:10), and at the end of the world 'they will come forth, those who have done good, to the resurrection of life, and those who have done evil, to the resurrection of judgment' (John 5:29; cf. Matthew 25:46)" (*Lumen Gentium* 48).

For Saint Paul the resurrection of the body and its relationship to the Risen Christ is a constant theme. "The one who raised the Lord Jesus will raise us also with Jesus and place us with you in his presence" (2 Corinthians 4:14). "We were indeed buried with him through baptism into death, so that, just as Christ was raised from the dead by the glory of the Father, we too might live in newness of life. . . . We know that Christ, raised from the dead, dies no more; death no longer has power over him. . . . Consequently, you too must think of yourselves as being dead to sin and living for God in Christ Jesus" (Romans 6:4, 9, 11).

OUR NEW LIFE HAS ALREADY BEGUN

We will someday be raised from the dead. What is equally marvelous is that we are already beginning the new life that will go on forever. The seeds of eternal life are already sown in us. Through baptism we have already put on the Risen Lord. In the Eucharist we nourish our growing spiritual life. This life, already now within us, will continue on after we walk through the doors of death in a way that we cannot even begin to imagine. Then it will reach a fullness that will be sustained forever.

Death is the end of man's earthly pilgrimage. It brings to an end the time of grace and mercy that God offers as we try to live out our earthly existence in keeping with God's divine plan. In this sense there is a finality to death. It brings to a close this chapter of our existence. In addressing this point the *Catechism of the Catholic Church* teaches that death is the end of earthly life but its dominion is limited. "In death, God calls man to himself. Therefore the Christian can experience a desire for death like Saint Paul's 'my desire is to depart and be with Christ' " (see section 1011 of the *Catechism*).

The *Catechism* is quite clear: there is no other earthly life beyond this one. "When 'the single course of our earthly life' is completed, we shall not return to other earthly lives: 'it is appointed for men to die once.' There is no 're-incarnation' after death" (section 1013).

In the final resurrection our bodies will be transformed. We do not know precisely how. "But someone may say, 'How are the dead raised? With what kind of body will they come back?' You fool!" (1 Corinthians 15:35–36). While we do not know what resurrected bodies will be like, of this we are certain: "For that which is corruptible must clothe itself with incorruptibility, and that which is mortal must clothe itself with immortality" (1 Corinthians 15:53).

Saint Paul seems to take for granted that all know and believe firmly that Christ rose bodily from the dead. His object was to convince his listeners that the resurrection also has an effect on them. Today the same exhortation might be in order. Theological questions naturally arise—they form the material of many weekly magazine articles from time to time. If Christ rose from the dead, where is his body? What physical substance is there in the kingdom of the risen? But these questions are secondary to the fact that Christ is risen. Since Christ is risen, our faith need not falter over little points we find hard to understand. Paul writes and the Church teaches. "But now Christ has been raised from the dead, the first fruits of those who have fallen asleep" (1 Corinthians 15:20).

Christ's resurrection from the dead is the pattern of our rising. The Scriptures recognize the mystery and glory of his new life, but they emphasize two points. One is the element of identity. The risen body of Jesus is the very body in which he suffered and died on the cross. "Look at my hands and feet, that it is I myself" (Luke 24:39). The other point is that his risen body is transformed. He became "a life-giving spirit" (1 Corinthians 15:45). So too shall it also be with all who rise to new life in Christ. We will be transformed. Each will rise as the same person, in the same flesh made living by the one Spirit. But the life of those who have risen will be richly enlarged, enhanced, and deepened.

THE LAST JUDGMENT

The *Catechism* tells us that the "how" of our resurrection "exceeds our imagination and understanding; it is accessible only to faith" (see section 1000). It then goes on to tell us that indeed "the resurrection of the dead is closely associated with Christ's Parousia: 'for the Lord himself will descend from heaven, with a cry of command, with the archangel's call, and with the sound of the trumpet of God. And the dead in Christ will rise first' " (1 Thessalonians 4:16).

The promises of Jesus' second coming are often framed in the colorful style of apocalyptic literature. The different images found in varying parts of Scripture are not themselves elements of the message of faith, but they express in vivid language what the faith does proclaim. They express the Christian belief that history as it is now, with its ambiguous intermingling of faith and unbelief, good and evil, will come to an end. God will be vindicated, evil will be overcome, and there will be a resurrection unto judgment and for the joyful life everlasting.

Our belief in the resurrection of the dead accounts for our ancient practice of praying for those who have died in anticipation of the resurrection, and also for our practice of burying the dead after having commended them to God in a solemn funeral liturgy. While we await the resurrection of the body, the earthly remains, which housed the gift of God's spirit and was a temple of the Holy Spirit, are treated with respect, buried with dignity, and recognized as that portion of the person awaiting resurrection.

Every time we visit a wake, attend a funeral, or pass by a cemetery, we are reminded of this simple and profound article of the creed—belief in the resurrection of the body. It is a sobering belief because it reminds us of the judgment yet to come, and at the same time it is a joyful belief that heralds life everlasting with God.

QUESTIONS TO THINK ABOUT:

1. What popular understandings of the last judgment do I see in movies and TV shows? How are those portrayals right? How are they wrong?
2. How does my belief in the resurrection of the body change my view of eternal life?
3. Do I look forward to the final judgment with fear or with joy? If I fear it, what can I do to change my fear to joy?

CHAPTER 32

Life Everlasting

"HERE WE HAVE NO lasting city, but we seek the one that is to come" (Hebrews 13:14).

All of God's created plan and all salvation history aim at a final fulfillment. Even now, the glory of Christ's ultimate victory is at work in this world. The kingdom of God is already beginning to be manifest. It ever so surely grows. Yet it must await the final action of God that brings down the curtain on this act of creation—our worldly existence—and opens onto life everlasting.

DEATH IS ENTIRELY NATURAL

The final article of the creed proclaims our belief in everlasting life. The *Catechism of the Catholic Church* begins this section by recalling for us the prayer of commendation in the order of a Christian funeral: "Go forth, Christian soul, from this world . . . May you live in peace this day, may your home be with God in Zion, may you see your redeemer face to face . . ." (Prayer of Commendation). This prayer follows a sequence of ritual and liturgical actions that witness the Church speaking for the last time Christ's words of pardon and absolution to the dying Christian, anointing him in preparation for the final journey, strengthened with the Body and Blood of Christ in holy viaticum.

In a sense, death is entirely natural. There is "a time to be born, and a time to die" (Ecclesiastes 3:2). Our lives are measured in time. We change; we grow old, and even death seems appropriate after a full life. "And the dust returns to the earth as it once was, and the life breath returns to God who gave it" (Ecclesiastes 12:7).

But the reality of death and its finality give an urgency to our lives. As the *Catechism of the Catholic Church* says, "Death puts an end to human life as the time open to either accepting or rejecting the divine grace manifested in Christ" (section 1021).

THE PARTICULAR JUDGMENT

The *Catechism* reminds us that while the New Testament speaks of judgment primarily in its aspect of the final meeting with Christ in his second coming, it also "repeatedly affirms that each will be rewarded immediately after death in accordance with his works and faith" (see section 1021). With death comes the particular judgment.

Implicit in that teaching of the Church is the recognition that the death of an individual marks an end to the period of trial. Then we are no longer pilgrims, for our journey is over. Christ's judgment comes upon us. It is the constant teaching of the Church that those who die in grace and in need of no further purification enter heaven promptly after death, and that those who die in a state of grace but in need of some purification enter heaven after that purgation or cleansing is completed. It is also the sad yet defined teaching that those who die in mortal sin enter their unending punishment promptly after death. The *Catechism of the Catholic Church* teaches that each person receives "eternal retribution in his immortal soul at the very moment of his death, in a particular judgment" (see section 1022).

Because individual judgment comes before the end of the world, the Church clearly distinguishes between a particular judgment and the final or last judgment in the resurrection of all the dead when Christ returns to claim his own and to present his kingdom to his heavenly Father.

WHAT AWAITS US IN THE PARTICULAR JUDGMENT?

At the moment of our death, we are everything that we have made ourselves to be by our own free acceptance or free rejection of the divine call and God's gracious gifts. In this sense we are already fashioning this judgment. By each free choice we make and by each decision we exercise for good or for evil, we mold our character and fashion our preferences. We become the result of the choices and decisions we make with our free will. God will not intervene to make us something other than what we have chosen to be. God will not force his friendship on us any more than he will violate our free will to turn us from evil choices. Consequently, if in this life we choose to live without God, always thinking first or only of ourselves and rejecting the presence and love of God in our lives, are we not already declaring our ultimate preference?

God's judgment will clearly indicate to each of us what we have made ourselves to be. What will follow in one sense is more a confirmation by Christ than a judgment that will catch us by surprise.

PURGATORY

Some die in grace and in the friendship of God, but burdened with venial sins and those imperfections that mar our spiritual life. The Church teaches that their souls are cleansed in a purgation that prepares them to enter into the presence of God. The *Catechism of the Catholic Church* tells us that "The Church gives the name *Purgatory* to this final purification of the elect which is entirely different from the punishment of the damned" (section 1031). This teaching finds a solid foundation on the practice of praying for the dead. In the second book of Maccabees the wholesome tradition of offering prayers for those who have died that they might be cleansed of their sins is affirmed. "Thus [Judas Maccabeus] made atonement for the dead that they might be freed from this sin" (2 Maccabees 12:46).

The precise form of the purgation has never been defined by the Church. Certainly a part of the pain is the very separation from God. Yet it is a suffering that can be borne, knowing that ultimately it will end. Saint Augustine in his commentary on the Psalms asked God to purify him in this life so that it would not be necessary for him after death to undergo purification, which he describes as cleansing fire.

HELL

Far more frightening than purgation is the possibility of eternal damnation. Hell is a reality. Scripture speaks of this eternal punishment and warns us against the deliberate malice that destroys a person from within and leads to eternal death. Christ spoke often of hell. When he talked of hell "the unquenchable fire" (Mark 9:43; compare Matthew 25:31 and Luke 16:22), the Lord spoke with compassion, to warn us away from the ultimate tragedy (see Mark 9:43–50)—this "second death" (Revelation 21:8) with its permanent separation from the everlasting life in God for which we were made (compare Matthew 25:31). Jesus spoke forcefully, in the images used in that time, of hell, "where their worm does not die, and the fire is not quenched" (Mark 9:48). In using these images our Lord called us to conversion and warned that those who deliberately persist in malice face a horrible end.

In the section on hell the *Catechism* tells us, "We cannot be united with God unless we freely choose to love him. . . . To die in mortal sin without repenting and accepting God's merciful love means remaining separated from him forever by our own free choice. This state of definitive self-exclusion from communion with God and the blessed is called 'hell' " (section 1033).

Faith teaches us that God is just and merciful, that no one is punished more harshly than he deserves. Yet the mystery of hell remains disturbing. We have every good reason to dread the possibility that persons created for eternal life could shape their wills in such a way as to reject God forever. We have as our one great consolation the recognition that Jesus, God's Son, chose to die on the cross to save us from such punishment—if we are willing before death to choose our Lord and Savior and set aside what would separate us from him.

HEAVEN

Those who come to eternal life will enjoy every manner of blessing, but at the core of their joy will be the possession of God himself. No longer shall we see him merely by faith, but we shall see God "face to face" (1 Corinthians 13:12). "We shall be like him, for we shall see him as he is" (1 John 3:2).

In describing the joys of heaven, the *Catechism of the Catholic Church* refers to the apostolic bull *Benedictus Deus* of Benedict XII (written in 1336), which teaches: "According to the general disposition of God, the souls of all the saints . . . and other faithful who have died after receiving Christ's holy Baptism (provided they were not in need of purification when they died . . . or, if they then did need or will need some purification, when they have been purified after death . . .) already before they take up their bodies again and before the general judgment . . . have been, are, and will be in heaven, in the heavenly Kingdom and celestial paradise with Christ joined to the company of the holy angels" (see section 1023 of the *Catechism*). Those who enter eternal life "see the divine essence intuitively and face to face, with no creature acting as a medium of vision for what they see, but with the divine essence showing itself to them plainly, clearly and openly." They are "truly happy and have life and eternal rest."

This blessed union with God that brings us perfect peace is far more than simply seeing or knowing God. In God's gracious gift to us of life everlasting, we will rejoice in God's infinite goodness. It is in that expectation that we pray that we will hear these words of our Lord at our own judgment, "Come, share your master's joy" (Matthew 25:21).

QUESTIONS TO THINK ABOUT:

1. Is a belief in the reality of purgatory frightening or consoling? Why?
2. If hell is a reality, should that change the way I live my life now?
3. How do I imagine heaven? What makes me imagine it that way?

CHAPTER 33

Amen—I Believe

HOW OFTEN THE WORD "amen" is on our lips. We say it at the end of grace before and after meals. We say it as we conclude morning and evening prayers. We pronounce it numerous times during the celebration of the Eucharist, particularly at the Great Amen, and when we receive a blessing, especially at the conclusion of Mass. It is our most frequent response in public and private prayer. As the *Catechism of the Catholic Church* concludes the study of Part One, The Profession of Faith, it devotes a whole section to the word "amen." It points out that the creed, like the final book of the Bible, ends with this Hebrew word, amen.

I BELIEVE

The last book of the New Testament—and, therefore, of the Bible—proclaims in its penultimate verse, "He who testifies to these things says, 'surely I am coming soon: Amen! Come Lord Jesus!' " (Revelation 22:20). Then the final verse is a prayer directed to God on our behalf: "The grace of the Lord Jesus be with all the saints. Amen" (Revelation 22:21).

The concluding words of the New Testament are an affirmation of faith in the Lord Jesus, in his return, and in his loving presence with us as we await his second coming. For as we learn in the *Catechism,* "In Hebrew, amen comes from the same root as the word 'believe.' This word stem expresses solidarity, trustworthiness, faithfulness. So we can understand why 'Amen' can express both God's faithfulness towards us and our trust in him" (section 1062). Our living response to God's revelation recorded in the pages of Sacred Scripture and professed in summary form in the creed is amen—I believe.

The process is timeless. God speaks to us and reveals who he is and that it is God who speaks. Out of this recognition on our part comes adherence both to God and what God says—an act of faith.

FAITH IS A GIFT FROM GOD

Revelation and faith are personal gifts of a loving God who acts freely in this world and in the human heart. In the Second Vatican Council's *Dogmatic Constitution on Divine Revelation,* we are instructed that, for faith to be shown, "The grace of God and the interior help of the Holy Spirit must precede and assist, moving the heart and turning it to God, opening the eyes of the mind and giving 'joy and ease to everyone in asserting to the truth and believing it' " (*Dei Verbum* 5). Reaching back over more than 1,400 years, the council reaffirms a statement of the Second Council of Orange in 529 that the act of faith is one done in "joy and ease."

We can affirm our belief regularly with as simple an effort as "amen" because God, by the gracious assistance of grace, makes it possible for each of us to have personal faith.

Faith is always free and personal. No one is forced to believe. It comes from the inner conviction that we have heard the word of God and God can neither deceive nor be deceived. What God reveals to us is the truth—a truth on which we can base our lives and direct our actions. Rather than force us against our will to accept and believe in him, God makes himself present in the world by his wondrous saving deeds and words and also in our hearts by his grace. God invites us to recognize him in the light of God's self-revelation.

FAITH AND FREE WILL

Here we touch the very heart of the mystery of faith in God and our own human free will. God reveals to us that it is God who speaks to us. Since with our limited human capability we have no way of verifying that it truly is God who speaks, we need to make a "leap" of faith. To do this requires God's grace.

At the same time, our free will must choose to accept that it is God who speaks to us and to adhere to God's word. While our free will may be touched by God's grace, this acceptance is still a human act of self-determination elevated by God's grace.

When we respond "amen" to God's word, to God's revelation, to God speaking to us, we are freely choosing God with minds illumined and hearts inflamed by God's grace.

The psalmist cries out, "The Lord is my light and my salvation" (Psalm 27:1). Saint Paul tells the Corinthians, "For God who said, 'Let light shine out of darkness,' has shone in our hearts" (2 Corinthians 4:6).

The inner light that opens our minds to accept God's word, solely and simply because it is God who speaks, is itself a grace from God. And once we know that it is God who speaks, we are prompted to accept his revelation as the truth. As we read in the first letter of John, "If we accept human testimony, the testimony of God is greater" (1 John 5:9).

FAITH IS THE PATH TO LIFE

Returning to the *Catechism of the Catholic Church,* we find the affirmation: "To believe is to say 'Amen' to God's words, promises and commandments; to entrust oneself completely to him who is the 'Amen' of infinite love and perfect faithfulness" (section 1064).

The believer, a Catholic convinced of his or her faith, can walk with serenity and confidence. Life may not be easy, and the trials we face may be formidable. Yet we are conscious of a great underlying truth that makes our daily life not only intelligible but also a source of joy and peace. It is God who speaks to us. Our God is a saving God. Through events in the history of salvation and through the divinely inspired words accompanying and clarifying those events, God makes himself and his saving plan known to us.

While we cannot fully grasp the transcendent mystery of God, he is eternal, perfect, and infinite. We are temporal, flawed, and finite. God, before whom we stand in awe and with an awareness of our own smallness, is holy. Yet in his greatness he has willed to be "God with us." In the confident assurance that we do not walk alone and make our way aimlessly through a meaningless reality, we can face each day with that peace of mind and that assurance of soul that belongs only to a person of faith. We can continually say, "Amen—I believe" in the face of difficulties, trials, disappointments, inconveniences, tragedies, and even death.

As we return to the last paragraph of the *Catechism*'s treatment of the profession of faith, we are assured, "Jesus Christ himself is the 'Amen.' He is the definitive 'Amen' of the Father's love for us" (section 1065).

While it is true that God dwells "in unapproachable light" (1 Timothy 6:16), nonetheless he enables us to know him so that he might give us the true fullness of life. Faith is not an academic exercise or an intellectual preoccupation. It is the path to life, to salvation, to everlasting glory. In a world that can offer so little that is not transient, ephemeral, and ultimately empty, the Church offers us in the proclamation of our faith the simple assurance that we are not alone. God is with us.

Each article of the creed that we affirm is not an intellectual proposition that we confirm as if we were piecing a puzzle together. Rather it is our personal recognition of a realm of spiritual reality at the core of which is God. We have come to know him through his manifestation to us in Christ Jesus, who is both God and one of us. The outpouring of the Holy Spirit is not a theological proposition, but a divine reality that offers us oneness with a totally transcendent yet completely loving and personal God. The Church exists in our midst not as a social response to human needs, but as the Spirit-animated expression of a whole dimension of human reality that eye cannot see, nor ear hear—nor has it even entered into the mind of humans to envision it.

As we conclude our review of the profession of faith we do well, as the *Catechism* instructs us, to reaffirm with an "Amen" that our faith is for us the beginning of new and eventually everlasting life. Amen—I believe!

QUESTIONS TO THINK ABOUT:

1. When I say "amen" at the end of a prayer, do I think about what that means?
2. Is my faith really a source of joy and peace? If not, what troubles me about it? Where would I go for help with those troubles?

CHAPTER 34

Liturgy

THE *CATECHISM OF THE CATHOLIC CHURCH* is divided into four sections:

- Part One, The Profession of Faith
- Part Two, The Celebration of the Christian Mystery
- Part Three, Life in Christ
- Part Four, Christian Prayer

Faith comes first because we are a people of faith. The Catholic Church is a faith community responding to the loving self-revelation of God by faith in God's word, through celebration of our share in God's life in the sacraments, in living out Christ's way in our daily activities, and finally through personal prayer with God.

We now begin our reflection on the second section, which explains the Church's faith as it is celebrated in the liturgy, essentially in the seven sacraments.

CELEBRATING OUR NEW LIFE

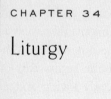

In knowing God we are invited into communion with God. This is the heart of Christian revelation. Saint Paul describes this divine transformation in the letter to the Galatians: "But when the fullness of time had come, God sent his Son, born of a woman, born under the law, to ransom those under the law, so that we might receive adoption. As proof that you are children, God sent the spirit of his Son into our hearts, crying out, 'Abba, Father!' So you are no longer a slave but a child, and if a child then also an heir, through God" (Galatians 4:4–7).

Since we are now adopted children of God, we can rejoice in the very life of God. We can celebrate the new life won for us by Christ in his death and resurrection. We do this in the spiritual action of the Church called *liturgy.* The word itself refers to the public work or service of the people. The *Catechism* tells us that "In Christian tradition it means the participation of the People of God in 'the work of God' " (see section 1069). In liturgy we encounter Christ with us in a way that actually transforms us, making us one with the Lord. What makes the sacraments unique is that they make the life-giving grace of God available to us.

Part Two of the *Catechism* begins with a reproduction of an ancient fresco found in a fourth century A.D. Roman catacomb. It depicts Jesus meeting the woman with the hemorrhage. Mark's gospel tells us that she was healed by touching the cloak of Jesus, through the power that "had gone forth from Him" (Mark 5:25–34). The caption explains that the sacraments of the Church continue the work of Christ as powers that go forth from the Body of Christ "to heal the wounds of sin and to give us the new life of Christ." It continues: "This image thus symbolizes the divine and saving power of the Son of God who heals the whole man, soul and body, through the sacramental life."

Christ joins the Christian community in this public worship of the Church, which is generally distinguished from private devotion or private prayer in that *it is Christ who ultimately offers the prayer.*

CHRIST IS PRESENT IN THE LITURGY

Liturgical prayer is more than community prayer. The Second Vatican Council, in its *Constitution on the Sacred Liturgy,* taught how the realities of prayer, community, and sacramentality converge in the liturgy. Here the Church speaks of the very presence of Christ in the liturgy. This first published document of the Second Vatican Council tells us:

"Christ is always present in his Church, especially in her liturgical celebrations. He is present in the sacrifice of the Mass, not only in the person of his minister, 'the same one now offering, through the ministry of priests, who formerly offered himself on the cross' but especially under the Eucharistic species. By his power he is present in the sacraments, so that when a man baptizes, it is really Christ himself who baptizes. He is present in his word, since it is he himself who speaks when the holy scriptures are read in church. He is present, finally, when the Church prays and sings, for he promised: 'where two or three are gathered in my name, there am I in the midst of them' (Matthew 18:20)" (*Sacrosanctum Concilium* 7).

We can readily see how significant liturgy is. We are a people formed by Christ into his new body—his Church. He calls us together so that we might not only profess our faith in him but also worship the Father as Christ's new body—members and head. While not diminishing the importance of personal and private prayer, liturgical prayer is meant to be the preeminent way in which we join ourselves to Christ in the worship of God.

Since that ultimate act of worship is the death and resurrection of Christ, it is just and fitting that the highest form of liturgical prayer would be the Eucharistic sacrifice. There the mystery of the death and resurrection of Christ is re-presented and renewed for us—and in such a way that we can actually be a part of what Christ has accomplished. The *Catechism* describes this action of the Church in these words: "As the work of Christ liturgy is also an action of his Church. It makes the Church present and manifests her as the visible sign of the communion in Christ between God and men" (see section 1071).

ALL THE CHURCH'S POWERS FLOW FROM THE LITURGY

Returning to the Second Vatican Council, we find another affirmation of the extraordinary work of the Church in the liturgy. When we know that in the liturgy the victory and triumph of Christ's death are made present, then we can understand two statements of the Second Vatican Council that might otherwise seem exaggerated:

1. "The liturgy is the summit towards which the activity of the Church is directed: At the same time it is the font from which all her powers flow" (*Sacrosanctum Concilium* 10).
2. "It is the primary and indispensable source from which the faithful are to draw the true Christian spirit . . ." (*Sacrosanctum Concilium* 14).

Here we come to the heart of what differentiates the liturgy from all other prayer. If the liturgy were merely symbolic ritual, the claims of the Church articulated in the *Catechism* and the council could not be sustained. They are true, however, because the liturgy continues and makes present the paschal mystery of Christ.

In the long sweep of history, there are three stages of the liturgy:

1. The actions of Christ achieving our redemption.
2. The liturgical re-presentation of that action in the sacraments, especially the Eucharist.
3. Finally, the culmination of the paschal mystery and all ritual symbolic and sacramental presentation in our union with the Father in Christ in glory.

What Christ accomplished, we continue to make present today until we are finally united to the Lord in a heavenly liturgy of praise and glory that will endure in its fullness forever.

THE LITURGY IS THE CLIMAX OF HISTORY

The Letter to the Hebrews points out how the crucified Christ replaced Aaron and appears now as the high priest of all humanity according to the order of Melchizedek (compare Hebrews 7 and Genesis 14:18). "But when Christ came as high priest of the good things that have come to be, passing through the greater and more perfect tabernacle not made with hands, that is, not belonging to this creation, he entered once for all into the sanctuary, not with the blood of goats and calves but with his own blood, thus obtaining eternal redemption. . . . For Christ [has entered] . . . heaven itself, that he might now appear before God in our behalf" (Hebrews 9:11–12, 24).

The Book of Revelation also describes this liturgy as the climax of history. "Then I saw standing in the midst of the throne and the four living creatures and the elders a Lamb that seemed to have been slain. . . . 'Worthy is the Lamb that was slain, to receive power and riches and wisdom and might and honor and glory and blessing!' " (Revelation 5:6, 12).

Liturgy, the most perfect ecclesial act of worship, is the action of the Church as it publicly worships uniting itself to its spouse and head Jesus Christ. It is for this reason that the council proclaims: "Rightly, then, the liturgy is considered as an exercise of the priestly office of Jesus Christ" (*Sacrosanctum Concilium* 7).

In concluding, this section of the *Catechism of the Catholic Church* reminds us that liturgy is also the "privileged place for catechizing the People of God" (section 1074). It is in the liturgy with its rich content of God's word and the unsurpassable sacrifice of Christ that we find unfolding for us the heart of the Church's teaching. In the next few chapters, we will address sacrament by sacrament the unfolding of the Church's public work—our liturgy.

QUESTIONS TO THINK ABOUT:

1. How well do I know the parts of the Eucharistic liturgy? If I remember some parts better than others, why do I remember those particular parts?
2. How can I help non-Catholic Christians understand the importance of the liturgy? How would I explain to them why the Church insists on this ancient tradition?

CHAPTER 35

Sacraments

THERE IS NOTHING MORE visible in the Church than her sacraments. Most of us relate to the Church and identify our membership in the Church by the frequency with which we celebrate the sacraments.

Sometimes we hear the rather sheepish excuse "I am not the best Catholic," usually meaning "I don't get to Mass very often." Yet even for the person who has drifted away from a fuller and richer participation in the life of the Church, the sacraments continue to be the most visible expression of communion with the Church. That may be one of the reasons why a baptism, confirmation, marriage, funeral, or Eucharistic celebration of anniversaries continues to have such an appeal for even less than fervent Catholics. The sacraments are the most visible sign of our participation in and identification with the Church.

SACRAMENTS ARE REAL

When we talk about the sacraments, we need to underline that what is taking place in the sacramental sign is *real,* even though it is a distinct and unique reality. It is true that all of us have different ideas of what is real, and for many people there is a temptation to consider only sensible things as real. Yet even here we recognize that there is a quality of existence beyond the concrete. Memories are real. We cherish them and many times relive them. Our historical reenactments, often in the form of memoirs and reflections, autobiographical and biographical, all bear testimony to the powerful reality of memory.

Imagination is also a form of reality, even though by definition we are able with a fertile and vivid imagination to expand the limits of our daily experience. Increasingly with new technology we deal with what is termed virtual reality. While it is not the same as what is actual in our lives, nonetheless virtual reality is a recognized form of existence and is part of a rapidly growing area of entertainment.

Sacramental presence is also a unique kind of reality. It is not limited to the concrete data and sensible materials of this world. At the same time, it is much more than memory, imagination, or virtual reality. Sacramental presence combines sensible, concrete, experiential elements with the spiritual and supernatural dimension of life.

A SACRAMENT ACCOMPLISHES WHAT IT SYMBOLIZES

To properly understand what a sacrament is, we need to recognize what we mean by a symbol and the various ways in which a symbol can be used.

Symbols and signs stand for something not present. They point the way. A wedding ring, for example, is a sign of marital love—but it is not the love itself. A lighted candle in church may be a sign of personal devotion, but it is not the devotion itself. A box of chocolates given on Mother's Day may be a symbol of a child's love for his or her mother, but it is not the love itself. Symbols serve a purpose. They speak to us of something beyond the symbol itself.

A sacrament is a very special kind of symbol or sign. What is unique about a sacrament is that it not only points to what is beyond it but also realizes what it symbolizes. In the sacrament of baptism, for example, the water symbolizes the washing away of sin and the restoration of new life, the dying with Christ and rising to share in his resurrection. At the same time, it also begins to accomplish what it indicates.

Because sacraments actually accomplish what they symbolize, they are unique signs. Because they put us in contact with God in such a way that God's grace touches us, they are holy signs. In a very real sense, the transcendent, spiritual, supernatural world of God, God's grace and everlasting life, intersects with this limited world—with its finiteness, failure, and limitations—in a sacrament.

The *Catechism of the Catholic Church* offers the following definition: "The sacraments are efficacious signs of grace, instituted by Christ and entrusted to the Church, by which divine life is dispensed to us. The visible rites by which the sacraments are celebrated signify and make present the graces proper to each sacrament. They bear fruit in those who receive them with the required dispositions" (section 1131).

CHRIST WAS THE FOUNDER OF THE SACRAMENTS

The sacraments were instituted by Christ—all of them and each of them. The *Catechism* describes the sacraments as "powers that come forth from the Body of Christ which is everliving and lifegiving. They are actions of the Holy Spirit at work in his Body, the Church" (section 1116).

The word "sacrament" comes from the Latin word for the Greek *"mysterion,"* the mystery of God in Christ in which Saint Paul sees the vast unfolding and action of God among us (see Colossians 1:26). In this mystery, Christ poured into the Church all the riches of grace and truth gained through his death and resurrection. The Second Vatican Council's *Constitution on the Sacred Liturgy* teaches us that the Church was born "from the side of Christ as he slept the sleep of death upon the cross" (*Sacrosanctum Concilium* 5).

The visible Church is also the great sacrament. It is a living continuation on earth of its divine founder. Jesus is truly the Son of God, but equally an individual man, the son of Mary. In a like manner, the Church is the presence of Christ and the Holy Spirit, a bearer of heavenly gifts, yet it is also very human in its existence upon the earth. Its sublime mission is carried out by human agents. In doing their work those human agents perform sacred ceremonies that we call the sacraments, using ordinary realities of human life: bread, water, wine, oil, gestures, and words. As Christ in his humanity could appear unattractive to those who did not understand the mystery concealed in his humanity (compare Isaiah 53:3), so the visible humanness of the Church might lead some to undervalue it and the importance of the sacraments.

Just as the Word took on a human body and became man, so too the Church, the continuing presence of the Risen Lord, takes on the flesh of the liturgy to continue the work of Jesus. The Church uses words, signs, symbols, and all forms of reality to accomplish her work—just as her divine founder did. As we saw in the previous chapter, we call this mysterious working of God's grace through human words and actions the liturgy.

The Church continues to do today what Christ accomplished in his death and resurrection. Even the means are the same. Signs, words, and symbols manifest and accomplish the work of salvation. This mystery we call *sacrament*.

THE SEVEN SACRAMENTS

The great sacrament, the Church, is the home of the seven sacraments that continue visibly to manifest and effect the saving work of Christ in our world and in the lives of the faithful. The Church confirms that there are seven sacramental rites instituted by our Lord Jesus Christ:

1. Baptism
2. Confirmation
3. Holy Eucharist
4. Penance
5. Anointing of the sick
6. Holy orders
7. Matrimony

In each of these sacraments, the spiritual realm of Christ's eternal kingdom intersects with our world and with each of us who receives a sacrament. The spiritual touches the material. The eternal intersects with the temporal. The transcendent crosses paths with the immanent. Is it any wonder that we speak of the sacraments as privileged moments of grace, as encounters with Christ, as channels of God's love?

Each of these rites has one or more visible material elements, like bread, wine, water, oil, or human actions. These material elements are illumined by sacred words and become signs of faith and instruments of Christ's own saving action. What is important to remember when we deal with a sacrament is the fact that the visible sign of each sacrament symbolizes the spiritual activity taking place and, at the same time, effects an outpouring of grace that Christ confers in the sacrament.

We must never underestimate the power of a sacrament. The efficaciousness of the sacrament does not depend on the worthiness of the minister, or even entirely on the disposition of the one receiving the sacrament. What makes a sacrament so extraordinary is that even though it is a veiled encounter, it is nonetheless a real one with God through Jesus Christ. Every time we receive a sacrament, we are united to God in praise, petition, and thanksgiving. At the same time, God comes to us bearing life and his life-giving gifts.

God chose to take created reality and raise it to the level of a sacrament so that through it the very love of God could touch us. It is up to each of us to avail ourselves of so extraordinary a gift—one that makes Christ present to us really and truly, even if hidden in the action we call sacramental.

QUESTIONS TO THINK ABOUT:

1. How does my understanding of the sacraments affect my daily life? For example, how does my view of marriage change when I remember that marriage is a sacrament?
2. Do I approach the sacraments as if I expected to find Christ there? What do I do to prepare myself to meet him?

CHAPTER 36

Baptism

THERE ARE THREE SACRAMENTS of Christian initiation by which we become a full and complete member of the Catholic Church: baptism, confirmation, and Eucharist. We begin our reflection with baptism.

Most Christians do not have a firsthand experience of their own baptism. We usually come to know it by participating in the baptism of others. This is so because according to one of the most venerable traditions in the Church, we are baptized as infants, usually soon after birth. This fact in itself should tell us something about the fundamental importance of the sacrament of baptism and why, even before we can learn much about human life, we are introduced into the divine life of the triune God.

A NEW CREATION

In the opening section on this sacrament, the *Catechism of the Catholic Church* speaks about baptism as the "plunge" into the waters symbolizing the catechumen's burial into Christ's death "from which he rises up by resurrection with him as 'a new creature' " (see section 1214). These words pick up a theme in the New Testament—found, among other places, in the second letter of Paul to the Corinthians, where we are told that "Whoever is in Christ is a new creation" (2 Corinthians 5:17).

When the waters of baptism are poured over the person being initiated in the Church, a whole old order begins to pass away and a new creation comes to be. The faith of the Church, clearly expressed in the New Testament, is that Christ came to establish a kingdom of the Spirit. Through his death and resurrection, Christ won for God a new people, a holy people, a people set apart—marked with God's Spirit. We who are members of the Church are that new people, and we are the beginning of a whole new creation.

HOW DOES THIS CREATION COME TO BE?

The beginnings are found in the Acts of the Apostles, which describes how, when the day of Pentecost came and the twelve were assembled in one place, "Suddenly there came from the sky a noise like a strong driving wind, and it filled the entire house in which they were. Then there appeared to them tongues as of fire, which parted and came to rest on each one of them. And they were all filled with the Holy Spirit . . ." (Acts 2:1–4).

Just as in the beginning, when God created everything and sent his Spirit to form out of nothing everything that was to be, so in his new creation God sends forth the Spirit to bring forth a whole new level of life in each believer—the life of God's own Spirit. There is a real parallel between the first creation and this new and marvelous creation of the Spirit.

The *Catechism* tells us that "This sacrament is also called the washing of regeneration and renewal by the Holy Spirit, for it signifies and actually brings about the birth of water and the Holy Spirit without which no one 'can enter the kingdom of God' " (section 1215). On the first Pentecost, with the outpouring of the Holy Spirit, God began the work of his Church. What results from this outpouring of the Holy Spirit is Christ's new body, the Church, the beginning of his kingdom on earth, the first manifestations of the new creation, which will reach its fullness in glory.

Baptism then is not just a personal initiation into the Church, but rather a continuation of the new creation coming to be all around us and in us through the power of God's Holy Spirit.

WE ARE BURIED AND RISE WITH CHRIST

How do we enter this kingdom and become a part of the new creation? How do we become a member of the Church? Baptism. Baptism is described as the gateway to life in the Spirit, and as the door that gives access to the other sacraments. Hence baptism becomes the first of the sacraments of initiation into the new order—the new creation. In a ritual that is both simple and profound, the person to be baptized is presented to the

Church. Then the waters of new life are poured over the person symbolizing and effecting a change that brings about new birth, new life, and a passage from sin and slavery into freedom and grace.

In explaining the mystery unfolding the sacrament of baptism, the *Catechism of the Catholic Church* looks to the old covenant for prefigures of baptism and then sees in Christ's baptism a type and model for our own. The Old Testament's signs of baptism show us that water is at once destructive and life-giving. So in baptism there is a destructive process: "Those who have been baptized are engrafted in the likeness of Christ's death. They are buried with him . . ." (Rite of Baptism for Children). Saint Paul explains: "We know that our old self was crucified with him, so that our sinful body might be done away with, that we might no longer be in slavery to sin" (Romans 6:6).

In the water of baptism, sin—personal and original—is washed away so that we can truly say that we have died with Christ and were buried with him. At the same time the water signifies an outpouring of the Holy Spirit, God's life-giving spirit, which brings us to a new and elevated level of life where we can say we have also risen with Christ. The new life implanted in our heart through the outpouring of the Holy Spirit in baptism is the life of God—a divine seed planted within us that needs to be nurtured, nourished, and cultivated so that it can grow and flower into life everlasting.

BAPTISM MAKES US GOD'S CHILDREN

The Rite of Baptism for Children in the general introduction tells us that "Baptism, the cleansing with water by the power of the living Word, makes us sharers in God's own life and his adopted children" (5). Baptism is both a rising with Christ and a new birth. As Saint Peter wrote: "Blessed be the God and Father of our Lord Jesus Christ, who in his great mercy gave us a new birth to a living hope through the resurrection of Jesus Christ from the dead . . ." (1 Peter 1:3). This new life as a child of God through baptism is told to us by Jesus himself: "Amen, amen, I say to you, no one can enter the kingdom of God without being born of water and the Spirit" (John 3:5).

We become adopted children. Jesus is the "only Son of God" (John 3:18). We receive our status by "adoption" (Galatians 4:5). Still, as Saint John assures us, this adoption is no legal fiction, as when children were legally adopted: "See what love the Father has given us, that we should become children of God: and so we are" (1 John 3:1).

Offspring share the nature of their parents. If we are truly children of

God in a sacramental, spiritual, and mystical sense, then we must share in some way in the nature and life of God. Scripture assures us that we do: "He has bestowed on us the precious and very great promises, so that through them you may come to share in the divine nature, after escaping from the corruption that is in the world because of evil desire" (2 Peter 1:4).

THE RITUAL OF BAPTISM

Whether the sacrament is administered to a child or to an adult, the essence of the sacrament remains the same. While the Church with great solemnity celebrates baptism at Easter, it also celebrates it throughout the year, particularly and most especially on Sunday. Baptism may be administered either by pouring baptismal water over the candidate's head three times, or by immersing the candidate three times in the baptismal water. While the water is applied, the celebrant speaks the baptismal formula: "[Name], I baptize you in the name of the Father and of the Son and of the Holy Spirit." The water and the words symbolize the new life of the Trinity to which one is called, by sharing in the death and resurrection of Christ.

The ritual continues with the anointing with sacred chrism, which is a perfumed oil consecrated by the bishop. It signifies the gift of the Holy Spirit to the newly baptized, who has become a Christian—that is, one who is anointed by the Holy Spirit, "incorporated into Christ who is anointed priest, prophet and king" (see section 1241 of the *Catechism*).

Bishops, priests, and deacons are the ordinary ministers of baptism. However, anyone, even a non-Christian in an emergency, can validly administer this sacrament by performing the rite with the serious intent to baptize in accord with the mind of the Church.

Given what is happening in the sacrament of baptism, it is not difficult to understand that it is a necessary sacrament. Heeding the words of the gospel (John 3:3, 5), that no one can enter the kingdom of heaven unless he or she is baptized, the *Catechism* notes, "The Church does not know of any means other than Baptism that assures entry into eternal beatitude. . . . God has bound salvation to the sacrament of Baptism, but he himself is not bound by his sacraments" (section 1257).

Finally, the Church speaks of a baptismal character. Saint Augustine introduced the word "character" into Christian theology when speaking about the uniqueness of baptism, confirmation, and holy orders. In the Scriptures, the word used to signify character is "seal," which also marks or identifies.

Saint John in his vision of heaven sees an angel with "the seal of the living God" (Revelation 7:2), which was to be used in marking the servants of God on their foreheads. (Revelation 7:3). On the other hand, Saint Paul speaks of our being sealed already and accepting the gospel: "In him you also, who have heard the word of truth, the gospel of your salvation, and have believed in him, were sealed with the promised Holy Spirit" (Ephesians 1:13).

It is Christ who spiritually marks out his own. In the sacrament of baptism, the minister, bishop, priest, or deacon claims the one to be baptized for Christ. He marks the baptized with a spiritual seal that indicates our permanent vocation, the call by Jesus Christ—a call to life everlasting.

As we conclude this reflection on the sacrament of baptism, we do well to cite once again the *Catechism,* which tells us that "Baptism constitutes the foundation of communion among all Christians, including those who are not yet in full communion with the Catholic Church" (section 1271). Baptism not only marks us as members of God's household and children of a new creation; it is also the basis for our own obligations to each other as members of the Church, and the starting point for our efforts to restore to Christ's Church that unity rooted in one baptism, one faith, and one Lord.

QUESTIONS TO THINK ABOUT:

1. As a baptized Christian, do I live my life as though I were God's adopted child?
2. Do I sometimes have trouble thinking of other Catholics as my brothers and sisters? How can I overcome that difficulty?

CHAPTER 37

Confirmation

CONFIRMATION IS ONE OF the three sacraments of initiation by which we become full, complete members of the Church. In baptism, we receive new life in the Spirit. In the Eucharist, we nurture that new life with the Body and Blood of our Lord. In confirmation, we receive the gifts of the Holy Spirit that enable us to live that new life in a public way that bears testimony to the grace of God alive within us. The three sacraments of initiation are intimately bound together, even though they may be received at different intervals in our lives.

TWO DIFFERENT TRADITIONS OF CONFIRMATION

The *Catechism of the Catholic Church* discusses the two traditions surrounding the administration of the sacraments of baptism and confirmation—the Eastern and Western traditions. "In the West the desire to reserve the completion of Baptism to the bishop caused the temporal separation of the two sacraments. The East has kept them united . . ." (section 1290). The Eastern Churches in union with Rome (the Western Church) have their own liturgical rite, theology, and administrative traditions. One of these includes the age for reception of confirmation.

All three sacraments continue to be the means of Christian initiation, but in the West the process was extended over a number of years, in order to allow for instruction in the faith. Baptism of a child takes place as soon as possible after birth. The other two sacraments of initiation are administered later in life.

The Western difference evolved as Christian families began to grow. Infants, the children of believing parents, were initiated into the Church so that they could grow in the faith as they grew in life—with the experience of the faith as a natural part of their development. To be born into a Christian family was much more common than to encounter Christianity for the first time as an adult.

As the *Catechism of the Catholic Church* points out, another factor in the evolution of the sacraments of initiation is found in the central role of the bishop in the process. In the early Church, as head of the local church, the bishop welcomed new members into the faith community. He was the minister of the sacraments of initiation. As the Church grew and priests assisted the bishops in the pastoral care of far-flung faith communities, the bishop's presence was reserved for the confirmation part of initiation.

CONFIRMATION IN AMERICA TODAY

Today, in dioceses around the United States, the age for the administration of the sacrament of confirmation varies. In some places, the emphasis is on a desire to return to the original order of the sacraments—baptism, confirmation, and Eucharist—thus necessitating the confirmation of the child at an early age. In other dioceses, the focus is on the personal appropriation of the faith. In these locales the age of administering the sacrament of confirmation is delayed sometimes as late as the final years of high school.

The diversity of age limits established for reception of confirmation represents a range of solid, pastoral judgments, all of which are valid and seek to express the living spiritual reality found in the sacraments of initiation.

A strong case is made that the sacraments of initiation should follow the natural pattern of human life, which involves birth, growth, and nourishment. Pope Paul VI wrote in the *Apostolic Constitution on the Sacrament of Confirmation:* "The sharing in the divine nature which is granted to all people through the grace of Christ has a certain likeness to the origin, development and nourishment of natural life. The faithful are born anew in baptism, strengthened by the sacrament of confirmation and finally are sustained by the food of eternal life in the Eucharist" (Introduction).

THE RITUAL OF CONFIRMATION

At whatever age the sacrament of confirmation is administered, the essence remains the same: the outpouring of the Holy Spirit—the reception of the gifts of the Holy Spirit through the laying on of hands.

In the Acts of the Apostles, we read: "Now when the apostles in Jerusalem heard that Samaria had accepted the word of God, they sent them Peter and John, who came down and prayed for them, that they might receive the Holy Spirit, for it had not yet fallen upon any of them; they had only been baptized in the name of the Lord Jesus. Then they laid hands on them and they received the Holy Spirit" (Acts 8:14–17).

To the laying on of hands described in the Acts of the Apostles there was added an anointing with oil. In imitation and fulfillment of the anointing in the Old Testament, the oil came to symbolize the coming of the Spirit, as a sharing of the gift first sent to the apostles. At times the laying on of hands was absorbed into the act of anointing, and at other times both actions were retained distinctly. It should be noted that today the anointing of the forehead is done by the laying on of the hand.

The *Catechism* teaches us the essential rite of the sacrament by quoting from the *Apostolic Constitution on the Sacrament of Confirmation.* In the Latin rite, "The sacrament of Confirmation is conferred through the anointing with chrism on the forehead, which is done by the laying on of the hand, and through the words: *'Accipe signaculum doni Spiritus Sancti'* (Be sealed with the Gift of the Holy Spirit)" (see section 1300 of the *Catechism*).

DEEPENING OF BAPTISMAL GRACE

The effects of confirmation are found in the outpouring of the Holy Spirit as was granted to the apostles on the day of Pentecost. The *Catechism* cites the following increase or deepening of baptismal grace as the work of confirmation: "It roots us more deeply in the divine affiliation . . . it unites us more firmly to Christ . . . it increases the gifts of the Holy Spirit within us; it renders our bonds with the Church more perfect; it gives us a special strength of the Holy Spirit to spread and defend the faith . . . as true witness of Christ . . ." (section 1303).

The challenge of the believer—fully initiated into the life of the Church—is to share in the mission of the Church to spread the gospel. The Second Vatican Council explains in the *Decree on the Apostolate of the Laity:* "In the concrete, their apostolate is exercised when they work at the evangelization and sanctification of men; it is exercised too when they endeavor to have the gospel permeate and improve the temporal order, going about it in a way that bears clear witness to Christ and helps towards the salvation of men" (*Apostolicam Actuositatem* 2).

For most Catholics, confirmation is the sacrament that completes initiation into the Church. It brings with it an outpouring of the gifts of the Holy Spirit: "wisdom, understanding, fortitude, knowledge, piety, and fear of the Lord" (section 1231). These gifts are ours not just as a personal possession, but as a means to proclaim God's presence in our world and to announce his kingdom at work in us, and in all who share the name Christian.

Given the importance of the sacrament of confirmation for the individual as well as for the Church, the celebration of this sacrament should be a particularly festive occasion in the parish. I rejoice when visiting our many parishes for the administration of the sacrament of confirmation, particularly when I find the parish community gathered around its young members to welcome them with great solemnity into full membership in the Church. It also provides an opportunity to recognize all of those who have prepared the young adults for the completion of their initiation into the Church and to challenge these new fully initiated members to a life of faith and service.

QUESTIONS TO THINK ABOUT:

1. How is confirmation celebrated in my diocese? What are the reasons given for that practice?
2. How well was I prepared for my own confirmation? What change did it make in my life as a Christian?
3. What advice would I give to a young person preparing for confirmation?

CHAPTER 38

The Eucharist

AFTER THE CELEBRANT SHOWS the consecrated host and the chalice of precious blood to the people at Mass, he genuflects in adoration and then joins the people in a proclamation that expresses the core of our Christian faith. "Christ has died, Christ is risen, Christ will come again."

Our faith teaches us that what we proclaim in the Eucharist, Christ's death and resurrection, is also re-presented in that very action by the power of God's love and goodness. This is the heart of our faith in the sacrament we call the Eucharist, the holy sacrifice of the Mass, the real presence of Christ.

AT THE CENTER OF THE CHURCH'S LIFE

The *Catechism of the Catholic Church* begins the article on the Eucharist with a reflection on the names by which the sacrament is identified. Here we read that each name "evokes certain aspects" of the sacrament. It is called "Eucharist because it is an action of thanksgiving to God" (section 1328). It is sometimes referred to as "the Breaking of Bread" because Jesus used this rite, above all, at the Last Supper (section 1329). The Eucharist is also called "the memorial of the Lord's passion and resurrection . . . the Holy Sacrifice" because it makes present the one sacrifice of Christ the Savior and includes the Church's offering (section 1330).

The Eucharist is at the center of the Church's life. In the celebration of this mystery of faith, Christ himself is present to his people. Rich in symbolism and richer in reality, the Eucharist bears within itself the whole reality of Christ and mediates his saving work to us. In short, when the Church gathers in worship of God and offers the Eucharistic sacrifice, not only is Christ really and truly present under the species of bread and wine, but he also continues his saving work of our salvation.

With great clarity, the Second Vatican Council's *Constitution on the Sacred Liturgy* teaches: "At the Last Supper, on the night he was betrayed, our Savior instituted the Eucharistic sacrifice of his body and blood. He did this to perpetuate the sacrifice of the cross throughout the centuries until he should come again, and so to entrust to his beloved spouse, the Church, a memorial of his death and resurrection: a sacrament of love, a sign of unity, a bond of charity, a paschal banquet in which Christ is received, the mind is filled with grace, and a pledge of future life is given to us" (*Sacrosanctum Concilium* 47).

RE-PRESENTING THE ONE GREAT SACRIFICE

In the Eucharist, Jesus has instituted the sacrament in which the very passion, death, and resurrection he would undergo would be made present again in our lives in a way that enables us to share in the benefits of the cross. We speak of our dying to sin and rising to new life because we participate in the mystery of Jesus' death and resurrection. The Church uses the word "re-present" to speak of what is happening in the Mass. The term "holy sacrifice" of the Mass is also exact because sacramentally, but really and truly, the death and resurrection of Jesus are once again made present.

It is true that there is only one sacrifice—the self-giving of Christ on the cross at Calvary. Once and for all Jesus, who was the victim for our sins, offered himself up for our redemption. "For this reason he is mediator of a new covenant: since a death has taken place for deliverance from the transgressions under the first covenant, those who are called may receive the promised eternal inheritance" (Hebrews 9:15).

This one great sacrifice was accomplished by Jesus, the priest and victim, who offered himself on the altar of the cross for our redemption. This sacrifice need not and cannot be repeated, but it can be re-presented so that we are able, sacramentally and spiritually, to enter it and draw spiritual nourishment from it.

The haunting words and melody of the hymn "Were You There When They Crucified My Lord?" come to mind as we reflect on the Eucharist as sacrifice. The hymn catches the sense of sacramental presence. While it is true that we cannot be physically present at Calvary, there is a real, sacramental, and spiritual sense in which we are present as we participate in the Eucharist. The merit obtained for us through the death of Jesus is applied to us in the very mystery that we call the paschal mystery—passover from death to life.

The beginning of this sacred mystery goes back to the struggle that is so much a part of the story of humanity—the struggle of good against evil. The Eucharist is our sign and pledge of the ultimate victory of God. "God was reconciling the world to himself in Christ" (2 Corinthians 5:19). God triumphed in Christ, winning victory over sin and Satan, over the bondage of the old law and death. Sin has reigned over us (Romans 5:21) and enslaved us (Romans 6:7), but through the passion of Jesus, the Father set us free and restored us to the "kingdom of his beloved Son, in whom we have redemption, the forgiveness of sins" (Colossians 1:13–14). "This is the cup of my blood, the blood of the new and everlasting covenant. It will be shed for you and for all so that sins may be forgiven."

THE INSTITUTION OF THE EUCHARIST

The origins of the Eucharist are found in the Last Supper. The *Catechism* teaches us that "in order to leave them a pledge of this love, in order never to depart from his own and to make them sharers in his Passover, he instituted the Eucharist as the memorial of his death and Resurrection, and commanded his apostles to celebrate it until his return; 'thereby he constituted them priests of the New Testament' " (section 1337). In the Last Supper, Jesus instituted a new memorial sacrifice. The true "Lamb of God" (John 1:29) was about to be slain. By his cross and resurrection he was to free not just one nation from bondage but all humanity from the more bitter slavery of sin. He was about to create a new people of God by the rich gift of his Spirit.

All was to be new. But first Christ would have to die on the cross and rise to new life. As a perpetual memorial to his death and resurrection, at the Passover meal with his apostles he took the bread, "said the blessing, broke it, and giving it to his disciples said, 'Take and eat; this is my body' " (Matthew 26:26). In like manner he took the ceremonial cup of wine, "gave thanks and passed it to his disciples, saying, 'this cup is the new covenant in my blood, which will be shed for you' " (Luke 22:20). Finally, he commanded them: "Do this . . . in remembrance of me" (1 Corinthians 11:24).

Like the Passover meal, this memorial sacrifice of the new law is both sacrifice and sacred meal. Both aspects remain inseparably a part of the same mystery. The Eucharist is an unbloody re-presentation of the sacrifice of the cross and an application of its saving power. The Lord is immolated in the sacrifice of the Mass when, through the outpouring of the Spirit and the words of consecration, he begins to be present in a sacramental form under the appearance of bread and wine to become the spiritual food of the faith.

What Sacred Scripture and Church teaching are describing is the central act of worship of the Church. And just as, individually, we are brought into union with Christ through our participation in the paschal mystery and our sharing in the Body and the Blood of Christ, so the Church as the new people of God comes to be in its celebration of the Eucharist. We are a people made one with Christ and one with each other precisely in the Eucharist. It is for this reason that the *Catechism* teaches "the Eucharist is the efficacious sign and sublime cause of that communion in the divine life and that unity of the People of God by which the Church is kept in being" (section 1325).

WHY ATTENDING MASS IS IMPORTANT

Later in the book, we will discuss reception of communion as an integral part of the celebration of the Eucharist. Here, however, it seems appropriate to note why the Church insists upon the faithful's attendance at Mass.

Since we are constituted God's family, God's people—his Church—precisely by our participation in the Eucharist, we cannot grow into Christ's new body as healthy and full members without sharing in the Eucharistic liturgy.

On each Sunday, which is a commemoration of Easter Sunday, the faithful come together not only to profess the faith but also to renew the life of Christ within them. We gather not as individuals isolated from each other and related only to God, but precisely as God's family interrelated to each other and through the Church. We are made one in the Eucharist.

For this reason, the Church calls upon believers to celebrate the great gift of God with us in the Eucharist every Sunday. To absent oneself from the Sunday Eucharist is to diminish one's own spiritual life—one's own communion with Christ's new body, the Church.

We celebrate Eucharist as a faith family—as the Church—on Sunday because it is here that we find our identity, our unity, and our very being as members of Christ's body, members of his Church.

QUESTIONS TO THINK ABOUT:

1. If the Eucharist is a re-presentation of Christ's sacrifice, how does that affect the way I think about the Mass? Does it give the Mass more importance?
2. How often do I miss Sunday Mass? Why? Do I often take advantage of the other opportunities to attend Mass in my parish?

CHAPTER 39

The Real Presence

ONE OF THE BEAUTIFUL celebrations I recall from my student days is held on Corpus Christi, the Solemnity of the Body and Blood of Christ, at Genzano, a small Italian hill town south of Rome, about a half-hour drive beyond Castel Gandolfo, the Pope's summer residence. In a tradition that goes back to 1778, one of the principal streets of this community is covered with flower petals depicting artful designs and religious scenes. It gives the impression of a carpet of tapestries. People work with great care and skill to cover the entire roadway, so that on the feast of the Body and Blood of our Lord, the Blessed Sacrament can be carried from one church to another along this "avenue of flowers." It is a fitting carpet for the Eucharist procession.

In the early 1940s a similar effort was begun in the town of Tarentum in the Diocese of Pittsburgh, using colored sawdust but with the same effect. I have experienced the joy of carrying the Blessed Sacrament along this beautifully designed and colorful carpet representing the faith, love, and devotion of the people who work so hard to prepare this "avenue for the Lord."

THE BODY OF CHRIST

While perhaps without as much exuberance, Corpus Christi processions take place in Catholic parishes all over the world. The format is simple but devout. The priest carries the Blessed Sacrament along a designated route, where the faithful gather to reverence the presence of Christ in the Eucharist and thank God for this great gift.

One of the ancient and outstanding visible signs of Catholic piety is devotion to the Blessed Sacrament and the public manifestation of faith in this unique and abiding presence of Christ in the Eucharist.

The faith of the Church in the real presence of Jesus in the Eucharist goes back to the words of Jesus himself, as recorded in the gospel of Saint John. In the Eucharistic discourse after the multiplication of the loaves, our Lord contrasted ordinary bread with a bread that is not of this world but which contains eternal life for those who eat it. He said: "I am the bread of life . . . I am the living bread that came down from heaven; whoever eats of this bread will live forever; and the bread that I will give is my flesh for the life of the world" (John 6:48, 51).

What Jesus offers us is his continuing, enduring presence every time we celebrate the Eucharist. The bread becomes his Body and the wine becomes his Blood. The way in which Jesus is present in the Eucharist cannot be explained in physical terms, because it transcends the ordinary necessities of space and measurement.

It is not as though Jesus took on a miniature body to be present in the Eucharist or as though he were present in a natural but hidden way beneath a layer of bread and wine. It is a supernatural mystery that the person who becomes fully present at Mass is the same Risen Savior who is seated at the right hand of the Father. In becoming present on the altar, Christ's condition does not change. He does not have to leave heaven to become present on earth.

In explaining this doctrine of the faith, the *Catechism of the Catholic Church* quotes the Council of Trent as it summarized our Catholic belief. "Because Christ our Redeemer said that it was truly his body that he was offering under the species of bread, it has always been the conviction of the Church of God, and this holy Council now declares again, that by the consecration of the bread and wine there takes place a change of the whole substance of the bread into the substance of the body of Christ our Lord and of the whole substance of the wine into the substance of his blood. This change the holy Catholic Church has fittingly and properly called transubstantiation" (see section 1376 of the *Catechism*).

DEVOTION TO THE EUCHARIST

The real presence endures after the celebration of the Eucharist liturgy. It is for this reason that there is a tabernacle in Church. Once communion has been distributed, the remaining hosts are placed in the tabernacle to provide "viaticum" (literally, food for the journey), communion for those who turn to the Church in their final hour, and also to provide a focal point for prayer and worship of Christ in his real presence.

With the passage of time, however, reverent reflection led the Church to enrich its Eucharistic devotion. Faith that Jesus is truly present in the sacrament led believers to worship Christ dwelling with us permanently in the sacrament. Wherever the sacrament is, there is Christ, who is our Lord and our God; hence he is ever to be worshiped in this mystery. Such worship is expressed in many ways; in genuflections, in adoration of the Eucharist, and in the many forms of Eucharistic devotion that faith has nourished.

The popularity of the feast of Corpus Christi (Body and Blood of Christ), with its joyful hymns and public processions, encouraged further development of Eucharistic devotions. At times the Blessed Sacrament is removed from the tabernacle in which it is ordinarily kept and placed upon the altar for adoration. These periods of exposition are sometimes extended into holy hours. One particularly popular parish tradition is a Eucharistic day, or the forty hours' devotion, with exposition of the Blessed Sacrament and a homily calling particular attention to this glorious, divine gift.

The Eucharist is inseparable from the celebration of the Mass. It is in this context that we understand the nourishing aspect of the Eucharist as food—the sacred banquet of communion with the Lord's Body and Blood. The *Catechism* reminds us that "the celebration of the Eucharistic sacrifice is wholly directed towards the intimate union of the faithful with Christ through communion. To receive communion is to receive Christ himself who has offered himself to us" (section 1382).

PREPARATION FOR THE EUCHARIST

To respond to the Lord's invitation to eat his flesh and drink his Blood, the believer must be prepared. Saint Paul urges us to examine our conscience. "Therefore whoever eats the bread or drinks the cup of the Lord unworthily will have to answer for the Body and Blood of the Lord" (1 Corinthians 11:27). Before we approach the table of the Lord it is important to reflect on our life, ask God's forgiveness for our failings, and, if necessary because of serious sin, avail ourselves of sacramental confession.

Recent polls indicate that a significant number of Catholics do not have a complete understanding of the Eucharist, and specifically the real presence of Christ in the Blessed Sacrament. Whatever the cause of such misunderstanding of the faith, each person who approaches the table of the Lord needs to recognize the significance of that action and the importance of spiritual preparation. It sometimes becomes the task of older members of the family to review with youngsters what is happening at Mass and whom we receive in holy communion. Grandparents have in some instances a unique and privileged role as teachers of the faith in an age where the awareness of the real presence seems to be diminished.

WHY NON-CATHOLICS CANNOT RECEIVE THE EUCHARIST

Often at weddings, funerals, and other religious occasions, where those who do not share our faith are present, there is the temptation to avoid any type of awkwardness by inviting non-Catholics to receive the Eucharist. Those who do not profess membership in the Catholic Church are not permitted to participate at the table of the Lord as if they were full members, sharers in the full sacramental life of the church. Reception of communion creates the public perception that the one receiving the Eucharist is a member of the Catholic Church.

To help both Catholics and those who do not share our faith respond appropriately, the National Conference of Catholic Bishops has issued guidelines for receiving holy communion. These remind Catholics of their need to be properly disposed, to have fasted for an hour, and to seek to live in charity and love with our neighbors. For other Christians, the text points out that "it is a consequence of the sad divisions of Christianity that we cannot extend to them a general invitation to receive communion. Catholics believe that the Eucharist is an action of the celebrating community signifying a oneness in faith, life, and worship of the community. Reception of the Eucharist by Christians not fully united with us would imply a oneness which does not yet exist and for which we must all pray."

At the end of this chapter, you will find the most recent edition of the National Conference of Catholic Bishops' *Guidelines for the Reception of Communion.*

As we reflect on the extraordinary gift of the Eucharist, both as the re-presentation of Christ's death and resurrection and also as our spiritual food, we are called to thank God that such an overwhelmingly generous gift was given to us. We are also called to challenge ourselves to receive our Lord reverently and frequently.

In a tradition that is enjoying a resurgence in some parishes, a number of people are once again coming to church early to prepare themselves quietly for the spiritual experience of the Eucharistic liturgy and the reception of our Lord in communion. This is one small practice that each of us can adopt as a way of strengthening our own faith and appreciating more deeply the mystery we are invited to enter as we approach the presence of God with us in the Eucharist. Those few minutes of quiet preparation have the spiritual effect of helping make our heart "an avenue for the Lord." Each Sunday we can quietly, in our hearts, prepare a way for the Lord every bit as beautiful as the flower and sawdust tapestries of Genzano or Tarentum. All it takes is a little time to recollect our thoughts, recall what we are doing, and thank God for the real presence of Jesus Christ in the Eucharist.

QUESTIONS TO THINK ABOUT:

1. Do I approach the Eucharist as though I really believed in the real presence of Christ?
2. How do I prepare to receive the Eucharist? What distracts me from preparing for it? How can I overcome those problems?
3. How might I explain to non-Catholics why they are excluded from this ritual?

GUIDELINES FOR THE RECEPTION OF COMMUNION

For Catholics

As Catholics, we fully participate in the celebration of the Eucharist when we receive holy communion. We are encouraged to receive communion devoutly and frequently. In order to be properly disposed to receive communion, participants should not be conscious of grave sin and normally should have fasted for one hour. A person who is conscious of grave sin is not to receive the Body and Blood of the Lord without prior sacramental confession except for a grave reason where there is no opportunity for confession. In this case, the person is to be mindful of the obligation to make an act of perfect contrition, including the intention of confessing as soon as possible (*Code of Canon Law,* canon 916). A frequent reception of the sacrament of penance is encouraged for all.

For Fellow Christians

We welcome our fellow Christians to this celebration of the Eucharist as our brothers and sisters. We pray that our common baptism and the action of the Holy Spirit in this Eucharist will draw us closer to one another and begin to dispel the sad divisions that separate us. We pray that these will lessen and finally disappear, in keeping with Christ's prayer for us "that they may all be one" (John 17:21).

Because Catholics believe that the celebration of the Eucharist is a sign of the reality of the oneness of faith, life, and worship, members of those churches with whom we are not yet fully united are ordinarily not admitted to holy communion. Eucharistic sharing in exceptional circumstances by other Christians requires permission according to the directives of the diocesan bishop and the provisions of canon law (canon 844 § 4). Members of the Orthodox Churches, the Assyrian Church of the East, and the Polish National Catholic Church are urged to respect the discipline of their own churches. According to Roman Catholic discipline, the Code of Canon Law does not object to the reception of communion by Christians of these churches (canon 844 § 3).

For Those Not Receiving Holy Communion

All who are not receiving holy communion are encouraged to express in their hearts a prayerful desire for unity with the Lord Jesus and with one another.

For Non-Christians

We also welcome to this celebration those who do not share our faith in Jesus Christ. While we cannot admit them to holy communion, we ask them to offer their prayers for the peace and unity of the human family.

CHAPTER 40

Order of the Mass

"AT THE LAST SUPPER, on the night he was betrayed, our Savior instituted the Eucharistic sacrifice of his body and blood." This firmly held teaching of the Church, repeated in the Second Vatican Council's *Constitution on the Sacred Liturgy* (47), is reaffirmed in the *Catechism of the Catholic Church* (see section 1323). Every time we celebrate Mass we do what Christ did at the Last Supper and what the Church has done at every Eucharist century after century from the rising to the setting of the sun in every part of the world.

Perhaps because we have such ready access to Mass and are so familiar with it, we can be tempted to take it for granted. Worse yet, we may be lax in our participation in this great gift. The more we learn about what actually takes place in the Eucharist, the more we should desire it.

THE ANCIENT TRADITION

One of the most intriguing aspects of the celebration of the Eucharist is the fact that it has changed so little over twenty centuries. The essential elements are found in the narrative of the institution of the Eucharist as recorded in the gospels. The liturgical structure of that celebration developed very rapidly in the early life of the Church and has changed only imperceptibly since. Even in many of the details, we find in the celebration of the liturgy today an identity with what went before us for so many centuries. Saint Paul speaks of this ancient liturgy in his First Letter to the Corinthians (see 1 Corinthians 11:24).

Christ commanded his disciples to prepare the large furnished room where he would celebrate the Passover meal with them and institute the sacrifice of his Body and Blood. As we learn in the *General Instruction of the Roman Missal,* the Church has always taken that command to mean that the Church is responsible for giving directions concerning the preparation of the minds of the worshipers and the place, rites, and text of the celebration of the holy Eucharist. The norms that are used in the missal for the celebration of the Mass according to the Roman Rite "are fresh evidence of the great care, faith, and unchanged love that the Church shows toward the Eucharist" (*General Instruction,* Introduction, 1).

In speaking about the continuity of the celebration of the liturgy today with the most ancient forms, the *Catechism* holds up for examination the text of Saint Justin Martyr. "As early as the second century we have the witness of Saint Justin Martyr for the basic lines of the order of the Eucharistic celebration. They have stayed the same until our own day for all the great liturgical families" (see section 1345 of the *Catechism*).

JUSTIN MARTYR

Saint Justin Martyr, who lived in the second century of the Christian era, was a devout follower of the Lord, convinced that he could bring others to the practice of the faith by explaining to them what Christians believe and how we worship.

He wrote to the pagan emperor Antoninus Pius, who reigned from 138 to 161, sometime around the year 155 explaining what Christians did when they celebrated the Eucharist. In the *Catechism* there is a step-by-step outline in the words of Saint Justin Martyr. Were you to take this text and line it up against the order of the Mass that we use today, you would find very little difference—and that only in the details (see section 1345 of the *Catechism*).

THE LITURGY TODAY

Today the order of the Mass calls upon the priest who will preside and the community with whom he will celebrate to come together, especially and particularly on Sunday. This is the day that commemorates the resurrection of Christ. Therefore for Christians it is the Lord's day, our holy day, the time to celebrate his death and resurrection as Christ asked us to do in his memory.

The liturgy is divided into two parts: the liturgy of the word and the liturgy of the Eucharist. It is in this first part that we find the readings, sometimes taken from the Old Testament or the letters of the New Testament, and always with a section from one of the four gospels. The Sunday readings are almost always three—one from the Old Testament, another from the New Testament, and a third from the gospels. Saint Justin writes, "The memoirs of the apostles and the writings of the prophets are read, as much as time permits" (see section 1345 of the *Catechism*).

In the instruction for the celebration of the Eucharist today, we read: "When the Scriptures are read in the Church, God himself is speaking to his people, and Christ, present in his own word, is proclaiming the Gospel" (*General Instruction,* Chapter Two, 9).

An integral part of the celebration of the liturgy of the word is the homily by the priest. The homily is a commentary on the readings or some other element of the faith and life of the Church. Since so much in our culture changes so rapidly, it is essential that the teaching of Christ be applied to circumstances of our day in a way that allows the believer to see the full implications of his or her profession of faith. The text from Saint Justin points out that "when the reader has finished, he who presides over those gathered admonishes and challenges them to imitate these beautiful things." Here too we see a direct correlation with the celebration of the Mass today. The general instruction tells us that "the homily, as an integral part of the liturgy, increases the word's effectiveness" (Chapter Two, 9).

At this point in the liturgy, the creed is recited as a summary profession of our faith. By reciting it, we acknowledge that what we have read is the word of God, and we announce our adherence to the teaching of Christ and the profession of his Church, so that we can proceed to celebrate the Eucharist worthily.

The priest then invites the faithful to offer their prayers for the needs of the Church, for the community, and for their personal concerns. This is called the prayer of the faithful. In the *Catechism,* we read Saint Justin's description: "Then we all rise together and offer prayers for ourselves . . . and for all others, wherever they may be . . ." (see section 1345 of the *Catechism*).

Saint Justin goes on to tell us that "then someone brings bread and a cup of water and wine mixed together to him who presides over the brethren." In this we recognize our own offertory procession and the offering of bread and wine mixed with water that constitutes the preparation of the gifts.

THE HEART OF THE EUCHARIST

What follows next is the very heart of the Eucharist. Using for the most part one of four Eucharistic prayers, the priest prays over the gifts, asks the outpouring of the Holy Spirit upon them, recites the narrative of consecration, elevates the host and cup for the faithful to reverence, and proceeds to call to mind the passion, resurrection, and glorious return of the Lord Jesus. Saint Justin describes this great prayer of thanksgiving and then notes, "when he has concluded the prayers and thanksgivings, all present give voice to an acclamation by saying: 'Amen.' "

According to Saint Justin there follows the communion of the Body and Blood of Christ and an indication that a deacon is assigned to bring the Sacred Species to those "who are absent." We read today in the *General Instruction of the Roman Missal* that at this point in the Mass "the priest then shows the eucharistic bread for communion to the faithful and with them recites the prayer of humility in words from the gospels. It is most desirable that the faithful receive the Lord's Body from hosts consecrated at the same Mass and that, in the instances when it is permitted, they share in the chalice. Then even through the signs communion will stand out more clearly as a sharing in the sacrifice actually being offered" (Chapter Two, 56 g, h).

When we compare the account from Saint Justin (found in the *Catechism* in section 1345) and the current order of the Mass (an extensive exposition is in sections 1348 through 1355), we see a convergence that reflects how sacred the Church holds this celebration to be, and how unchanged it has come down to us through so many centuries. In concluding its teaching on the Eucharist, the *Catechism* reminds us that it is also "the pledge of the glory to come." "There is no surer pledge or clearer sign of this great hope in the new heavens and new earth 'in which righteousness dwells' than the Eucharist" (section 1405).

The *Catechism* closes by quoting Saint Ignatius of Antioch. "Every time this mystery is celebrated, 'the work of our redemption is carried on' and we 'break the one bread that provides the medicine of immortality, the antidote for death, and the food that makes us live forever in Jesus Christ' " (Saint Ignatius of Antioch, Letter to the Ephesians, 20:2; see section 1405 of the *Catechism*).

QUESTIONS TO THINK ABOUT:

1. Why is it important that the order of the Mass is so ancient? Does it link us more closely to the apostles?
2. Have I ever paid real attention to the order of the Mass before? What makes the order of these ceremonies so important? Where would I go to get a better understanding of the Mass?

CHAPTER 41

The Sacrament of Penance and Reconciliation

ONLY IN STORYBOOKS DO people live "happily ever after." The much more sobering and sad fact of real life is that we all make mistakes. None of us is perfect. We do not always live as we should. Each one of us can recognize in our lives moments of joy and sorrow, occasions of great acceptance and accomplishment, as well as times of rejection and frustration. We are capable of marvelously good actions, and we know that we also sin. We do not live happily ever after.

In reflecting on the sacraments of healing, the *Catechism of the Catholic Church* reminds us that we have received new life in Christ. Yet we carry this life "in earthen vessels" and it remains "hidden with Christ in God" (2 Corinthians 4:7; Colossians 3:3; see section 1420 of the *Catechism*).

Aware of our human frailty, Christ, the divine physician of our souls and bodies, has willed that his Church continue in the power of the Holy Spirit, to bring about his work of healing and salvation. That work is done through the two sacraments of healing: Penance and the Anointing of the Sick (see section 1421 of the *Catechism*).

We will follow the lead of the *Catechism* and begin with a reflection on the sacrament of penance and reconciliation. We do this because the Second Vatican Council's *Dogmatic Constitution on the Church* tells us: "Those who approach the sacrament of Penance obtain pardon from God's mercy for the offense committed against him, and are, at the same time, reconciled with the Church which they have wounded by their sins and which by charity, by example, and by prayer labors for their conversion" (*Lumen Gentium* 11).

RETURNING TO OUR FATHER

The sacrament of reconciliation is the story of God's love that never turns away from us. It endures even our shortsightedness and selfishness. Like the father in the parable of the prodigal son, God waits, watches, and hopes for our return every time we walk away. Like the son in the parable, all we need do to return to our Father is to recognize our wrong, our need, and God's love.

Jesus continues to speak to us of our noble calling to holiness and of his loving forgiveness. He offers us reconciliation if we ask for it. This saving, healing, and restoring action takes place in the sacrament of reconciliation, which is still often called penance or confession.

In fact the *Catechism* recognizes the many names of this sacrament. Sometimes "it is called the sacrament of conversion because it makes sacramentally present Jesus' call to conversion . . ." (section 1423). But it is also better known as the sacrament of penance "since it consecrates the Christian sinner's personal and ecclesial steps of conversion, penance and satisfaction" (section 1423).

For many of us it still continues to be known as the sacrament of confession "since the disclosure or confession of sins to a priest is an essential element of this sacrament" (section 1424). At the same time the *Catechism* reminds us that it is called the sacrament of forgiveness "since by the priest's sacramental absolution God grants the penitent 'pardon and peace' " (section 1424). Finally it is also called the sacrament of reconciliation because it reconciles sinners to God and then to each other (section 1425).

As a sacrament, reconciliation is distinct from baptism, although reconciliation's purpose is to restore or renew our baptismal holiness and reconcile us with God and the Church. A Catholic who has committed grave sin needs to ask for forgiveness in this sacrament provided by Christ in order to be restored to spiritual wholeness. The sacrament of penance renews once again our baptismal innocence.

THE EXPECTATION OF MERCY

At the heart of the sacrament of reconciliation is the mercy of God. The priest, who is Christ's minister in penance, listens to the confession in the name of the Lord, to discover in the penitent's openness, sorrow, and will to conversion the grounds for a judgment of forgiveness. It is in the person of Christ that the priest hears the confession of guilt.

Such a confession is made with the full expectation of mercy, compassion, and ultimately absolution. Each of us approaches this foreshadowing of the judgment seat of God aware of our failings, yet fully expecting the mercy of God. And God does not fail us. In the name of Christ, the priest speaks the judgment of the Savior's mercy: "I absolve you from your sins in the name of the Father and of the Son and of the Holy Spirit."

The *Catechism* reminds us that the sacrament of reconciliation must be seen within the context of conversion. "Jesus calls to conversion. This call is an essential part of the proclamation of the kingdom . . ." (section 1427). And even if our conversion is ongoing and only partial, we are still subject to the effort that will someday reach completion. Saint Peter's conversion, the *Catechism* points out, after he denied his Master three times "bears witness" to Jesus' infinite mercy.

The importance for us of the sacrament of penance is that it really does restore and renew our baptismal holiness. A Catholic who has committed grave sin is obliged to ask forgiveness for it in this sacrament. Once we do and receive sacramental absolution we are restored again to holiness—to an innocence before God. So powerful is the grace of this sacrament that the Rite of Penance reminds us that "frequent and careful celebration of this sacrament is also very helpful as a remedy for venial sins. This is not a mere ritual repetition or psychological exercise, but a serious striving to perfect the grace of baptism so that, as we bear in our body the death of Jesus Christ, his life may be seen in us ever more clearly" (Introduction, 7).

FOUR ASPECTS OF THE SACRAMENT

The Church has long identified four aspects of the sacrament of penance: contrition, confession, absolution, and satisfaction (some act of penance). The Rite of Penance says that "the follower of Christ who has sinned but who has been moved by the Holy Spirit to come to the sacrament of penance should above all be converted to God with his whole heart. This inner conversion of the heart embraces sorrow for sin and the intent to lead a new life. It is expressed through confession made to the Church, due satisfaction, and amendment of life. God grants pardon for sins through the Church, which works by the ministry of priests" (Introduction, 6).

Once we have sorrow for our sins, we are obliged to confess them to the priest, who stands in the person of Christ and his Church. At the judgment of the priest, we receive absolution and the imposition of a penance by way of satisfaction. These familiar steps are the elements of the sacrament of reconciliation. At the core of the sacrament is our confession of our sins and the absolution of the priest.

THREE RITES OR RECONCILIATION

Today the sacrament of reconciliation finds expression in three forms: the rite for the reconciliation of individual penitents, the rite for reconciliation of several penitents with individual confession and absolution, and the rite of reconciliation of penitents with general confession and absolution.

The first rite is the most familiar form of penance. It usually takes place in the private confessional or reconciliation room at the church. Yet even in this "private" form of confession, the social and communal element is still expressed, since the priest represents the Church in the act of reconciliation.

A second form, sometimes referred to as a communal penance service and often celebrated in Advent and Lent in preparation for the great feasts of Christmas and Easter, consists essentially in a communal celebration of the Word in preparation for confession, which is then administered in the form of private, individual confession. Communal celebration shows more clearly both the social impact and the common experience of sin and the ecclesial nature of penance and reconciliation.

A third form, which is called general confession and absolution and is used only in extraordinary situations, involves one priest giving general absolution to a group of penitents who have not made a personal confession to the priest. The Rite of Penance reminds us that those who receive pardon for grave sins by a common absolution are strictly bound to go to individual confession within a year following reception of general absolution.

The deepest joy of the guilty is in their deliverance from sin in a new Passover that frees them from separation from God. Renewed, refreshed, and reconciled in this sacrament once more, we who have sinned are a "new creation." Once more we are made new.

QUESTIONS TO THINK ABOUT:

1. If the Church asks me to do penance, do I approach that penance with dread or with joy?
2. How often do I take advantage of this sacrament of mercy?
3. Do I harbor any secret sins that I try to keep from God?

CHAPTER 42

Anointing of the Sick

ON THE CEILING OF the Sistine Chapel are some marvelous fresco paintings by Michelangelo. One of them depicts God the Father in the act of creation reaching his hand toward the outstretched hand of the inert form of Adam and passing on life, giving life.

There is another outstretched hand that also gives life. On the cross Christ stretched out his arms and died, so that in the act of dying he could restore the spiritual life that was lost to each of us in sin.

THE HEALING HAND OF CHRIST

In that first great act of creation, God gave life. In that gift, the Father gave us the possibility of friendship with himself—a relationship that was lost by the Fall, by sin. Sin continues to mar our relationship with God. The hand of God that gave us life is now extended a second time in Christ to restore, to heal, to mend whatever is broken in our life, our spiritual life that relates us to God.

When we talk about the wonderful gift of healing that is the sacrament of anointing of the sick, we reflect on the healing hand of Christ—the hand that was outstretched on the cross to win us ultimate redemption, but a hand that was also outstretched to the sick as he walked this earth. That action continues now in the anointing hand of the priest.

The sacrament of anointing of the sick is, as the words of Saint James make clear, for the sick and infirm. "Is anyone among you sick? He should summon the presbyters of the church, and they should pray over him and anoint him with oil in the name of the Lord, and the prayer of faith will save the sick person, and the Lord will raise him up. If he has committed any sins, he will be forgiven" (James 5:14–15).

The *Catechism of the Catholic Church* cites this text (as does the Council of Trent) as an indication that the apostolic Church had its own rite for the infirm—a sacred anointing of the sick instituted by Christ as truly and properly a sacrament of the New Testament (see section 1510 of the *Catechism;* compare Council of Trent, *Doctrine of the Sacrament of Extreme Unction*).

There is nothing more frustrating than being sick. From a common cold to a serious incapacitating illness, nothing so speaks to us of our own limitations. Sickness runs from annoying inconvenience—like a headache—to grave life-threatening cases involving major surgery or incurable diseases. It can take the form of old age resulting from the simple passing of years, or a sprain from the exuberance of youthful energy. In each case sickness tells us of our limitations—serious limitations.

Our reaction to infirmity is to seek alleviation. With an instinctive understanding of the human person, the Church from its beginning has provided spiritual as well as corporal remedy for our illness. We are not just flesh and bone. We are spirit, mind, and body.

THE IMPORTANCE OF THE SACRAMENT FOR THE COMMUNITY

In a very real sense, the sacrament of the anointing of the sick has a very important community dimension. In illness, particularly one as we near the end of our lives, we should never have to stand alone. We should not have to face infirmity without the consolation of others. In the ritual that we just noted in the Letter of Saint James, the sick person is instructed to call for the elders of the Church. These "presbyters" represent the community and the community's concern. Such concern is further highlighted in the "prayer of faith" that Saint James said will reclaim the one who is ill—the prayer arising from the community of faith, the Church gathered around the sick person precisely to invoke "the name of the Lord."

How is this sacrament celebrated? The *Catechism of the Catholic Church* reminds us that "the Anointing of the Sick is a liturgical and communal celebration, whether it takes place in a family home, a hospital or church, for a single sick person or a whole group of sick persons" (section 1517).

Increasingly today, there is an effort to bring people together for a communal anointing of the sick, usually in the parish church. Since infirmity and age constitute legitimate reasons for receiving this sacrament, a parish can easily provide a setting for a number of parishioners to receive the anointing of the sick regularly. It can serve the purpose of the sacrament and at the same time build up the faith community itself.

WHO MAY BE ANOINTED

The Rite of Anointing tells us that there is no need to wait until a person is at the point of death. All that is required is a prudent judgment about the seriousness of the illness. The sacrament may be repeated if the sick person recovers after anointing, or if during the same illness the danger becomes more serious. A sick person should be anointed before surgery when a dangerous illness is the reason for the intervention (*Rite of Anointing,* Introduction, 8–10).

Out of solicitude for the spiritual welfare of the faithful, the Church in the Rite of Anointing tells us that "old people may be anointed if they are in weak condition even though no dangerous illness is present. Sick children may be anointed if they have sufficient use of reason to be comforted by this sacrament" (*Rite of Anointing,* Introduction, 11, 12). The faithful "should be encouraged to ask for the anointing and, as soon as the time for the anointing comes, to receive it with faith and devotion, not misusing this sacrament by putting it off" (*Rite of Anointing,* Introduction, 13).

The image in Mark's gospel account of the woman with the hemorrhage comes quickly to mind when we speak of the sacrament of anointing of the sick. The woman, who is depicted in the reproduction of the mosaic that opens this section of the *Catechism,* was eager to touch only the Lord's cloak. "If I but touch his clothes," she thought, "I shall be cured" (Mark 5:28). The sick person today "touches" Christ the divine physician and experiences his power through sacramental anointing. The results may not always be evident physical healing, but the spiritual restoration is at work.

The *Catechism* reminds us that "only priests (bishops and presbyters) are ministers of the Anointing of the Sick" (see section 1516). In the administration of the sacrament, however, the Christian community—while represented by the priest—is encouraged to be present in the person of friends and relatives who may assist in the reading and prayers. The actual anointing is done only by the priest. The anointing is a laying on of hands, now with blessed oil, together with the prayer that accompanies it.

WHEN WE SUFFER, WE SUFFER WITH CHRIST

No small part of the sign value of the anointing of the sick is the reminder that our own weakness and suffering are made valuable in the sight of God through our loving acceptance of God's will. Saint Paul recalls for us: "The Spirit itself bears witness with our spirit that we are children of God, and if children, then heirs, heirs of God and joint heirs with Christ, if only we suffer with him in order that we may also be glorified with him" (Romans 8:16–17).

Eventually all physical remedies fail. In the life cycle of our present human condition, life begins, grows, matures, declines, and ends in death. Communion received by the dying is called viaticum, "food for the journey," the spiritual food one takes for the last journey. The *Catechism* teaches us "in addition to the Anointing of the Sick, the Church offers those who are about to leave this life the Eucharist as viaticum. Communion in the body and blood of Christ, received at this moment of 'passing over' to the Father, has a particular significance and importance. It is the seed of eternal life and the power of resurrection, according to the words of the Lord: 'He who eats my flesh and drinks my blood has eternal life, and I will raise him up on the last day' " (section 1524).

As the *Catechism* concludes its presentation on sacraments of healing, it reminds us that, "just as the sacraments of Baptism, Confirmation and Eucharist form a unity called 'the sacraments of Christian initiation' so too it can be said that Penance, the Anointing of the Sick and the Eucharist as viaticum constitute at the end of Christian life 'the sacraments that prepare for our heavenly homeland' or the sacraments that complete our earthly pilgrimage" (section 1525).

We have here no lasting city, but rather seek that home that is our true and final one with God. The sacraments of healing are a reminder that we need to concentrate every bit as much on our spiritual journey toward our final destination as we do on our daily passage through the cares and concerns of our earthly life.

QUESTIONS TO THINK ABOUT:

1. Do I encourage those who are ill or elderly to receive the sacrament of the anointing of the sick? Have I assisted at a communal anointing of the sick in my parish?
2. When I'm sick, how easy is it for me to accept God's will? What help from my friends, family, and Church makes that acceptance easier?

CHAPTER 43

The Sacrament of Orders

THE HEADING UNDER WHICH we find the sacrament of holy orders in the *Catechism of the Catholic Church* is "the sacraments at the service of communion." The *Catechism* points out that the sacraments of initiation "ground the common vocation of all Christ's disciples, a vocation to holiness and to the mission of evangelizing the world" (section 1533). At the same time it tells us that "two other sacraments, Holy Orders and Matrimony, are directed toward the salvation of others" (section 1534).

THE DIVISION OF LABOR IN THE CHURCH

In the sacrament of baptism, a person is differentiated from the world and becomes a member of Christ's Church. As such, the person shares in the mission of the Church and is identified as part of God's priestly people. The first letter of Peter speaks of the baptized faithful as "a chosen race, a royal priesthood, a holy nation, a people of his own" (1 Peter 2:9).

Each baptized person, as a member of the Body of Christ, is identified with Christ, who is King, Prophet, and Priest. This spiritual quality or identity we call the priesthood of the laity. Thus we can speak of every Christian being in some way a priest. The Second Vatican Council's *Dogmatic Constitution on the Church* tells us: "Though they differ from one another in essence and not only in degree, the common priesthood of the faithful and the ministerial or hierarchical priesthood are nonetheless inter-related. Each of them in its own special way is a participation in the one priesthood of Christ" (*Lumen Gentium* 10).

Other members of the body of the faithful are called to minister to the Church. The sacrament of orders allows these faithful to participate in Christ's mission in a unique way. It makes the recipient an authentic, authoritative, and special representative of Christ as head of the Church. For Christ, at the Last Supper, instituted the ministerial priesthood as a distinct sacrament, and the priesthood of the ordained is different and distinct from the common priesthood of the faithful. Because of the call to minister in the person of Christ to the whole body, the *Catechism* identifies holy orders as a sacrament at the service of communion.

Saint Paul points out that the Holy Spirit is the source of the division of labor in the Church. The offices are quite distinct (see 1 Corinthians 12:4–11; Romans 12:4–8). The division of work follows a design set by God. Some are called to serve as priests, others to serve in other roles—and all are called to build up the Church of Christ (compare 1 Corinthians 12:27–31).

AN IDENTIFICATION WITH CHRIST

Christ is the true, invisible head of his Body, which is the Church. Yet just as that Body of Christ is made visible and manifest in all of the members throughout the world, so too is it manifest in the presence of Christ, the head of the Church—specifically in the priesthood, which carries on the ministry of Christ.

The Second Vatican Council's *Decree on the Ministry and Life of Priests* tells us that the priestly office "is conferred by that special sacrament through which priests, by the anointing of the Holy Spirit, are marked with a special character and are so configured to Christ the Priest that they can act in the person of Christ the Head" (*Presbyterorum Ordinis* 2).

In explaining how the priest can function as Christ, the Church speaks of the priesthood as an identification with Christ on the most fundamental level. In their reception of holy orders, priests are "consecrated to God in a new way." They become "living instruments of Christ the eternal priest," so that they may be able to "accomplish His wonderful work of reuniting the whole society of men with heavenly power" (*Presbyterorum Ordinis* 12).

Because of sacred ordination, the priest stands in the midst of the Church as its leader—its head. He also then functions in the name of the whole Church specifically when presenting to God the prayers of the Church and, above all, when offering the Eucharistic sacrifice.

As we identify the work of the priest, we see that it is completely tied to the continuation of the unique work of Christ. That work is preeminently achieved in Christ's death and resurrection, which won our redemption. Hence the priesthood is intimately tied to the Eucharist, which continues to make present the life-giving effects of the great Passover. On the same first Holy Thursday on which he instituted the sacrament of the Eucharist, Christ conferred priesthood on the apostles: "Do this in remembrance of me."

In instituting the sacrament of the Eucharist, our Lord created what would be a living representation of his own death and resurrection. At the same time, he charged some to see that this sacred mystery would be performed forever in his memory. The Church sees the origin of holy orders in the will of Christ and his explicit acts on that first Holy Thursday. Thus it is true to say that holy orders and the great Christian paschal mystery are inseparable. Christ the priest offered himself for our salvation. The Eucharist is the continued re-presentation of that sacrifice. The priesthood is a special human participation in that divine work.

PRIESTHOOD IS THE WILL OF CHRIST

All of this is the plan of God unfolding in Christ. Priesthood is not an afterthought of the Christian community, but rather the explicit will of Christ. Because of this, the Church teaches that holy orders do not take their origin from the community, as though it were the community that "called" or "delegated" priests. The sacramental priesthood is truly a gift for this community that comes from Christ himself, from the very fullness of his own priesthood.

In his first letter to all the priests of the Church on Holy Thursday 1979, Pope John Paul II reminds us that the fullness of Christ's priesthood "finds its expression in the fact that Christ, while making everyone capable of offering the spiritual sacrifice, calls some and enables them to be ministers of His own sacramental Sacrifice, the Eucharist—in the offering of which all the faithful share—in which are taken up all the spiritual sacrifices of the People of God" (April 8, 1979).

The *Catechism* points out that the origin of the word "orders" is rooted in Roman antiquity, where it referred to a special governing body. Those ordained to holy orders are incorporated into Christ so that they might lead God's holy people. This hierarchy—from the Greek *hier archos,* holy ordering—assumes the responsibility of furthering the work of Christ: to teach, to lead, and to make holy.

DEGREES OF THE MINISTRY

The Second Vatican Council's *Dogmatic Constitution on the Church* reminds us that the divinely instituted ecclesiastical ministry is exercised in different degrees by those who even from ancient times have been called bishops, priests, and deacons (see *Lumen Gentium* 28). From the earliest days, Catholic teaching, the voice of the bishops, and the constant practice of the Church have recognized that there are two degrees of ministerial participation in the priesthood of Christ: the episcopacy and the presbyterate. The diaconate, the *Catechism* affirms, "is intended to help and serve them" (section 1554). Holy orders is manifest in its fullness in the episcopate—bishops, who are successors to the apostles. The sacrament is also manifest in priests or presbyters, who are coworkers with the bishop. Finally, holy orders is seen in the diaconate, which exists to assist those in priestly orders.

The order of presbyter grows out of the realization that the bishop is not able to be present in every part of the church over which he presides. In this regard, the *Catechism* quotes the Second Vatican Council: "The function of the bishops' ministry was handed over in a subordinate degree to priests so that they might be appointed in the order of the priesthood and be *co-workers of the episcopal order* for the proper fulfillment of the apostolic mission that had been entrusted to it by Christ" (*Presbyterorum Ordinis* 2; see section 1562 of the *Catechism*).

The ordination of deacons is to provide in the Church those who will be of service to the priests and especially the bishop. The *Catechism* quotes first from the *Dogmatic Constitution on the Church* and then from *The Apostolic Tradition* of Saint Hippolytus. The council reminds us: "At a lower level of the hierarchy are to be found deacons, who receive the imposition of hands 'not unto the priesthood, but unto the ministry' " (*Lumen Gentium* 29). Following Hippolytus we read, "At an ordination to the diaconate only the bishop lays hands on the candidate, thus signifying the deacon's special attachment to the bishop in the task of his 'diaconia' " (*Apostolic Tradition* 8).

In keeping with a tradition going back to Christ's selection of his apostles and affirmed in the Church as the explicit will of Christ, only men can be ordained to the priesthood. It is important that we recognize the issue as one of sacramental theology, not civil rights. At the same time we must also note that the Church makes great effort, particularly today, to underline the dignity of women in the Church and their role in the life of the Church apart from sacred orders. While the Church does not have the power to ordain women, it is clearly calling on all the members of the

Church to recognize the important role that women have in the life of the Church, and to recognize and highlight that role and the dignity of women.

While holy orders exists to be of service to the faithful, it should also call forth from them a spirit of support, understanding, and solidarity. Perhaps the most important thing we can do for our priests as they labor on behalf of the Church is to recognize our need to be open to their teaching, their leadership, and their sacramental ministry, and to embrace them in a solidarity of prayer and loving support.

QUESTIONS TO THINK ABOUT:

1. What priests have influenced my life the most? How did they exert that influence?
2. How would I feel if my brother or my son entered the seminary to study for the priesthood? Would I support his call?
3. Do I support the priests in my parish as well as I ought to support them? What could I do to be more open to their leadership?

CHAPTER 44

Marriage

THE PREPARATIONS FOR MARRIAGE are usually extensive, and the celebration itself is a moment of great joy—not only for the couple but also for their families and friends. It should be this way. A marriage marks the beginning of two lives coming together to share a whole new reality: their lives as a couple, a husband and wife.

THE CONSENT OF THE COUPLE IS AT THE HEART OF THE CEREMONY

The marriage ritual clearly describes what is happening, not only for the couple but also for the Church. The bride and groom stand before the priest. He addresses them in these words: "My dear friends, you have come together in this church so that the Lord may seal and strengthen your love in the presence of the Church's minister and this community . . ." We are reminded that this man and woman ask the Lord to seal their love publicly in the presence of the Church. The couple declares that they have come freely and without reservation to give themselves to each other and lovingly to accept children from God if this be God's plan.

The essential element of the wedding ceremony is the consent of the couple. In fact, of all the seven sacraments, this is the only one, in the Western Church, conferred not by a sacred minister but by the participants themselves. The priest is present to witness the marriage in the name of the Church and to bless it, but the wedding itself takes place through the public consent of the couple. It is for this reason that the priest invites the man and woman to declare their consent: "Since it is your intention to enter into marriage, join your right hands, and declare your consent before God and his Church." (In the Eastern Churches, the sacrament is conferred by the blessing of the priest.)

In a tradition-laden formulary used in dioceses in the United States, the consent of the groom and the bride is expressed in words that proclaim that they promise each other, "To have and to hold, from this day forward, for better, for worse, for richer, for poorer, in sickness and in health, until death do us part."

After receiving their consent, the priest invokes God's blessing on their decision and reminds everyone present that what God has joined, human beings "must not divide." Everything about the wedding calls attention to its public nature and its permanency.

In another ancient tradition that continues to this day, rings are blessed and exchanged as a sign of the couple's love and fidelity. The ring is worn to announce to all that the two now form one family and are lifelong partners.

MARRIAGE IS AT THE SERVICE OF COMMUNION

What is a part of the human condition from the beginning according to God's creative plan—the coming together in a covenant for lifelong support and procreation of children—has been raised by Christ to the level of a sacrament. The love that brings a couple together becomes a channel of grace. The marriage bond that they form in the exchange of vows becomes an instrument of God's saving action among us.

Thus, marriage is viewed by the Church as a sacrament at the service of communion. Not only does the individual who receives the sacrament together with his or her spouse benefit from this sacrament but so too does the new reality they create—a family—and through that family the community and the Church.

The *Catechism of the Catholic Church* speaks of the goods and requirements of conjugal love, highlighting the unity and indissolubility of marriage, fidelity, and its openness to fertility, and the communion of love that embraces their entire life. Such lifelong commitment in mutual support is a blessing that is enriched with the passage of each year. It requires commitment, faithfulness, and sacrifice on the part of each of the spouses.

The *Catechism* points out, "By its very nature conjugal love requires the inviolable fidelity of the spouses" (see section 1646). This follows from the gift they make of themselves to each other, which has to be definitive if it is to endure in the face of difficulties.

Finally, the *Catechism* addresses the openness to offspring with a quotation from the *Pastoral Constitution on the Church in the Modern World:* "By its very nature the institution of marriage and married love is ordered to the procreation and education of the offspring and it is in them that it finds its crowning glory" (*Gaudium et Spes* 48).

THE DOMESTIC CHURCH

As the spouses come together to exchange vows publicly and have their marriage witnessed and blessed by the Church, they form a family. With the passage of time and the blessing of God, this family should grow stronger in love for God and one another. Their focus on love, faith, prayer, and their spiritual communion reflects the very life of the Church itself. For this reason we refer to the family as the "domestic Church."

The Second Vatican Council revived the use of this ancient expression and calls the family *"ecclesia domestica"* (*Lumen Gentium* 11). Following this line of thought the *Catechism* points out: "It is here that the father of the family, the mother, children, and all members of the family exercise the priesthood of the baptized in a privileged way 'by the reception of the sacraments, prayer and charity' " (*Lumen Gentium* 10; see section 1657 of the *Catechism*).

MARRIAGE IS INDISSOLUBLE

In a society where family life is collapsing and our social order is unraveling, the Church's teaching on the indissolubility of marriage and the obligation of parents to their children is a timely remedy. Today we see children generated by parents who take no responsibility for them. We observe the spread of surrogate families and the proliferation of gangs and individuals who feel alienated. We experience the growing expectation that somehow the state or society is supposed to assume the responsibilities of the family. In a time like this, the wisdom of the Church's teaching becomes more apparent.

The family is under assault today because marriage is frequently devalued within our culture. As members of the Church, we are obliged to be all the more attentive to the challenges that weaken marriage as a social institution and as an expression of God's plan for the well-being of the human race. Divorce, temporary live-in arrangements, sexuality as a form of entertainment, and the general diminishing of respect for the natural order of two-parent families all directly challenge the vision of family life revealed in Sacred Scripture, proclaimed by the Church, and experienced throughout human history.

The Church firmly proclaims and has always taught that a sacramental marriage between Christians in which there has been true matrimonial consent and consummation is absolutely indissoluble except by the death of one of the partners. As a sacrament recalling Christ's undying love for the Church, it creates and expresses a binding tie that endures for life, no matter what happens between the spouses.

Marriage, like all the sacraments, has important and highly visible social and ecclesial implications and is carefully regulated by Church law. Just as baptism, for example, to be valid requires water and the invocation of the name of the Trinity, as well as the proper intention on the part of the minister, so also does marriage require a proper intention, freedom, and capacity on the part of its ministers, the bride and groom, and the observance of the "proper form" of marriage by Catholics as required by the Church's law.

Since these laws touch the sacramental life of the Church—her core reality—they are not to be taken lightly, lest a marriage be invalidly celebrated. Only when a marriage is invalid from the beginning does the Church through its tribunals declare its nullity. (For more on this subject, see Chapter 75.)

The celebration of marriage between two Catholics normally takes place within Mass. In the liturgy of the Eucharist, in which salvation history rises to its climax, the newly married couple enters the sacramental source of the paschal mystery so as to "eat this bread and drink the cup" and to "proclaim the death of the Lord until he comes" (1 Corinthians 11:26). Here they find the pattern for their own married life. Even in ceremony, the Church seeks to enshrine and consecrate marriage by her most sublime possession, the mystery of faith.

In the human love that brings a woman and man to marriage, we already hear God speaking to us of the beauty and fidelity of love, its transforming power, and its creative energy. In the sacrament of matrimony, God speaks to us of the fullness of human love. Our limited experience of love is only a sign and beginning of a love that changes us into children of God, who share his own wondrous and unending life of love. Christ's love for the Church is the pattern for married life. "Love one another as I love you!" (John 15:12).

QUESTIONS TO THINK ABOUT:

1. How have secular cultural attitudes toward marriage influenced my own thinking? Do I find it hard to accept the teachings of the Church on marriage?
2. How could I help other Christians understand the importance of the Christian view of marriage?
3. How does married love help us understand the love of God?

CHAPTER 45

Family Life

EVERYONE RECOGNIZES THAT FAMILY life in our country is breaking down. With its collapse, we are witnessing the unraveling of the fabric of society on the local, regional, and national levels.

THE ORIGINAL CELL

Why is the family so essential? The *Catechism of the Catholic Church* reminds us that "The family is the original cell of social life" (section 2207). It is the natural society in which a husband and wife come together in love and give themselves to each other in love and in the gift of life.

From that "original cell," the whole human community grows in an ever-widening set of relationships. It begins with a husband and wife, then grows to include their children, the wider family, and eventually all those other communities—educational, cultural, social, economic, and, of course, political—of which they become a part.

If the original cell or the foundational building block is damaged in any way or even destroyed, neither the body of which it is a cell nor the edifice of which it is the foundation can long endure.

WHY FAMILIES ARE COLLAPSING

Some might ask why this condition has reached such a critical point today. There have always been failed marriages and irresponsible parents in the past. Today, however, I believe we are recognizing an extensive and perhaps overwhelming collapse of individual families precisely because our society no longer supports the basic and essential values on which families rest and our community is built.

If we look to the teaching of the Church, we find a vision of family life that is not always replicated in the secular society in which we live. In the apostolic exhortation of Pope John Paul II on the family (*Familiaris Consortio*) and the 1994 *Letter to Families in the International Year of the Family,* as well as in the teaching of the *Catechism of the Catholic Church,* we find a beautiful vision of marriage and family that corresponds to God's plan, to our true happiness, and to what we are called to sustain as faithful members of the Church.

In contrast, it is precisely the rejection of these principles that has resulted in a society where children no longer have a relationship with both of their parents, parents take no responsibility for the children they generate, and marriages are of such short duration that children experience a variety of adult figures in their lives without the necessary rapport with a caring and loving father or mother.

THE ORIGINAL PLAN OF CREATION

At the core of the Church's teaching on family life is God's plan for the human race set forth so majestically in the Book of Genesis. Male and female God created them—in the image and likeness of God he created them. God looked on all that he made and he found that it was good (see Genesis 1:26–27).

The original plan of creation called for the man and the woman to come together and form a society of mutual support. "It is not good for the man to be alone. I will make a suitable partner for him" (Genesis 2:18). This partnership was to be a permanent one—to allow both partners the mutual support and care they would need to get through life and to provide the enduring context in which their children could be raised, educated, nurtured, and prepared for life on their own as the next generation of family life.

This teaching was confirmed explicitly by Jesus himself. In order to test him, some asked whether it was lawful for "a man to divorce his wife for any cause whatever" (Matthew 19:3). Jesus replied, "Have you not read that from the beginning the Creator 'made them male and female' and said, 'For this reason a man shall leave his father and mother and be joined to his wife and the two shall become one flesh'? So they are no longer two, but one flesh. Therefore, what God has joined together, no human being must separate" (Matthew 19:3–6).

A HARD SAYING

Among the "hard" sayings of Jesus, this has become a particularly challenging one for many people today. Statistics show that one of every two marriages in this country ends in divorce, and the rate continues to climb. Perhaps what Jesus was recognizing for all of us was that it is impossible to sustain a loving, permanent relationship through all of the difficulties of life without the firm commitment that, in spite of all of the trials and tribulations, the partnership will endure. In a society that so lightly sets aside personal commitment, we should not be surprised that marriage is in a state of decline.

It would not be far off the mark to say that our secular society's denial of the intimate connection between sexual activity and the marriage bond is responsible for most of the unraveling of family and, therefore, community life in our time. If sexual activity and the generation of children are for personal satisfaction alone, we can expect an ever-growing number of children who cannot identify in any meaningful sense with their parents, and parents who are not in any realistic sense participants in sustaining, educating, and developing their offspring.

The Church proclaims another entirely different vision of the family. It is the "domestic Church." A Christian family constitutes a specific manifestation and realization of ecclesial communion. It is a sign and an image of that communion of the Father, the Son, and the Holy Spirit just as the Church itself and every believer are to be a realization of the love of God within us through the power of the Holy Spirit.

The Church's picture of family life includes the personal commitment of the partners in the marriage. It also includes openness to the generation of new life if it is God's plan for their marriage—the joyful acceptance of the responsibility and privilege of raising children and helping them to grow in wisdom, age, and grace. Finally, it includes the recognition that this action is a graced response to the love of God. That recognition elevates married life to the level of sacramental participation in Christ's own redeeming action, allowing parents to participate in the building up of the Body of Christ by bringing new life into the world and into the Church.

This is summed up in the *Catechism of the Catholic Church,* where we read: "The conjugal community is established upon the covenant and consent of the spouses. Marriage and family are ordered to the good of the spouses, to the procreation and the education of children" (section 2249).

We should neither be surprised nor dismayed if those whose views of life are different from ours and who hold another set of values continue to push contrary views. We hold a vision for our country. We need also to be active and engaged in the struggle if we hope to preserve family life and its importance for our country, our community, our Church, ourselves, and our children.

We must always be ready to defend the family and always confident that whatever we say or do that supports wholesome and healthy family life ultimately benefits both our nation and God's family among us—the Church.

QUESTIONS TO THINK ABOUT:

1. How is the modern secular view of family life reflected in my own parish? What can we do to counteract the influence of that view?
2. How well does my own family represent the ideal of the "domestic Church"? What can I do to help it come closer to that ideal?
3. How can we help heal broken families in our parish?

CHAPTER 46

Sacramentals

AT THE ENTRANCE TO most Catholic churches, there is a holy water font—sometimes as large as a baptistry and at other times small enough to fit just the fingers on our hand. On entering any church, we bless ourselves with the sign of the cross by tracing the symbol of our redemption on our forehead, chest, and shoulders. The holy water in the font is also a reminder of our baptism into the death and resurrection of Christ.

Throughout the liturgical year and every aspect of our life, a variety of physical, visible, tangible realities are used to turn our attention to the realm of the Spirit and the world of grace. In addition to holy water and the sign of the cross, the blessings, the ashes used at the beginning of Lent, the palm, the blessing of throats, the rosary, and the stations of the cross are some of the more familiar sacramentals.

SACRAMENTALS ARE INSTITUTED BY THE CHURCH

Sacramentals are closely allied to the sacraments, but they are not the same. A sacrament is an outward sign—something visible, sensible, and discernible that achieves what it signifies and has been elevated by Christ to the level of actually conferring grace.

The *Catechism of the Catholic Church* tells us that sacramentals are instituted by the Church. "These are sacred signs which bear a resemblance to the sacraments. They signify effects, particularly of a spiritual nature, which are obtained through the intercession of the Church" (section 1667). While sacraments and sacramentals are similar, they are also very distinct. They both use "outward signs"—discernible, natural realities—to address a spiritual dimension of life. The sacraments are instituted by Christ, but sacramentals are instituted by the Church. The efficacy of the sacraments is through the power of Christ. Sacramentals invoke the intercession of the Church.

WHY SACRAMENTALS WERE CREATED

Why would the Church create sacramentals? The answer is found in why Christ created the sacraments. We are people made up of body and soul, physical matter and spirit. When God chose to reveal himself to us, he came among us as one of us in a visible, audible, sensible manner so that we could grasp that which was beyond us—the transcendent, the spiritual, the immaterial. When God became one of us in Christ Jesus, the incarnation became the norm for the action of the Church.

Just as the Eternal Word of God took on flesh and became visible among us, so too Christ would institute his Church and the sacraments, which would be visible and at the same time spiritual. In like manner the Church continues to use material realities to speak to us of the far more substantial spiritual order—the order of grace. The *Catechism* tells us "there is scarcely any proper use of material things which cannot be thus directed towards the sanctification of men and the praise of God" (section 1670).

BLESSINGS

Some of the most familiar sacramentals are blessings. We should begin and end each day with the sign of the cross just as we should initiate and conclude all of our activities "in the name of the Father and of the Son and of the Holy Spirit." The sign of the cross is a summary of our faith and a renewed personal profession of our Christian belief. We invoke the Holy Trinity and recognize the Father's loving presence in our lives, the redemption won for us by Christ on the cross, and the enduring new life of the Holy Spirit within us.

Regularly we ask for blessings on our lives, homes, and religious articles, for activities of particular importance to us, or when we are sick or experience a special need. All of the blessings of the Church, many of which are found in the *Book of Blessings,* symbolize the faith dimension of our life and call upon the Church to intercede before God on our behalf.

SACRAMENTALS ASSOCIATED WITH THE LITURGICAL CALENDAR

Some sacramentals are tied closely to the liturgical year and our presence in Church. Holy water recalls our baptism and the purification that calls us to put on a new person whose mind and heart is of Christ. Sometimes the Eucharistic liturgy will begin with the sprinkling rite so that the water touching us will evoke a remembrance of our baptismal commitment and challenge us to renew our baptismal promises.

Of the sacramentals associated with the liturgical calendar, blessed palm and blessed ashes are two of the most popular. It is not unusual to see people lined up in and even outside the church waiting to receive the familiar sign of repentance on Ash Wednesday. Another long-standing Catholic tradition is to take the blessed palm received at church on Palm Sunday and place it in a visible location at home. One tradition calls for the palm to be inserted between the corpus and the cross of a crucifix that hangs in a particularly visible part of the home.

Candles have always played an important part in the devotion of the faithful. Beginning with the paschal candle solemnly blessed, lighted, and placed in the sanctuary during the Easter Vigil, and including the countless votive lights in churches throughout the world, the candle is the symbol of Christ. He is the light of the world. We walk in his way according to his light.

On the feast of the Presentation of the Lord, February 2, the Church blesses candles to be used throughout the year. In many places, there are processions marking this event. On the next day, the feast of Saint Blaise, February 3, the newly blessed candles are used as the priest imparts a blessing over the throats of the faithful. Invoking the name of a saint in the use of a sacramental, whether it be the blessing of throats, the procession of a statue, or the sharing of Saint Anthony's bread, is a recognition that we form one communion with the saints. Their intercession is both welcome and encouraged.

Votive candles of all sizes have played a significant role in the devotional life of Catholics for centuries. The lighting of candles before the Blessed Sacrament or at various shrines and chapels is a pious and praiseworthy effort to keep our needs and prayers before the Lord even when we are caught up in other activities that may distract us. The candle burning brightly says in effect "Lord, even if I should forget you, please do not forget me."

The scapulars, medals, medallions, and particularly blessed crosses that we wear make our personal commitment to Christ visible to others. In the same way that the invisible character of our baptismal grace distinguishes our soul, so too an outward sign in the form of a medal or cross marks us publicly as followers of Jesus.

THE ROSARY AND THE STATIONS OF THE CROSS

Two immensely popular sacramentals that allow not only for personal piety but also for a communal expression of our devotion are the rosary and the stations of the cross. Quietly and individually or collectively and vocally, we can in the stations of the cross trace the suffering and death Christ endured for our salvation. The fourteen stations of the cross are found in most churches and begin with the condemnation to death of Jesus by Pilate and culminate with Jesus being placed in the tomb.

There is no set format for the prayers as one moves from station to station reflecting on the passion and death of our Lord, but a particularly popular "Way of the Cross" was composed by Saint Alphonsus Liguori. His version was first published in Italian in 1761 and in his brief introduction to this devotion Saint Alphonsus wrote: "The pious exercise of the Way of the Cross represents the sorrowful journey that Jesus Christ made with the cross on his shoulders, to die on Calvary for love of us."

Consisting primarily of five sets of ten "Hail Marys," the rosary offers us an opportunity to reflect on the whole life of Christ. The recitation of the rosary through its entire fifteen decades takes us from the annunciation of the coming of Christ through all of the joyful, sorrowful, and glorious mysteries of our salvation. It culminates in Christ's resurrection and the pledge of eternal life for each of us already gloriously manifest in the Blessed Virgin Mary as queen of heaven.

There is no particular time or place when the rosary is more appropriate. It can be said anywhere at anytime. A particularly appealing location for reciting it is during long drives or times spent in the car in congested traffic.

Given the wide range of sacramentals, there are certainly some that are spiritually appealing and meaningful for each believer. The Church encourages us to use these signs of our faith to nourish our Christian life so that they might be symbols of Christ's life growing within us.

QUESTIONS TO THINK ABOUT:

1. Which sacramentals have the most meaning for me? Why those particular ones? What do they symbolize to me?
2. How would I explain the sacramentals to a non-Catholic? How would I help others understand their value?

CHAPTER 47

The Rosary

NEXT TO THE CROSS itself, the most ubiquitous symbol of Catholic devotion is probably the rosary. Usually in the shorter five-decade form, "the beads" are the basis for the private prayer life of countless millions of people throughout the Church in every land. Interestingly enough, the rosary has its origin in the formalized public prayer of the Church called the Liturgy of the Hours.

A MINIATURE OF THE LITURGY OF THE HOURS

In the *Catechism of the Catholic Church,* we learn that "medieval piety in the West developed the prayer of the rosary as a popular substitute for the Liturgy of the Hours" (2678). In response to the scriptual injunction to pray ceaselessly at every hour, the Church developed a liturgy that calls for a series of prayerful interludes throughout the day. These include the office of readings to be prayed at any time, morning and evening prayer, a midday prayer, and finally night prayer.

Since the Liturgy of the Hours follows the liturgical calendar, all of the major commemorations of our redemption that invoke the life of Jesus and his mother Mary are highlighted. The liturgical year begins with Advent and the annunciation of the coming of Christ. It continues through Christmas and the birth of Christ, into the Lenten period and Holy Week, commemorating the suffering and death of Christ. Finally, it climaxes in the Easter and Pentecost season, as we celebrate the resurrection of Jesus, the outpouring of the Spirit on his Church, and our hope to share eternal life with Christ in glory.

In a concise and miniature re-presentation of the Liturgy of the Hours and the liturgy calendar, the rosary takes us through the mysteries of Christ's redemption. We make the journey mystery by mystery in increments of approximately fifteen minutes.

THE STRUCTURE OF THE ROSARY

At the heart of the structure of the rosary is the "decade." A decade corresponds to each of the fifteen mysteries commemorated in the rosary. Ten Hail Marys are said for each decade; they are preceded by an Our Father and followed by a Glory to the Father.

While reciting a decade of the rosary, one is expected to meditate on the particular mystery for that decade and on its meaning in our life. Thus we proceed bead by bead, using the words in the New Testament to engage us as we turn our mind and heart to the mystery before us.

The entire rosary is divided into three chaplets: the joyful, the sorrowful, and the glorious mysteries. To "say a rosary" commonly means to pray one chaplet of five mysteries, although it is not uncommon for some people to spread out the entire rosary of fifteen decades across their day.

According to a long-standing tradition, the joyful mysteries of the rosary are prayed on Monday and Thursday, the sorrowful mysteries on Tuesday and Friday, and the glorious mysteries on Wednesday, Saturday, and, of course, Sunday, which is the day on which the Church celebrates the resurrection of Jesus from the dead every week.

Commonly a chaplet begins with the recitation of the Apostles' Creed, followed by an Our Father and three Hail Marys—all offered as a petition for an increase in faith, hope, and love. It is particularly fitting that the recitation of the rosary begins with the Apostles' Creed because it is precisely our faith that will form the object of our meditation during the rosary. The creed recalls for us the major elements of our faith: belief in the Father, the Son, and the Holy Spirit, and belief in Christ's Church.

WHY PRAY THE ROSARY?

The rosary is an exceptionally versatile instrument of prayer. It can be prayed privately as an individual or collectively as a small community. It combines vocal prayer with meditation and can be utilized in almost any setting. I find, as do so many others, that reciting the rosary while driving not only converts a time-consuming activity into a moment of communion with God, but also helps reduce the frustrations and temptations to impatience and anger that are increasingly a part of driving in urban settings.

For many of us the rosary also satisfies another human need: to pray to God in private. This form of prayer—individual private prayer—was commended by Jesus in the Sermon on the Mount: "When you pray, go to your inner room, close the door, and pray to your Father in secret. And your Father who sees in secret will repay you" (Matthew 6:6).

Jesus himself lived always in a prayerful spirit and turned easily to explicit prayer. He also taught the apostles to live their lives in a spirit of prayer. They should "watch and pray." The Lord seemed even to have commended prayer as a constant activity: "Then he told them a parable about the necessity for them to pray always without becoming weary" (Luke 18:1).

From the example and teaching of Jesus, it is clear that a Christian should be a person of prayer. All who know that their existence and life of grace come from God can recognize the need to remain in communion with God.

This point is important because there are always people who find prayer difficult. We are easily distracted, and perhaps are not as generous as we ought to be in the time we give to prayer. In encouraging us to turn our hearts to God in prayer, the Church reminds us that the very act of praying can be an acknowledgment of one's weakness and dependence on God in such a way that we stand humbly before God in obedience to his will for us.

Such prayer flows from one's filial relationship with God. It is the loving, obedient response of a child to a father's love. Any life lived in faith, hope, and love will have to express itself to God in prayer.

Personal prayer is essential to living the Christian life, as the words of the Lord clearly indicate. This is the daily link to God that transforms both our character and our life. Personal prayer helps prepare each of us as a Christian for the public prayer to which we are all called—liturgical prayer. Regular private daily prayer is the best preparation for a full, rich participation in the public prayer of the Church. Praying the rosary is an example of this regular private daily prayer.

THE MYSTERIES OF THE ROSARY

As we mentioned earlier, there are fifteen mysteries of the rosary that form the fifteen decades around which we focus our prayer while reciting the Hail Marys.

The joyful mysteries:

1. The annunciation
2. The visitation of Mary to Elizabeth
3. The nativity of our Lord
4. The presentation of Jesus in the temple
5. The finding of the child Jesus in the temple

The sorrowful mysteries:

1. The agony of Jesus in the garden
2. The scourging at the pillar
3. The crowning with thorns
4. The carrying of the cross
5. The crucifixion and death of Jesus

The glorious mysteries:

1. The resurrection of Jesus
2. The ascension of Jesus into heaven
3. The descent of the Holy Spirit upon the apostles
4. The assumption of Mary into heaven
5. The coronation of Mary as queen of heaven

There is a long-standing tradition in the Church that encourages us to offer each decade of the rosary for a particular intention. In this way we are able to call to mind and place before God our needs and those of our loved ones, our petitions for the good of the Church and our human community. Perhaps you might frequently include as an intention for one of your decades the intentions of our Holy Father, the Pope.

QUESTIONS TO THINK ABOUT:

1. How often do I pray the rosary? Where might I make time to pray the rosary more often?
2. Why do I pray the rosary?
3. For what intentions did I offer each decade the last time I prayed the rosary? Why did I make those choices?

CHAPTER 48

Christian Funerals

A NUMBER OF YEARS ago, a book entitled *The American Way of Dying* called attention to the extravagant way in which Americans lavish all types of creature comforts on a corpse. Unlike the tradition of memorializing a person or his or her accomplishments with a monument or even a rather ostentatious tomb, the current practice seems to provide for the "comfort" of the deceased person as if, the book goes on, "to deny that death has occurred."

Perhaps it is an expression of our increasingly secular age that funerals no longer mark a passage from this life to a life to come but rather signal a lack of faith in eternal life.

DEATH IS A CHANGE, NOT AN END

Our Catholic faith presents us with another completely different view of human mortality. As the preface for the funeral Mass tells us, we believe that in death "life is changed, not ended." In the firm faith and expectation of the resurrection, we bury our dead. Funerals are acts of faith and not declarations of despair.

In an earlier age, before the Christian era, the classical Roman practice for concluding a funeral service included the salutation *"ave atque vale"*—hail and farewell. It symbolized the last greeting and then the departure of the deceased into an "everlasting sleep." But that last greeting was unbearably sad. The deceased had passed beyond all hearing—in fact all being.

Our Catholic faith calls us to a belief that life exists after death. Christ is risen from the dead, and so too shall we rise. The pledge of everlasting life is a part of our heritage. As the prayer for the Mass for the dead relates: "When the body of our earthly dwelling lies in death we gain an everlasting dwelling place in heaven."

When Lazarus died, his sisters Martha and Mary sent for Jesus. "When Jesus arrived, he found that Lazarus had already been in the tomb for four days . . . Martha said to Jesus, 'Lord if you had been here, my brother would not have died. But even now I know that whatever you ask of God, God will give you.' Jesus said to her, 'Your brother will rise.' Martha said to him, 'I know that he will rise, in the resurrection on the last day.' Jesus told her, 'I am the resurrection and the life; whoever believes in me, even if he dies, will live, and everyone who lives and believes in me will never die. Do you believe this?' She said to him, 'Yes, Lord, I have come to believe that you are the Messiah, the Son of God, the one who is coming into the world' " (John 11:17–27). Our Catholic faith urges us to profess as Martha did that "I have come to believe." Our funerals reflect that belief.

THE CHRISTIAN FUNERAL

Part Two of the *Catechism of the Catholic Church* deals with "The Celebration of the Christian Mystery," where we have reviewed and reflected on the liturgical life of the Church, her sacramental patrimony, and the mystery of Christ's presence with us in the sacramental ministry. It seems fitting that this section should close with an article on Christian funerals. From baptism through every stage of the believer's life, Christ has been present in his Church: blessing, anointing, healing, saving, ministering, instructing, guiding, and caring for each of his disciples. There is no more appropriate conclusion to a Christian life than a Catholic funeral in the deceased one's parish church, followed by burial in ground made hallow in anticipation of our sharing in Christ's resurrection.

Any reflection today on Christian funerals causes us to comment on some more recent trends in our country. Currently, as funerals become part of an ever-increasing conglomerate business, the relationship of one's death, funeral, and burial to one's faith life and Church becomes more tenuous.

Increasingly, "one-stop shopping" offers Catholics a package that excludes some of our most cherished traditions of burying the dead. We need to make sure, when we make arrangements for our own death or that of a loved one, that a funeral Mass in church and burial in a Catholic cemetery are part of our agreement. Too often, these are now presented as unnecessary "extras" and "added burdens" to the bereaved.

As part of a tradition going back to the earliest days of the Church, we bring our dead to the parish church for the final farewell and celebration of the Eucharist. Most fittingly this takes place in the parish church because it is there that the follower of Christ received baptism into new life, was confirmed in the gifts of the Spirit, and was regularly nourished (weekly, even daily) with the Body and Blood of Christ at the Eucharist. It is in the parish church that we seek absolution, are married, celebrate first communion, and mark with our families the great events of our lives.

How appropriate it is, then, to be brought at the end of our life down the aisle of the same parish church. The Christian family, which is manifested in the parish, joins our family and friends in bidding us farewell and in asking God's mercy on us as we pass through the doors of death into what we pray will be a realm of eternal light, rest, and peace.

As the body is brought to the entrance of the church, the priest greets the family and mourners and sprinkles the coffin with holy water as a sign and reminder of our baptism into Christ's death and resurrection. A pall is placed over the coffin as a sign of the new life we have put on in Christ and as a pledge that we will one day be clothed in glory.

The *Catechism of the Catholic Church* teaches us: "The Church who, as Mother, has borne the Christian sacramentally in her womb during his earthly pilgrimage, accompanies him at his journey's end, in order to surrender him 'into the Father's hands.' She offers to the Father, in Christ, the child of his grace, and she commits to the earth, in hope, the seed of the body that will rise in glory. This offering is fully celebrated in the Eucharistic sacrifice; the blessings before and after Mass are sacramentals" (section 1683).

I am often struck by how calm, reflective, and peaceful the family and mourners become as the Eucharistic liturgy begins. The holy sacrifice of the Mass calls us beyond ourselves out of our own grief and loss into the sacramental and transcendent presence of God—the God who wipes away every tear and makes all things new.

The ritual for the burial of the dead reminds us that the homily is to provide an instruction on our faith in the resurrection. More and more I am convinced of the wisdom of this instruction. There is a temptation to use this time to present a eulogy—a summary of the person's life in praise and recognition of his or her accomplishments. Given the number of people present who are less aware of the teaching of the faith they profess than they are of the accomplishments of the deceased, the importance of using this time to explain what is happening in the context of our faith is all the more evident.

Pastorally, I find it serves the interest of everyone involved to reserve a time at the end of Mass—after the final prayer but before the final commendation—for those remarks, reflections, and remembrances that speak to us of the great gift that the deceased has been and of the value of his or her life. In this way both the human and faith dimensions of the believer are properly celebrated.

At the conclusion of the Mass, the priest sprinkles the coffin with holy water and incenses it, because it has been a temple of the Holy Spirit and will be called to bodily resurrection on the last day.

Finally the body is taken to the gravesite for internment. Catholic cemeteries continue to provide a ministry in the Church that recognizes the uniquely Christian understanding of death. They also provide us with holy ground where we can with some regularity remember our dead, recall their goodness to us, and ask God's blessing on them. We pray for the dead with the full awareness that we too shall follow in their steps.

QUESTIONS TO THINK ABOUT:

1. What makes a Christian funeral different from a secular funeral?
2. It is always difficult to accept the passing of a loved one. Why do we mark a death with a funeral, rather than simply trying to forget about it?
3. Have I made clear my wishes for my own funeral? Do I know the wishes of my loved ones?

CHAPTER 49

Life in Christ

As we make our way through the *Catechism of the Catholic Church* we have arrived at Part Three: Life in Christ. Remember that the *Catechism* is divided into four parts. The first takes us through our profession of faith and a study of the articles of the creed. The second deals with the celebration of the Christian mystery and a review of the liturgy and sacramental life of the Church. The third (this section) deals with our life in Christ, or how we live out our faith—a commitment expressed in the Ten Commandments. Finally, the fourth is a section on Christian prayer woven around the Lord's Prayer and its petitions.

THE NEW LAW

As each of the other sections opens with an illustration from some artwork of antiquity, so too does this one on "Life in Christ." The piece chosen to introduce this portion of the *Catechism* is taken from a sarcophagus discovered underneath the main altar of the Basilica of Saint Peter in Rome and dates from the year 359. In this carving, we see Christ in glory seated on his heavenly throne surrounded by the apostles Peter and Paul. Each of the apostles looks to Christ, from whom they receive the scrolls of the new law.

The carving reminds us that, as Moses had received the old law from God on Mount Sinai, now the apostles, represented by their two leaders, receive from Christ, the Son of God, the Lord of heaven and earth, the new law; no longer written on tablets of stone, but engraved by the Holy Spirit on the hearts of believers.

As we begin this section of the *Catechism,* it is important for us to recall that the law of Christ, the law of love, is more than a set of regulations imposed from outside us and against which we measure our actions. Rather, it is the power of God's Spirit moving our hearts to follow Christ, his way, his will, his love. Saint Paul in his Letter to the Philippians reminds us that we should put on the same attitude that was in Christ Jesus (see Philippians 2:5).

The words from Pope Saint Leo the Great that begin this section of the *Catechism* remind us of our call to holiness: "Christian, recognize your dignity and, now that you share in God's own nature, . . . remember who is your head and of whose body you are a member" (section 1691 of the *Catechism;* Sermo 21 on the birth of the Lord).

OUR NEW LIFE

Our call to holiness is rooted in the gift of new life we receive through Jesus Christ in the outpouring of the Holy Spirit. Saint Leo does not exaggerate when he says that we share in God's own nature because we receive in the Holy Spirit the very Spirit of God. We become children of God by adoption, by an outpouring of the Spirit that allows us to call God our Father.

Our parents, working with God, give us life—our human life. The basis of who we are and what we do is centered on this wondrous gift of human life. All our rights and obligations flow from the fact that we have received this gift. All the things we can accomplish in life—all our joys, achievements, and hopes—are intimately tied to the fact that we are living human beings made in the image and likeness of God. Take away this gift and there is nothing.

Together with this human life, and elevating it, is a new life that we receive in baptism. Not that we have two lives, but now our human life is transformed and raised to a dignity that lets us live and move and have our being as children not just of human creation but of divine sonship. Everything else in our spiritual life, all of our aspirations for life eternal, are rooted in the precious gift of new life that comes to us in Christ.

It is this mystery that we shall explore as we study what it means to say that Christ comes to give new life. "I came so that they might have life and have it more abundantly" (John 10:10). He offers us a life richer than any we could ever otherwise have, a life so radically new that we must be born again to have it (see John 3:3–8).

The new life that we receive in baptism, that we nurture through the sacraments, and that someday will flower into eternal life in glory was part of God's plan from the beginning. God "chose us in him, before the foundation of the world, to be holy and without blemish before him. . . . In all wisdom and insight, he has made known to us the mystery of his will in accord with his favor that he set forth in him as a plan for the fullness of times, to sum up all things in Christ, in heaven and on earth" (Ephesians 1:4, 8–10).

Perhaps the most dramatic statement of the intensity of our new life in Christ is found in Saint Paul's Letter to the Galatians. Here he tells us that when the fullness of time came, God sent his son "so that we might receive adoption" (Galatians 4:5). By the utter graciousness of God's goodness, God chose to take us, fallen, frail creatures, and raise us to a level of unique relationship with himself that reflects his unity with and love for his own son. All of this was done through the power of the Holy Spirit. "As proof that you are children, God sent the Spirit of his son into our hearts, crying out, 'Abba, Father!' So you are no longer a slave but a child, and if a child then also an heir, through God" (Galatians 4:6–7).

PREPROGRAMMED TO KNOW GOD

In order to understand how it is that we can be elevated to life in Christ and therefore share in some sense the very life of God, we need to go all the way back to the beginning. God created us, and did so in God's image and likeness. We have a human soul—a spiritual reality capable of loving and knowing God. Already built into our human nature are immaterial faculties: our will and our intellect. They can carry us beyond the limitations of physical reality and make it possible for us to *know,* and therefore to know *God;* and to love, and therefore to share God's life, which itself is love.

In a sense, we were preconditioned, preprogrammed if you will, to move beyond the limitations of this material and finite world and somehow identify ourselves with a spiritual and eternal being. The *Catechism of the Catholic Church* tells us: "Endowed with 'a spiritual and immortal' soul, the human person is 'the only creature on earth that God has willed for his own sake.' From his conception, he is destined for eternal beatitude" (section 1703).

How would we be transformed so that the capability we have would become real? Jesus answers this question in his discussion with Nicodemus in the third chapter of John's gospel. We would be born again, this time of water and the Holy Spirit. God's Spirit would come upon us in a way that we are made one with God.

The whole teaching on the mystical body of Christ is a reminder that our life is to be transformed by our union with him. His life, his mind, and his Spirit are to be ours. For "we are members of his body" (Ephesians 5:30). It is for this reason that the Church teaches us that we are called to holiness. We are created with all of the capability of oneness with Christ. God sent Christ to help us respond to that call and then poured out the Holy Spirit on us to give us the power to live the new life.

Anyone who has ever received a gift—or even given one—that has on it the warning "batteries not included" knows how useless even the most intriguing appliance or toy can be without the power to make it work. There is nothing to make a potentially delightful mechanism function. The batteries provide the energy that allows the cellular phone, pager, razor, flashlight, pocket calculator, computer, or electronic game to function.

We have been created with a remarkable capability to know and to love with immense potential, which allows us to move beyond ourselves and to touch the divine. But all of this remains lifeless without the gift of the Holy Spirit—the divine energy that makes possible our union with Christ.

Our new spiritual life is just the beginning. The new life, the divine energy we have within us, will go on forever and reach its fullness in glory. There is a continuity between the new life in Christ we now share partially, sacramentally, but truly, and the fullness of that life we will one day experience in glory.

QUESTIONS TO THINK ABOUT:

1. How is the new law the fulfillment of the old law?
2. How does our reason help us know God?
3. What does it mean for a Catholic to be "born again"? How is that different from what certain non-Catholic "born-again Christians" mean by "born again"? How would I explain the Church's understanding to them?

CHAPTER 50

Christian Freedom

WE KNOW THAT WE are free. Freedom is a human quality that we experience even if some aspect of it is limited. From earliest childhood, as we become more aware of our surroundings and our relationships with other people, we recognize that we make choices.

Decisions to do one thing rather than another or to make one choice over another are part of being human. As a child, a young person, or an adult, we are profoundly conscious of the ability and need to make choices. This capacity is not something outside us, nor is it given to us by another person or the government. It is an expression of our very human nature. Even in the most extreme state of physical or emotional confinement, we are conscious of our capacity to make choices. These choices determine who we are.

WHAT IS FREEDOM?

What does it mean to say that we are free? The answer to this deep human inquiry has always been important. But it is particularly important today, since so much emphasis is placed on "freedom of choice."

What, then, does it mean to be free and to choose freely?

Under the heading "Freedom and Responsibility," the *Catechism of the Catholic Church* defines freedom as "the power, rooted in reason and will, to act or not to act, to do this or that, and so to perform deliberate actions on one's own responsibility" (section 1731). This is our starting point. We are free because God in creating us has given us the power of intellect to know what is good and the ability to choose what is good.

FREEDOM TO MAKE THE RIGHT CHOICE

The object of our intellect is truth. When something is presented to us as true, the intellect accepts it without question—two and two are four. One can deny this mathematical principle only at the expense of denying the truth. As our range of knowledge expands and we are less certain of the correct answer, we must make a choice based on the best knowledge available to us. A multiple-choice test becomes difficult when among the choices are several that seem to be equally true. It is only when we have sufficient information to know which answer is correct that our intellect chooses it and we make the right choice.

Coupled with the intellect is our human will. God created us to love what is good and to choose what we know to be good. The problem of choosing the good arises when we are not sure which of the options before us is truly good. This is the dilemma that every child faces standing before the cookie jar. On the one hand, we recall our mother's instruction not to take another cookie. We want to obey her because we value, respect, love, and revere her. We know that she intends our well-being and loves us. On the other hand, there is the cookie—waiting, enticing, and challenging us to accept it as a much better "good." How many times does the cookie win out? Is it because we reject our mother and all she means to us, or is it simply because at this particular moment the allure of the cookie is overwhelming and seems to be a better good? For that moment the desire for the cookie overwhelms every other consideration.

Although these examples are simplifications, they nonetheless speak of a profound human experience rooted in our human nature. God created us to know the truth and to love it, so that our intellect would lead us to know what is right and our will would urge us to choose what is good.

The choices we make form us as human beings. One of the reasons parents spend so much time, effort, and energy teaching children good from bad, right from wrong, what is safe and what is harmful, is because we all know that the choices we make will affect us in some way. Not everything a child would like to put in its mouth is nourishing. A youngster needs to be taught what is healthy and what is unhealthy. The common, basic, maternal instinct to move a child's hand away from an open flame is not intended primarily to impair freedom of choice but to help this human being know what is truly good for him or her.

Freedom is not exercised in a vacuum. There is a context for all our human actions. On the most primitive human level, that context is the perception of what is good for our life. In the wider range of human experience, we recognize that how we relate to God is a fundamental human good, because without it we cannot achieve our true human fulfillment and come to be with God now and forever.

As the *Catechism* teaches us, "By free will one shapes one's own life. Human freedom is a force for growth and maturity in truth and goodness; it attains its perfection when directed toward God, our beatitude" (section 1731). As we are free, so we are responsible. Freedom is not just about making choices but about making right choices. To place one's hand in an open fire is to exercise human freedom irresponsibly.

KNOWING HOW TO CHOOSE

How do we know what choice to make? How do we know how to exercise our precious gift of human freedom in a way that makes each act of the will a responsible decision within the context of God's loving creation, the natural moral order that flows from it, and our call to holiness and union with God?

Choice always has an object. We choose something. To walk into a dark room and select items without knowing what they are is hardly a full, free, responsible act of freedom. Some light will help us to make a better choice. The greater the light—the more clearly we see the object—the more responsible our choice should be. So it is with each human act. Our freedom is rooted in our capacity to know what is good and to choose it because it is good. Wrong choices are made because people see a particular object or action as good for them here and now even though it may be a severely limited good.

One of the most striking examples of a wrong exercise of freedom is the choice to kill an unborn child—abortion. For the persons making such a choice, the understanding of what they are doing may be clouded, or their desire for an immediate, limited good may urge them to choose something that clearly contradicts the larger and more important good: the value and dignity of every human life. Abortion for convenience is a striking example of the abuse of free will by placing a lesser good (our personal, immediate convenience) over a far greater good (the dignity and value of each human life).

Why are so many bad choices made? Much is the result of bad information. We receive our information and formation from many sources. After viewing much of today's entertainment and information, one could conclude that the true ultimate norms of human existence are personal gratification through sexual activity, the accumulation of wealth, and the exercise of power to control others. In sharp contrast with this view is the teaching of Christ and his Church. But this voice is often muted or overwhelmed by the loud and insistent voices of the secular society in which we live. It is for this reason that we need to inform our conscience with the wisdom of God.

Through its teaching office, the Church offers clear, consistent, and insistent teaching on the major moral issues that we face today. There *is* an answer to the question of what is right and what is wrong. When we exercise our freedom and make choices, we as Catholics need to do so in the light of Christ's revelation and his teaching continued in the Church and applied to our daily circumstances.

In making a good choice, a number of elements should be present. The *Catechism* teaches us that our choice must be deliberate, consider all available information, and be guided by the teaching of Christ. Choice must also be free. It cannot be so overwhelmed by emotion or the passions that our action is not truly a human act. Finally, our freedom must be exercised in relationship to all those around us and specifically in our relationship to God. Prayer and openness to God's grace are sure and safe means that enable us to make right choices confidently.

QUESTIONS TO THINK ABOUT:

1. What are some good examples of the irresponsible exercise of freedom in today's society?
2. How would I answer the argument that freedom means doing whatever you want?
3. What limitations need to be placed on our freedom from outside? What limitations should we place on our own freedom?

CHAPTER 51

Responsibility Before God

FREEDOM IS A CHERISHED gift. We value our personal freedom and make great effort and even sacrifices to protect it. To know how to use it, we need to recognize that true freedom is responsible freedom.

At issue is not what we are *able* to do but what we *ought* to do. God created us free and gave us the ability to make choices. Personal freedom is manifest in the exercise of that power.

GOOD AND BAD CHOICES

Each one of us is free to make choices. Our decisions are important because they shape our life. Good choices take us in one direction; bad choices have devastating results. When we make choices we enter the world of morality. Some things cry out to be done, and often we know we can and should do them. But there are also things we know we should not do. We live responsibly when we care about what is truly good and when we acknowledge the authority of God to direct our choices. Morality is another word for living a good, full, decent life according to right choices. The *Catechism of the Catholic Church* reminds us that "Freedom makes man *responsible* for his acts to the extent that they are voluntary" (section 1734).

A part of growing up is learning that we are not free to do whatever we want, whenever we want, and to whomever we want. Life carries with it not just the exercise of freedom but also responsible decisions that are the result of our freedom.

RESPONSIBILITY MEANS PUTTING LIMITS ON OUR FREEDOM

When we consider responsibility, we come face to face with limitations. Sometimes these limitations are imposed upon us from outside, and sometimes they come from within us.

Smokers today increasingly have their freedom limited and their choices curtailed. This does not mean that a person who chooses to smoke is less a human being because she or he cannot do so in public buildings. What it does indicate is that society has chosen to limit the expression of freedom in this area. In effect, what society has done is recognize a good to be achieved and impose this good even though there are some individuals whose liberty is curtailed in the pursuit of that good. Personal freedom, in this example, is constrained by limitations imposed from outside the person.

Some smokers have chosen to give up smoking on their own. They recognize the value of lungs not clogged with smoke. This decision should be easier to follow because it is not imposed from outside but rather comes from within the person.

There are issues far more significant than smoking—issues that go straight to the core of human living. Human experience over the millennia tells us that some things are right and others wrong. God's revelation has helped to make these distinctions clearer. "You shall not kill." "You shall not commit adultery." "You shall not steal." "You shall not bear false witness." A person attempting to live a moral life needs to make these commandments a personal rule not just because God says so but also because they are valued as expressions of what is truly good for us. This is what we mean by internalizing moral rules or appropriating moral imperatives.

THE VOICE OF CONSCIENCE REMINDS US OF THE LIMITS

The voice of conscience reminds us of the rightness and wrongness of some actions even when we freely and deliberately choose the wrong ones. This quiet voice of right and wrong grows out of our human nature, which was created by God in a way that urges us to respond to his plan for correct human living. It takes a great deal of energy and effort to silence this voice of conscience and drown out the echoes of right and wrong heard deep within our soul.

The temptation is strong, however, to deny what we know is right and to manipulate the voice of conscience. That is why Christ provided a clear and insistent voice to hold up to us God's law and its implication for our moment in history. The teaching of the Church explicitly distinguishes, day in and day out, right from wrong, good from evil. The urging of the magisterium should not be seen as a voice outside us, but rather as an amplification of that quiet voice of conscience within us.

We have always recognized that boundaries can be placed and enforced from within us—that is, from our own conscience and free decision to follow God's way—or they can be enforced from without. This is why we have laws, courts, police, and jails. Not everyone exercises freedom in a responsible way.

THE DANGERS OF IRRESPONSIBLE FREEDOM

We should be concerned that we as a society are moving farther and farther away from the very concept of constraint—personal, interior restraint based on God's law and our understanding of that law. If we succeed in removing the internal constraint, all that will be left is the external restraint of force in a society that will have to rely on more jails, more police, more laws.

The doctor-death message expressed by Dr. Kevorkian suggests that every individual is the lord and final arbiter of life. It is an extreme version of the theory that personal freedom is absolute, has no boundaries, and is responsive to no law other than the will of the individual. The reason why the Church speaks out in defense of human life and against physician-assisted suicide is because we know from human nature, human experience, and God's law that God is the author of life, the lord of life, and the giver and taker of life. Once we transfer the authorship of life from God to ourselves, there is nothing to prevent human freedom from establishing its own law of life and death according to whatever is politically correct at the moment.

Another example of a misunderstanding and abuse of freedom is the proposal that legislation be created to endow "same sex unions" with the same status as marriage. Here we find the thesis advanced that human beings should determine and rename the most fundamental human relationship in creation. Marriage is defined as the communion of a man and woman in marital love. This definition is not imposed on us from outside but grows out of human nature, confirmed and affirmed by God's holy revelation. The presumption that we are free without any bounds whatsoever to change this reality is a false application of human autonomy.

The Church's well-known and often-stated opposition to abortion grows out of the concern for human life, out of God's order for the human race, and out of our understanding of the rightness of the created order. Simply stated, it is not right to take the life of an innocent person. The assertion that we are free to choose to kill an unborn child and that there should be no constraint or restraint flies in the face of millennia of human experience. It is also wrong because it proclaims human authority over the lives of others and substitutes human beings for God as the author, lord, and judge of life.

The same is true for the rejection by the Church of capital punishment. Given the highly complex and sophisticated nature of human society today and its well-organized structure, it is not only feasible but relatively easy to constrain even the most vicious person who exercises the most irresponsible freedom of choice by taking the lives of other innocent people. It is not necessary to take the life of this person in order to restrain him or her.

At issue today in so many legislative and moral debates is the question of responsible boundaries for human freedom. On the one hand, we insistently hear the claim that the only restraint on human freedom is that imposed by political correctness determined by the majority of people. On the other hand, the ancient and wise voices of faith and reason tell us that some constraints and boundaries are good when they follow God's plan, given to us in creation and revealed to us in God's law. We should not be too quick to abandon the truth that we are bound personally by the voice of God within us to use our freedom responsibly.

In the *Catechism* we read that *"the right to the exercise of freedom,* especially in moral and religious matters, is an inalienable requirement of the dignity of the human person. This right must be recognized and protected by civil authority within the limits of the common good and public order" (section 1738).

Today as we consider the many problems our society faces, the violence that haunts our communities, and the disintegration of family life, we need to be all the more attentive to the truth that we are bound personally by the voice of God within us and the law of God revealed to all. The use of our freedom must be in conformity with that law and in a responsible, caring, and loving manner.

QUESTIONS TO THINK ABOUT:

1. Do I see my personal freedom as a gift from God to be put at God's service?
2. What limits do I impose on my own freedom? Why do I impose those limits?
3. Which limits on freedom ought to be enforced by the state? Which ones ought to be left to the conscience of the individual?

CHAPTER 52

Christian Morality

NOT TOO LONG AGO, at a meeting that involved a large number of young people who had been in and out of the correctional system, one of the youngsters told of how being involved in "drugs on the street" is enticing as a way of life. One of the adults present suggested that perhaps the youngster's view of right and wrong was so impaired by the environment in which he grew up as to be nonexistent.

The young but astute "street kid" shot back, "Everybody knows the difference between right and wrong."

Challenging this response, the adult continued, "Then why do you do what is wrong?"

The reply from the young person echoes the entire human condition. "I know what's right, but I get more out of what's wrong."

OUR CHOICES HAVE CONSEQUENCES

In a sense, we create the world in which we live. Each of us has the power to make decisions, and the cumulative effect of those choices results in the goodness or badness of our society. Every action we take has an impact not just on us but on the world. All we need to do is look around us, pick up a daily paper, or watch the evening news to verify that there is much that is not right. A great deal of what is wrong is the result of the attitude and moral climate of our times. There are some who insist that this age has lost its "moral compass."

As soon as we begin to speak of morality, there are those who object on the grounds that each person's opinion is his or her own and equal to that of anyone else. For some, there can be no objective and commonly agreed-upon moral norm. For such persons, morality is an illusion. How many times have we heard that morality is a completely personal and subjective choice? This position is probably the most widespread and pernicious challenge to morality that our society has ever faced. The issue today in much of our public discourse—and certainly on talk shows—is: "Do values have any value?"

As Christians, we recognize that there is more to life and human action than fleeting personal preference. Human existence is not a meaningless show of smoke and mirrors. Each one of us knows deep down at the very core of our being that there is such a thing as right and wrong—that, while the wrong choice may be alluring at the moment, it is a choice with lasting consequences. While individually we may not know the answer to every moral question, we are aware that there are answers—answers that oblige all of us.

There is right and wrong, human freedom, and the choice that each of us makes. At the core of human freedom is knowing and doing what we "ought" to do rather than what we "can" do. It is the voice of conscience that keeps reminding us what we ought to do even though there are enticing reasons to do otherwise.

When we look at the morality of human acts, the *Catechism of the Catholic Church* tells us we must consider a number of factors. "The object, the intention, and the circumstances make up the 'sources,' or constitutive elements, of the morality of human acts" (section 1750).

THE OBJECT OF THE CHOICE

In making a good moral choice, the first thing we need to consider is what we are choosing. All choice involves an object. We choose this rather than that. Given the basic human inclination to choose what is good for us, our choice will always be directed to a perceived good. The problem arises when there is a whole range of choices and each of the objects has some real or perceived goodness.

A little boy may return to the cookie jar against the expressed wishes of his mother because, at that moment, the taste of another cookie is a "good" that he seeks. One can excuse a child for setting aside all the other goods, including obedience to his mother, precisely because the child is still young and irresponsible. The same should not be said for adults. The person who helps himself to another's wallet because it happens to be close at hand and because the additional cash is a "good" greatly to be desired is expected to know better and to behave accordingly.

THE INTENTION OF THE CHOICE

We must judge if something is or is not "in conformity with the true good" (see section 1751 of the *Catechism*). We must not only know that what we are choosing is good, we must have the intention of choosing something good. When we set out to do something we must will to do the right thing. But our will cannot turn what is wrong into something good. "A good intention (for example, that of helping one's neighbor) does not make behavior that is intrinsically disordered, such as lying or calumny, good or just. The end does not justify the means" (section 1753). The objective moral order exists independently of the power even of our free will.

Today we often see examples of an appeal that the end does justify the means. The killing fields of Cambodia were justified by the decision of a few to "make a better society." As appalling as such reasoning may be, it is basically the same that is used to defend abortion, physician-assisted suicide, distribution of condoms in high schools, and in some lands child labor and religious persecution.

THE CIRCUMSTANCES OF THE CHOICE

The third element in determining the morality of an action is the circumstances. Here perhaps more than anywhere else, examples are presented with such emotional force that moral reasoning can be subverted. As the *Catechism* teaches us, the circumstances, including the consequences, "are secondary elements of a moral act. They contribute to increasing or diminishing the moral goodness or evil of human acts (for example, the amount of a theft)" (section 1754).

Circumstances do not create good and evil. The objective moral order determines what is right and wrong. Circumstances, however, may cause the goodness or evil of an action to be accentuated. For example, it is a good deed to offer a person in need some financial help. The goodness of the act may be dramatically increased if the person making the gift is doing so out of his or her own extremely limited resources. Jesus praises the "widows' mite" precisely because the circumstances greatly enhanced the generosity intrinsic to the gift.

THE CHURCH CAN HELP US KNOW RIGHT FROM WRONG

Christian morality is not only for Christians. It is for everyone, because all are called to follow God's law manifest in the natural moral order, revealed in the Ten Commandments, and made complete in Christ. Christian morality is the authentic, central, and integral form of morality. It is the fullness of teaching on the human condition before God. Apart from faith in Christ, the great questions about the reality of freedom, the rationality of conscience, and the value of pursuing human good unselfishly cannot be fully answered. It is for this reason that we look to Jesus and listen to his Church.

Where do we go to know right from wrong in all of the myriad forms that moral issues appear today? Jesus has not left us orphans. The pledge of the Holy Spirit in the fourteenth chapter of John's gospel is verified today as it has been for twenty centuries in the teaching office of the Church. In the many issues before us today, when decisions are presented with a range of good attached to each of the multiple choices, we need to listen to the sure and Spirit-led voice of the teaching office. It guides us in issues as complex and emotional as artificial insemination, physician assisted suicide, exploitation of the powerless, and the range of social justice, bioethical, and medical-moral dilemmas that manifest the complexity of the human condition.

It is true that morality is rooted in the natural moral order, because that order follows from God's creation. But it is equally true that God chose to reveal the moral order in the old covenant, through the Decalogue, and in the new covenant through Christ. When the Church calls the faithful to specific moral teaching, it does so with the full weight and authority of Christ, who has empowered his Church to speak for him. At the same time, the Church presents cogent and compelling reasons for her teaching based on an appeal to human nature and the natural moral order that we all share.

Life is complex. Moral decisions are difficult. But we need not fear, because we have a sure moral guide. Christ reveals to us the way. He sends the Holy Spirit to guide us and he enlightens his Church in a way that we can with confidence and trust follow its teaching in matters of faith and morals.

QUESTIONS TO THINK ABOUT:

1. If someone tells me that morality is relative and subjective, how do I respond?

2. Have I ever done a bad thing for good reasons? How would I solve the problem differently if I could do it over again?
3. How does the Church's teaching on moral values challenge many modern sensibilities? How can I help others to understand the wisdom of the Church's teaching?

CHAPTER 53

Moral Conscience

"When the fullness of time had come, God sent his Son, born of a woman, born under the law, to ransom those under the law, so that we might receive adoption. As proof that you are children, God sent the Spirit of his Son into our hearts, crying, 'Abba, Father!' " (Galatians 4:4–6).

THE INCLINATION TO GOD

God the Father so loves us that he sends his Son, Jesus Christ, to be one with us, precisely so that we ultimately can become adopted children of God. Our relationship to the Father in grace builds on that relationship that rests on our very creation.

Deep within us, within every human being, is planted the inclination to God who created us. There is also, as a part of that inclination, a natural desire for the goodness that is a reflection of God's call to each of us to draw more closely to him.

We who have an intellect and will, rather than simple instinct, are drawn to God by seeds planted deep within our intellect and will that urge us to know the truth and to love what is good. Yet the question remains: How does orientation to goodness find expression in the day-to-day experiences that form us, our character, and our world?

The *Catechism of the Catholic Church* defines conscience as "a judgment of reason whereby the human person recognizes the moral quality of a concrete act that he is going to perform, is in the process of performing, or has already completed" (section 1778). The *Catechism* quotes the Second Vatican Council's *Pastoral Constitution on the Church in the Modern World,* which teaches us: "Deep within his conscience man discovers a law which he has not laid upon himself but which he must obey. Its voice, ever calling him to love and to do what is good and to avoid evil, sounds in his heart at the right moment. . . . For man has in his heart a law inscribed by God. . . . His conscience is man's most secret core and his sanctuary. There he is alone with God whose voice echoes in his depths" (section 1776; *Gaudium et Spes* 16).

MORAL CONSCIENCE REVEALS SELF-EVIDENT TRUTH

Since we have been created by God in his image and likeness, the traces of our Creator remain with us. Resounding in the very core of our being is the remembrance of God's plan for us, etched in our human nature by the hand of the Creator who fashioned it. Everything within us strains to do what is right, to know what is true, to love what is good.

When Thomas Jefferson was asked to prepare a draft of the Declaration of Independence, he said he tried to reflect the "American mind." He turned to the simple recognition that our rights—to life, liberty, and the pursuit of happiness—are rooted "in nature and nature's God." He made the case, as we continue to do today, that this was self-evident.

Jefferson's thesis grows out of an even more ancient understanding of human nature. The Catholic Church has long understood that moral conscience is more than an exercise of free will. It is a human action grounded in our very human nature, which itself is the result of the action of a provident and loving God.

When we come face to face with the concrete limitations and challenges of daily life, we have to make multiple choices concerning what is identifiably true and really good. This action occurs not just according to our limited judgment but according to God's eternal plan, manifest in our human nature and revealed to us in his commandments—and most specifically in Jesus.

CONSCIENCE IS THE VOICE OF GOD

Some writers speak of conscience as the voice of God speaking something deep within us. It is a part of our nature that we are called to obey and that ultimately orients us always toward God. Its day-to-day expression, however, is far more concrete.

Conscience is best described as a judgment of practical reason about a specific, concrete action. Because it is the voice of God and corresponds to our most profound leanings toward God, we are obliged to follow our conscience. To act against conscience is to act against the only sure norm we have to measure whether what we are about to do is right or wrong. Even if our conscience turns out to be mistaken, which it can be, we are still obliged at the moment of choice to follow conscience.

But we are not born with a conscience fully aware of every answer to every moral question. We must not think of it as an internal pocket calculator of the soul programmed to respond to every question, every dilemma, every moral conflict. This wondrous echo of God the Creator within us urging us to live in communion with God's plan needs to be enlightened or informed. For this reason, the Church speaks of an informed conscience. Where do we turn to provide our conscience with the information that it needs to make the choices that keep it always directed toward God?

Judgments of conscience are the outcome of a person's honest effort to avoid being arbitrary or unresponsive in pursuing true human values. When we are able to set aside our personal prejudices or the biases that may close our hearts to the truth, then the choices we make are right. Then conscience is true and upright, and a person attains what he or she is implicitly or explicitly seeking: the knowledge of God's design and will. That is why Saint Paul not only observes the universality and naturalness of the phenomenon of human conscience in all times and places but also insists on the fact that conscience bears witness to the demands of God's law (see Romans 2:15).

Unfortunately, we are all aware of the facetious remark but all too often observable phenomenon: "Don't bother me with facts, my mind is already made up." The most glaring example of this is the phenomenon of abortion in the United States. One of the reasons why the aftermath of an abortion, the remains of an aborted child, is shunned by the media is because this evidence would undermine the whole pro-abortion, pro-choice argument.

The Church has constantly taught that to say a conscience judges correctly is to say its judgments are right and correspond to God's judgments. When one "enters into his own heart" sincerely seeking the true direction and standard for love, then "God, who probes the heart, awaits him there" (*Gaudium et Spes* 14). If one really cares for the search for the true and good, then, in the quiet reflection of conscience, "he is alone with God whose voice echoes in his depths" (*Gaudium et Spes* 16).

CONSCIENCE ACKNOWLEDGES GOD'S LAW

Conscience, then, is not a device for making exceptions to objective requirements of morality. On the contrary, as the Second Vatican Council's *Declaration on Religious Liberty* teaches, "through the mediation of conscience man perceives and acknowledges the imperatives of the divine law" (*Dignitatis Humanae* 3; compare *Gaudium et Spes* 16). This "divine law" is "eternal, objective and universal" and is the "highest norm of human life" (*Dignitatis Humanae* 3). Fidelity to conscience is fidelity in the search for truth. Insofar as our search is successful, we turn aside from blind choice and wishful thinking; we are guided by "objective norms of morality" (*Gaudium et Spes* 16).

In our search for the "objective norms of morality" so that we are able to inform our conscience and keep it from error, we turn obviously to the word of God. While there is planted in our human nature a natural moral law that urges us and inclines us to do good and avoid evil, in God's infinite mercy God chose to speak directly to us: first in the prophets and in the law and finally in his Son (see Hebrews 1:1). In this way, God revealed to us his plan for human living. As the *Catechism* explains, "in the formation of conscience the word of God is the light for our path; we must assimilate it in faith and prayer and put it into practice. We must also examine our conscience before the Lord's Cross" (section 1785). A conscience that knows its own power and dignity aspires to attain "the contemplation and appreciation of the divine plan" (*Gaudium et Spes* 15).

The *Catechism* goes on to remind us how important our right choices are. While God is sovereign master of his plan for our lives, he makes use of our cooperation. For God, our loving Father, "grants his creatures not only their existence, but also the dignity of acting on their own . . . and thus of cooperating in the accomplishment of his plan" (section 306). Is it any wonder that we stand in awe of so great a Father? He not only brings us into being but loves us and plants within us the voice of conscience to see that we remain always faithful to him in our life's journey.

QUESTIONS TO THINK ABOUT:

1. What does "liberty of conscience" usually mean in the modern world? Is the popular view consistent with the true purpose of conscience?
2. How is moral conscience related to free will?

3. How would I resolve the conflict if I believed my own conscience contradicted the teaching of the Church? Where would I look for help?
4. Do I ever find myself purposely ignoring the voice of my conscience? Why? What are the consequences when I ignore my conscience?

CHAPTER 54

The Human Virtues

THE CLOSEST THAT MOST ancient philosophers ever got to an understanding of God was in their discussions on the human virtues. This should not be surprising. The most that philosophy—human reason—can tell us about God is that he exists. Without God speaking to us, we have no way of reaching him, let alone coming to know him. Yet in the greatest of God's handiworks—human beings—we see some signs of the glory of God. So when philosophers turned their attention to human perfection, they came as close as they could to some small glimpse of God.

WHAT IS VIRTUE?

Much of the writing of Plato involves the challenge of virtuous living. His dialogues are replete with inquiry about what constitutes true virtue. When Aristotle addressed this same theme, in a more systematic manner, he faced essentially the same questions.

For the greater part of Western civilization, education was directed to helping the student identify virtue and then developing a life based on it. Even at the beginnings of our own country, education was seen as an endeavor to form the virtuous citizen. The practical knowledge of how to do this or that was presumed to be secondary to the more important knowledge of why we would do anything in the first place. Perhaps the collapse of so much of our public school educational effort reflects how far we have moved from this ancient and time-honored human intuition.

In his work on the beatitudes, Saint Gregory of Nyssa wrote that the goal of the virtuous life "is to become like God" (compare section 1803 of the *Catechism*). How do we do this? How is it that we can become more like God through our actions, dispositions, choices, and deeds?

PRACTICE MAKES VIRTUE

Saint Paul, perhaps out of his own youthful experience of sports, describes the struggle for a virtuous life in terms of sporting events, particularly the foot races that were so much a part of athletic competition in his time and that continue to form a significant part of Olympic competition in our day. At the core of virtuous living is practice. The old adage "practice makes perfect" is applicable not only to one's golf stroke, tennis swing, or hundred-meter dash but also the acquisition of virtue.

Some time ago I was intrigued by interview after interview of victorious athletes at the Olympic games. One by one they explained how they had set aside everything else in life to concentrate their full energies, attention, and prowess on developing their God-given gifts and honing their expertise in a particular area to a precision that would make them the best. Each repeated as if part of a choric refrain: "practice, practice, practice!"

Life is much like that experience. The virtuous life depends on our developing, honing, focusing, and orienting our response to God. The *Catechism of the Catholic Church* defines human virtues as "firm attitudes, stable dispositions, habitual perfections of intellect and will that govern our actions, order our passions, and guide our conduct according to reason and faith" (section 1804). While it is true that we are born with attitudes and dispositions that lead us to live a virtuous life, these habits of the heart need to be practiced with such regularity that they become our continuous, constant, and spontaneous response to life. We define character by the practice of virtue. The strength of our character will reflect the perfection of our virtue.

When addressing virtues, the *Catechism* begins with the human virtues and then treats the three theological virtues. We will follow the same pattern here, mindful that the moral or human virtues are acquired by human effort while the theological virtues are a gift from God. Both human or moral and theological virtues, however, demand practice to reach perfection.

THE HUMAN VIRTUES

The four human or moral virtues are *prudence, justice, fortitude,* and *temperance.* They are sometimes called the cardinal virtues, from the Latin word *cardo* or hinge. They are the virtues on which are supported all the other manifestations of good human activity. Some of the greatest teachers in the Church have used the four cardinal virtues as the focus around which to cluster all proper human activity and against which to weigh the rightness or wrongness of human actions.

Prudence is described as "the virtue that disposes practical reason to discern our true good in every circumstance and to choose the right means of achieving it . . ." (see section 1806 of the *Catechism*). Prudence helps us to avoid extremes. The ancient and wise saying *In medio stat virtus* can be translated in a variety of ways, but essentially it tells us that virtue avoids extremes. When the great Church teacher Origen took literally the injunction of the Scriptures, "If your eye is an occasion of sin to you, pluck it out," and mutilated himself, that was an extreme act. Prudence calls us to the middle road between extremes.

Because prudence urges us to deal with situations as we find them and avoid extremes, it is sometimes called the pastoral virtue that pastors apply when dealing with people or situations that require patience, guidance, and wisdom in helping to move the situation and the person beyond where they are and far closer to God. While there may be a temptation to denounce all who sin and the human condition that seems so hostile to virtue, such denunciation may not always effect the change of heart that a calmer, slower, more patient pastoral approach may achieve.

Justice is the moral virtue that consists "in the constant and firm will to give their due to God and neighbor" (section 1807). Perhaps another way of defining justice is to recognize that "to each belongs his own." We are obliged to give what is due to God, our neighbor, and ourselves. Justice is also described as a "social" virtue. All community, whether it is family or the wider educational, cultural, social, economic, or political variety, demands justice from its members if it is to succeed. The practice of virtue creates the peace and harmony that brings together people and allows them to prosper while sharing the efforts of collective communal life.

Civil law and the judicial system deal in large part with the virtue of justice because it is clear that a minimum level of justice has to be sustained for any civil society to survive. "Agreements must be kept" is the basis for much of the interchange that permits commerce, business, finance, and in general economic development.

Fortitude is the moral virtue "that ensures firmness in difficulties and constancy in the pursuit of the good" (section 1808). There is no age limit to courage—to fortitude. We have all, I am sure, witnessed very young, not-so-young, and quite elderly courageous people. Fortitude is the virtue that allows us to remain constant in our pursuit of what is good and gives us the strength to resist temptation that would pull us in other directions.

The last of the cardinal virtues is *temperance,* which the *Catechism* describes as the moral virtue "that moderates the attraction of pleasures and provides balance in the use of created goods." In creating us, God endowed human life with many good instincts and desires. All of these need to be kept in balance and within what the *Catechism* describes as "the limits of what is honorable." The tempered person directs the sensitive appetites to what is good and maintains again what the *Catechism* describes as "a healthy discretion" (section 1809). Perhaps another word for temperance is moderation in all things. Its practice involves the balanced use of the many goods God has given us so that their use remains ordered and at the service of the development of a good, wholesome, well-rounded, complete person.

QUESTIONS TO THINK ABOUT:

1. If practice is important to virtue, how am I practicing? What can I do to build up my moral virtues?
2. How do I follow the middle way of prudent religious practice? To which extreme am I most frequently drawn?
3. How can we harmonize justice with prudence? Is the strictest justice always the prudent course?
4. How am I most tempted to deviate from temperance? Do I have intemperate desires for alcohol? For chocolate? What can I do to help build up my temperance?

CHAPTER 55

The Theological Virtues

THERE ARE THREE THEOLOGICAL virtues: *faith, hope,* and *love.* In addition to the human or moral cardinal virtues, God blesses us with the theological virtues, which, in the words of the *Catechism of the Catholic Church,* "adapt man's faculties for participation in the divine nature: for the theological virtues relate directly to God" (section 1812).

Saint Paul writes to the Corinthians, "So faith, hope, love remain, these three; but the greatest of these is love" (1 Corinthians 13:13). These three virtues are gifts from God that relate us to God. Without the generous outpouring of these gifts, we would remain closed in on our limited, finite, human world.

FAITH IS A GIFT FROM GOD

Over one of the entrances to the Basilica of the National Shrine of the Immaculate Conception in Washington is carved a definition of faith taken from the letter to the Hebrews: "Faith is the realization of what is hoped for and evidence of things not seen" (Hebrews 11:1). By the virtue of faith, God enables us to share in the light of his own knowledge, so we may know him and his saving word.

Faith itself is a gift from God. We cannot believe in God except through the urging of the Holy Spirit. Yet we are capable of supporting and strengthening our faith life by the actions we take to build up our friendship with the Lord. It takes two to carry on a conversation, even when one of the participants is God.

When Jesus led the apostles to faith, he first invited them to friendship with himself. As they came to know him, they began to realize the richness of the kind of life that they had not known and that they longed to share in its fullness.

The task of the *Catechism* in presenting the faith is to show something of the richness of the life to which Christ calls us in faith, and to show how effectively the new life of Christ fulfills the desires and longings of the human heart. Our effort in this book itself is precisely to allow us to grow more secure in our faith through the knowledge of what Jesus teaches us—but also to grow more deeply in our faith through our loving response to the goodness of God to each of us.

FAITH AND REASON

When Jesus invited people to faith, he clearly respected their intelligence. His words were accompanied by signs of their truth: in the wisdom of his teaching, in the goodness of his life, in the power of the deeds he performed. So too the theological virtue of faith does not act in a vacuum. Rather it builds on and strengthens the movements of the human heart and mind to know and love God.

Normally people need good reasons to clear their way to faith. While there is no conflict between intelligence and belief—between faith and reason—we need to recognize that human reason alone is not sufficient to establish personal faith. No one can be driven to personal faith by dialectics. For faith involves believing God, not complex argumentation. Nonetheless, our intelligence can stimulate the pursuit of personal faith.

The encyclical letter *Fides et Ratio* (*Faith and Reason*) by Pope John Paul II describes faith and reason as "two wings on which the human spirit rises to the contemplation of truth." The metaphor highlights the relationship between faith and reason and the importance of the efforts of the human mind to understand the gift of revelation.

The theological virtue of faith is indispensable. The gospels portray the progress of Saint Peter toward faith. He has seen Christ's goodness, wisdom, and power. He has come eventually to have more firm views about Christ and who he is. But when the Lord's invitation led Peter from opinion to a ringing profession of faith, Christ told him that his new confident conviction was not the result of mere human insight. "Blessed are you, Simon son of Jonah. For flesh and blood has not revealed this to you, but my heavenly Father" (Matthew 16:17).

HOPE GIVES US QUIET CONFIDENCE

The *Catechism of the Catholic Church* describes hope as "the theological virtue by which we desire the kingdom of heaven and eternal life as our happiness, placing our trust in Christ's promises and relying not on our own strength, but on the help of the grace of the Holy Spirit" (section 1817). This is the virtue that keeps us from discouragement and sustains us during times when we feel abandoned. It is the gift from God that opens up our heart in expectation of all that we have been promised.

In the virtue of hope, God gives an unshakable confidence in himself. Saint Paul speaks in the name of every Christian: "For I am convinced that neither death, nor life . . . nor height, nor depth, nor any other creature will be able to separate us from the love of God in Christ Jesus our Lord" (Romans 8:38–39). In the face of so much challenge to the truth of the Church's teaching, each of us needs the quiet confidence that hope gives us—a confidence to proclaim what we believe, comfortable in the fact that it is true.

THE GREATEST OF THESE IS LOVE

As Saint Paul teaches and we recognize, the greatest of these three theological virtues is love. "Poured out into our hearts through the Holy Spirit" (Romans 5:5), it enables us to cling with our whole hearts to God with an energy and life that he himself communicates. It is in love that we actually identify with God, who, as Saint John teaches us, is love. "Beloved, let us love one another, because love is of God; everyone who loves is begotten by God and knows God. Whoever is without love does not know God, for God is love" (1 John 4:7–9).

There is a proper order of love. After love of God comes love of self. Christ commanded: "You shall love your neighbor as yourself" (Mark 12:31). But the love of self that is set as the standard for love of one's neighbor is a right love of self, a love governed and guided by love of God. One who does not have a right love of self, a love that flows from a grateful love of God, is not able to love one's neighbor correctly. All of us should think of our own salvation, our own pursuit of the truly good, as our first responsibility.

Christian self-love, which grows out of a grateful love of God and blossoms into unselfish love of neighbor, is supported by certain indispensable virtues. While love itself is a theological virtue and hence a gift from God, it is also supported by distinctly Christian virtues—ways of acting that have their origin in Christ's vision of human life.

The first of these is humility, one of the most distinctive of Christian virtues. Paradoxically, it exalts us by leading us to acknowledge our true status—we are creatures and every good in us is God's gift and should glorify God, not our own small ego. Humility does not require pretense or sham; rather it recognizes and is grateful for God's many gifts, even extraordinary talents one may happen to possess. Christ taught humility by words (see Matthew 5:3, 18:4) and by example. "Learn from me, for I am meek and humble of heart" (Matthew 11:29).

Saint Paul's beautiful words on the virtue of love are found in his letter responding to problems of order in the church of Corinth. Members of that church with diverse gifts and duties were contending with one another instead of cooperating. For example, some claimed that their particular gift of speaking in tongues was superior, others that their particular gift of prophecy was better.

Paul explained that just as each part of the human body had its own function, each member of the Church has his or her own role to play. No part of the body is independent. Each part needs the others; even the noblest needs the least noble. Therefore the gifts over which members of the Church were contending, gifts that will pass away, are far less important than the gifts that unite them, gifts that will last. "Faith, hope, and love remain, these three; but the greatest of these is love" (1 Corinthians 13:13).

Love vivifies the body of Christ: "If I speak in human and angelic tongues but do not have love, I am a resounding gong or a clashing cymbal. And if I have prophetic powers and comprehend all mysteries and all knowledge; if I have all faith so as to move mountains but do not have love, I gain nothing" (1 Corinthians 13:1–2).

THE GIFTS AND FRUITS OF THE HOLY SPIRIT

In concluding its teaching on the virtues, the *Catechism* lists the gifts and fruits of the Holy Spirit. It seems, therefore, appropriate to conclude this article with the same. We pray that God will bestow them on all of us.

The seven gifts of the Holy Spirit are Wisdom, Understanding, Counsel, Fortitude, Knowledge, Piety, and Fear of the Lord.

The fruits of the Holy Spirit are Charity, Joy, Peace, Patience, Kindness, Goodness, Generosity, Gentleness, Faithfulness, Modesty, Self-Control, and Chastity.

QUESTIONS TO THINK ABOUT:

1. What have I done recently to strengthen my faith life? Am I holding up my end of the conversation with God?
2. How has God helped to keep hope alive in times of struggle? What can I do to strengthen hope in others?
3. How does proper Christian self-love lead to love of my neighbor? What help would I need to build up that proper self-love?

CHAPTER 56

Sin

ALL OF CREATION, GOODNESS, and love are God's handiworks, but sin is most assuredly ours. God looked on all that he had made, including us, and proclaimed that it was very good. Yet into this world, created in goodness and out of God's love, Adam and Eve and each of us continuously introduced that human rebellion that claims the name "sin."

GOD'S MERCY TO SINNERS

But even in our failure God did not abandon us. Saint John tells us that God "so loved the world that he gave his only Son, so that everyone who believes in him might not perish but might have eternal life. For God did not send his Son into the world to condemn the world, but that the world might be saved through him" (John 3:16–17). Christ's love for us would be manifest in a way beyond our wildest imagination. For "though he was in the form of God," he "did not regard equality with God something to be grasped. Rather, he emptied himself, taking the form of a slave, coming in human likeness; and found human in appearance, he humbled himself, becoming obedient to death, even death on a cross" (Philippians 2:6–8).

The *Catechism of the Catholic Church* teaches us that "the Gospel is the revelation in Jesus Christ of God's mercy to sinners" (section 1846). The central focus of our new life is Christian love. Sin is the opposite of this love. Above all, it is hostile to that great love of God that calls us to growth in what is good.

SIN COMES ABOUT THROUGH OUR FREE WILL

Just as we can strive freely to see things from God's point of view and to act in accord with his will, so too we can freely choose to ignore God's plan and the role he invites us to play in it. This has been true from the beginning of history. We can be grateful to God, our Creator and Redeemer, and stand in awe of his power and holiness, or we can be ungrateful, ignore God, and violate his plan and holy will. We can determine to model our life on the life of Christ, or we can reject that model in favor of another pattern, one of our own making.

In short, just as we can accept the invitation God has issued to adopt us as members of his own family, we can refuse this offer in favor of a selfish and isolated life. Such a refusal of God's gift to us of himself is sin. Our refusal to recognize that we are to acknowledge the authority of the Lord who made us and calls us to life is pride—the root of all sin.

How is it possible that we can sin? How can it be that some things we do offend God? The answer to these questions lies in our free will. God created each of us in God's own image and likeness—with a will that is free. Every person makes choices. Some choices are good and others are bad. There may be many circumstances affecting each choice, but the simple fact remains that each of us has the enormous power to choose to do as he or she wants. Even if our choice runs against God, God's will, God's plan, and God's call, we are still free to make the choice. For this reason, we must be particularly attentive to what we choose. Choice is a gift. What we choose is a responsibility.

THE DEFINITION OF SIN

For a precise definition of sin, we turn to the *Catechism:* "Sin is an offense against reason, truth, and right conscience; it is failure in genuine love for God and neighbor caused by a perverse attachment to certain goods" (section 1849). Sin is basically a personal offense against God, a turning from God. For this reason it is important to distinguish between actions that are done with knowledge and freedom and those that are not. Some actions that are in themselves wrong are done without personal guilt because the doer acts in ignorance or without freedom. The actions in these cases are to be distinguished from sin in the strict sense, sometimes called formal sin, in which we freely and knowingly do what we judge to be wrong. A formal sin is a deliberate violation of the known will of God.

Sin is first of all the rejection of simple, ordinary human reason. There is a way in which we are supposed to act. There is a direction to life that we can recognize. Deep within us is the voice of conscience that calls us to act in a way that corresponds to that natural moral law that is a part of God's creation.

Some sins are directed against the very kingdom that God came to establish: sins against love, peace, justice, kindness, and understanding—all the elements of the kingdom of God. But there are also sins of passion. A person can get so caught up in the desires of the flesh that they overwhelm every other consideration. There are also sins against truth. We can distort, hide, cover, spoil the reality of God's truth in our lives in such a way that we create a world of error and falsehood that leads to division and hatred. All of these are sins against truth.

There are also sins against the unity that God plans for the human family. These sins are rooted in racism, in divisions of people against other people for reasons that have nothing to do with what is good and bad but rather with superficial things such as where they were born, the color of their skin, how they speak, and the names they might have. We find these types of sins all around us, sins that disrupt and tear apart the very fabric of the human family.

MORTAL AND VENIAL SIN

There are many kinds of sin, but in the tradition of the Church the two major classifications are mortal and venial. There is a sharp distinction between mortal and venial sin. A mortal sin is one that separates a person from friendship with God and deepens alienation from God. Formal mortal sin, which is incompatible with divine love, destroys the life of grace in the soul. Venial sin weakens but does not destroy the gift of grace.

As Pope John Paul II teaches us in the postsynodal apostolic exhortation *Reconciliatio et Paenitentia* (*On Reconciliation and Penance*), "There is no middle way between life and death." Everyone is either in the state of grace and in friendship with God or is separated from the grace of God and not on the way to eternal life. "Some sins are intrinsically grave and mortal by reason of their matter. That is, there exist acts that *per se* and in themselves, independent of circumstances, are always seriously wrong by reason of their object. These acts, if carried out with sufficient awareness and freedom, are always gravely sinful" (17).

Certain specific kinds of actions are in themselves always materially mortal sins. These are so seriously wrong that they exclude one who deliberately commits them from the kingdom of heaven. The Church does not teach that the passages in Scripture that list mortal sins list *all* the possible mortal sins, but rather teaches that there are kinds of gravely evil acts that are strictly forbidden by God, and that one who knowingly and deliberately does such acts is freely and consciously turning away from God.

In the letter of Paul to the Galatians, sin is described as the struggle between the life of the Spirit and the desires of the flesh. "I say, then: live by the Spirit and you will certainly not gratify the desire of the flesh. For the flesh has desires against the Spirit, and the Spirit against the flesh; these are opposed to each other, so that you may not do what you want" (Galatians 5:16–17).

Not all sin is mortal, although all sin is serious. The *Catechism* speaks of venial sin. This type of sin does not deprive one of the life of grace and friendship with God. It is not a turning away from God, but a shortcoming, a hesitation or misstep as it were, in one's efforts to follow Christ.

Yet the *Catechism* reminds us that "sin creates a proclivity to sin; it engenders vice by repetition of the same acts. This results in perverse inclinations which cloud conscience and corrupt the concrete judgment of good and evil. Thus sin tends to reproduce itself and reinforce itself, but it cannot destroy the moral sense at its root" (section 1865).

OUR SINS CAN ALWAYS BE FORGIVEN

Where sin abounds, God's mercy more graciously abounds. God's forgiveness is open to us. Thanks to the boundless infinite mercy of God, each of us can be absolved of our sin through the sacrament of reconciliation.

Our reflection on the existence of sin in our own lives should not lead us to despair, but rather to rejoice in a God who so loves us that he freely forgives us. Long before we stand before his judgment throne, we can present ourselves and freely receive forgiveness at God's seat of mercy—the sacrament of reconciliation. How blessed we are even in our fallen condition to know that we have the ready and sure assurance of God's mercy and absolution—no matter what the sin—as long as we are willing to sorrowfully admit our failure, confess our sins, seek absolution, and do penance.

QUESTIONS TO THINK ABOUT:

1. Many people reject the notion of sin entirely. How would I try to convince them that sin is real?
2. Are there particular sins that weigh heavily on my conscience? Have I sought God's mercy through the sacrament of reconciliation?

CHAPTER 57

The Seven Capital Sins

THERE IS A TYPE of sin that over the centuries has been designated as a "deadly" or "capital" sin. Tradition names seven of them: pride, gluttony, avarice, lust, sloth, envy, and anger. The *Catechism of the Catholic Church* lists these as the capital sins that "Christian experience has distinguished, following Saint John Cassian and Saint Gregory the Great" (see section 1866). These seven sins or vices lead us away from, and harden our resistance to, God's grace.

A TENDENCY TO SIN

The context, background, and foundation for our discussion of the seven deadly sins is the simple recognition that our human nature is tainted. We have a fallen human nature, which, while not destroyed, is certainly weakened in its relationship to God. Even with the grace of God and the indwelling of God's Holy Spirit, we struggle with sin.

Saint Paul in his letter to the Romans confronts the whole human condition and reminds us: "We know that the law is spiritual; but I am carnal, sold into slavery to sin. What I do, I do not understand. For I do not do what I want, but I do what I hate. . . . For I do not do the good I want, but I do the evil I do not want. Now if I do what I do not want, it is no longer I who do it, but sin that dwells within me" (Romans 7:14–15, 19–20).

Deep within us there is a tendency to sin, to struggle against God so that even with the best of intentions we sometimes sin. It is sin within us that pulls us down. This is the context in which we address the whole question of the capital sins—the deadly vices.

Why are they called capital? They have received this name because they are a source from which any other sins and tendencies to vice and to evil flow. When we repeatedly give in to these vices and commit actions that respond to their urging, we leave ourselves open even more readily to walk in that path that carries us away from God. Since that path leads to spiritual death, these vices are called deadly. They are like venom that slowly paralyzes and eventually kills.

PRIDE

The first of these capital sins is *pride.* The virtue that helps us overcome it is humility. Pride is clearly evident in all of human history. It is defined as the need, the tendency, of persons to exalt themselves, their gifts, their ability over others and even over God's plan.

One example of pride and the corresponding lack of humility is our failure to recognize that it is from God that we have received every good gift, ability, talent, and capacity in the first place. Pride is the unnatural, unbalanced exaltation of ourselves.

In the gospel, we read of the two men who went up to the temple to pray. One walked straight down to the front of the temple and stood there thanking God that he was not like the rest of people. He followed the law, he was upright, just—and considerably taken with himself. In the back of the temple, the other man simply knelt and asked God's forgiveness for his own unworthiness. Surely both men had gifts and failings. Jesus asked, "Which of the two do you think went home justified?"

Pride is the exaltation of self when our Lord calls us to the simple recognition that whatever we have, whoever we are, and whatever good gifts we possess are all from God.

GLUTTONY

The second capital sin is *gluttony.* Its counter-virtue is temperance. Essentially, gluttony is our failure to practice restraint. It places a priority on physical satisfaction and mental gratification. The temptation we give in to is to satisfy the physical desire for food or drink and to do so in a way that is unbalanced and completely disproportionate to our basic human need.

Temperance on the other hand is the virtue that controls our wish to overindulge in what we eat and drink. In a nation where reports annually show that we are the most overweight population on the planet and where a whole industry exists creating low-calorie food and drink, gluttony has not completely gone out of style.

AVARICE

Avarice is the third of the capital sins. This vice is also one of imbalance—this time, however, dealing with the goods of the earth. The counter-virtue is liberality.

Instead of accumulating the goods of the earth, building up vast stores of wealth beyond what we truly require, the virtue of liberality or detachment recognizes that we need only a certain number of things to live, and even to live well. There should be a limit to what we accumulate. The confines should be set by our heart.

The hoarding of things for the sake of having them is a vice very much at home in a consumer society. Need is not so much the norm by which we shop. In fact shopping itself becomes the need. Detachment teaches us that there are limits to what material goods can actually provide us, and that—more important—our individual worth is not determined by the number of possessions we have.

LUST

Lust is the next of the capital sins, and it too is in the category of an unbalanced attachment to a physical aspect of reality. In this case the attachment is to sexual activity and to the pleasure derived from it. The counterbalancing virtue is chastity.

One of Jesus' great concerns in the Sermon of the Mount is that we avoid treating people as objects. Lust does just that. It makes another person an object of personal satisfaction. It is clearly one of those sins that leads us away from God and from other people. Lustful relationships can never be enduring personal relationships.

SLOTH

The next capital sin we encounter is *sloth* or *acedia.* Sloth can be a spiritual sin, or it can be an attitude toward the way we address just about anything. "Laziness" is a good translation of *acedia.* It is spiritual laziness that constitutes a capital sin.

It takes diligence in the care of our spiritual life to pay attention to God within us, to God's Spirit urging us, to all the opportunities of grace that are around us every day. Sloth lets our care for the physical, our comfort, our creature needs override our diligence for our spiritual life. Couch potatoes exist in the spiritual order. Overwhelmed by the habit of doing little, we may be tempted to do nothing. We are called, on the other hand, to diligence in the things of the Spirit.

ENVY

Then comes *envy*—a sin that looks resentfully at the good things other people have received or achieved. Envy sees the ability of other people, their talents, gifts, diligence, and energy, as reasons to dislike both the person and their achievements. The counter-virtue is love.

We are called to rejoice that other people are doing well, are happy and successful. Envy says "that is not right because it is not mine." Love rejoices in good things that come to other people. Saint Paul writes to the Corinthians, "Love is patient, love is kind. It is not jealous, love is not pompous, it is not inflated, it is not rude, it does not seek its own interests, it is not quick-tempered, it does not brood over injury, it does not rejoice over wrongdoing but rejoices with the truth. It bears all things, believes all things, hopes all things, endures all things" (1 Corinthians 13:4–7).

ANGER

The last of the deadly sins is *anger.* Here we encounter an expression, living out, or manifestation of a feeling of resentment toward someone else. This can take many forms, sometimes outright and at other times far more subtle. It can even be expressed in silence. Passive resistance to the good things going on around us is as much an expression of anger as is a good, classic, foot-stomping tantrum. Anger boils over and expresses itself in a way that says, "I am going to act out my envy of the good things that others have."

The response and counterbalance to anger is the meekness of soul that Jesus speaks about in the beatitudes. He talks about the right temperament in rejoicing with the good that other people have received. Meekness does not mean that we do not speak up and act out of love of God and love of neighbor. Meekness is the right ordering of our appreciation for the good things God has given us and others, and the simple recognition that it all comes from God and should be a source of joy and satisfaction for everyone, not resentment and anger.

WITH GRACE, WE CAN OVERCOME SIN

We are all aware that the seven capital sins are hardly rare. What we need to recognize is that they are truly deadly. They are sins from which other evils flow. They attack our spiritual life at its very root.

As Christians, we must live in the realization that deep within us is a tendency to sin. But we have also been washed clean in the Blood of Jesus Christ. The Spirit of God dwells within us, and if there is a struggle going on between the Spirit of God and the temptation to sin, the struggle to overcome vice and to live a virtuous life before God is one that we can surely win. No matter what the struggle, God's grace is sufficient for us. All we need do is ask for it and prepare ourselves to receive it.

QUESTIONS TO THINK ABOUT:

1. How is proper self-esteem distinct from the sin of pride?
2. How does sloth show itself in my spiritual life? What has it caused me to avoid doing that I ought to have done?
3. Which of the seven capital sins is my own weakest point? What am I doing to overcome that weakness?

CHAPTER 58

The Person and Society

SOME OF THE CLEAREST expressions of the Christian commitment come from the mouths of children. Perhaps that is one of the reasons why I so much enjoy visiting our Catholic schools and parish religious education programs. It gives me a chance to interact with our young people.

On one such occasion I had been present for part of a math class, where small packages of candy were used to teach some rather intricate mathematical principles. A student gave me one of the packages that had been a part of the demonstration. As I thanked him, I told him that I was going to share this with the priest who had accompanied me so that he, the youngster, could keep a pack for himself. The budding young mathematician looked at me and replied: "You're supposed to share." So we are. It is the basis of our communal life and social obligation.

NO MAN IS AN ISLAND

We are social beings. Community with others not only helps us secure such basic goods as knowledge and life itself but also is a basic element in our well-being and fulfillment as persons. As the poet John Donne once wrote, "No man is an island entire of itself; every man is a piece of the continent, a part of the main." Each of our lives is deeply affected by the society in which we live; each has a duty to share in the task of shaping and conserving a just and humane social order. As the *Catechism of the Catholic Church* points out, "The human person needs to live in society.

Society is not for him an extraneous addition but a requirement of his nature" (section 1879).

THE FAMILY IS THE ROOT OF SOCIETY

Sharing is at the very core of good human relations. Each of us enters this world as part of a society—the family, the original cell of human society. As we grow, we experience an interaction with our parents and other members of the family that permits us to appreciate the value of others, their importance to ourselves, and our relationship with them.

Anyone who has grown up in a family with several siblings knows the give-and-take that is a part of family life. That we do not always have it our own way and that the needs of others may come before our own are lessons learned in the family. But it is more than just a process of socialization. It is the fulfillment of our human vocation. "Through the exchange with others, mutual service and dialogue with his brethren, man develops his potential; he thus responds to his vocation" (section 1879).

What begins in the family is rapidly expanded, but we can never underestimate the importance of the family as the first building block of community. As Pope John Paul II pointed out in his 1994 *Letter to Families,* "The history of mankind, the history of salvation, passes by way of the family" (23). Both our human culture and our knowledge of the gospels are transmitted to us in the context of our family, and usually find anchor and support there throughout our lives.

As we grow, we experience other communities, including the educational, for example at school; the cultural or social, such as athletics and community activities; the economic, employment and its rewards; and, of course, the political—the activities and structures that represent us as a city, state, or nation. At the same time, we experience the Church as an essential and vital part of our life.

SOCIAL TEACHING

Over more than a hundred years, the Church has produced a body of teaching known as the Church's social teaching—that teaching which calls us to an awareness of our obligations to each other. Social teaching is an essential part of the Church's message. Christ himself taught us that we should not selfishly seek earthly treasures, but rather, as children of one Father, we should share property generously, show special solicitude for the poor and afflicted, and seek to structure our earthly life in such a way that the kingdom of God may begin to appear in our midst.

The Church's social teaching is a working out of certain elementary requirements of Christian faith, hope, and love. This whole social teaching rests on two fundamental principles. First, we cannot find fulfillment unless we have some community with others, a community in which we serve and are served, love and are loved. Second, we cannot find personal fulfillment without making our own deep personal commitment to God. We are indeed social beings, but we are much more than that. We are social beings who are also persons with transcendent dignity, persons called to an immediate personal relationship with God.

Any effort to build a good and just society holds up before the eyes of its members our dual obligations: to God and to our neighbor. "You shall love the Lord, your God, with all your heart, with all your soul, and with all your mind. This is the greatest and the first commandment. The second is like it: You shall love your neighbor as yourself" (Matthew 22:37–40).

At the core of the Church's social teaching is the simple realization that we are brothers and sisters, children of the same God. We owe each other a realistic and active love. We have a duty to accept personal responsibility for concrete actions that work toward the shaping of a society in which there will be justice, freedom, and peace.

YOU'RE SUPPOSED TO SHARE

Human goods reflect God's goodness and the basic human goods are common goods that pervade all of human life. They are common too in the sense that all men and women can share in them. Finally, it is because we have a good in common that we can work together and be joined in authentic friendship, in unselfish shared pursuit of what is truly good.

The common good is understood in the *Catechism* as " 'the sum total of social conditions which allow people, either as groups or as individuals, to reach their fulfillment more fully and more easily' (*Gaudium et Spes* 26). The common good concerns the life of all" (section 1906).

We come together at a variety of different levels to share our talents and abilities, so that out of the effort might come something larger than ourselves that benefits all of us. Because of that, we inherently recognize the claims of society on ourselves. This includes the economic society in which we live.

Increasingly, the social teaching of the Church has focused on the economic condition of our brothers and sisters. Since the goods of the earth were created for the benefit of all, and since work is the way in which each of us has access to a share of the goods of the earth, such basic realities as the condition of workers and the economic life of the community become the object of the Church's study and teaching.

The *Catechism* reminds us that socialization, while in itself a good thing, "also presents dangers. Excessive intervention by the state can threaten personal freedom and initiative" (section 1883). It is for this reason that the Church offers guidance. The teaching of the Church has elaborated the principle of subsidiarity, according to which a community of a higher order should not interfere in the internal life of a community of a lower order, depriving the latter of its functions. Rather, communities of a higher order should support the work of lower-level communities and help to coordinate their activity for the common good (see section 1883 of the *Catechism*).

The main elements of the Church's teaching on social economic matters are rooted in the sublime dignity of the person and the destiny of the person. They are rooted in the principles of freedom, personal development, equality, subsidiarity, and participation in the life of the community.

At the heart of all of the Church's social teaching addressing the complex reality in which we live is the simple, basic realization that "you're supposed to share." All of the goodness of God manifest in creation is destined for all people. Social justice is another word for that sharing so essential to human development. Since none of us is an island, sharing is our natural condition.

QUESTIONS TO THINK ABOUT:

1. If the family is the basis of society, is my own family a good start? What could be improved in the way I relate to my family? Where would I look for help in improving it?
2. Do I share my property generously? How could I be more generous?
3. How do I support the Church's ministry to the poor?
4. When I vote in local elections, am I thinking primarily of my own benefit or of the common good?

CHAPTER 59

Social-Justice Issues in America

THOSE WHO LIVE IN the United States can be justifiably proud of the attention we pay collectively to many of the social-justice issues of our day—Social Security, Medicare and Medicaid, various forms of temporary government relief to those in need, and a host of laws regulating life in our country to provide a more equitable distribution of benefits. All of this is balanced with the desire to maintain the maximum amount of personal independence and freedom. For many, this takes its most concrete form in the annual "Tribute to Caesar" rendered in the form of federal, state, and local taxes.

The *Catechism* describes how a society ensures social justice when it "provides the conditions that allow associations or individuals to obtain what is their due according to their nature and their vocation" (section 1928). We are called to recognize first of all that there is such a thing as the common good, which transcends the temptation of individuals to focus exclusively and solely on their personal benefit. At the same time, the *Catechism* tells us that legitimate authority is a natural part of communal life, and that the exercise of authority, when done legitimately, is to be respected.

At the core of a good and just society, one in which there is a proper exercise of authority directed to the common good and respectful of the rights of individuals, is respect for the human person. "Respect for the human person entails respect for the rights that flow from his dignity as a creature. These rights are prior to society and must be recognized by it" (see section 1930 of the *Catechism*).

CALL TO RESPECT LIFE AT ALL TIMES

Time has proved the great wisdom of Pope Paul VI's statement, "If you want peace, work for justice." This important and succinct message was enriched by Pope John Paul II when he said, "If you want justice, respect life. If you want life, embrace the truth—truth revealed by God" (Homily, St. Louis, January 28, 1999).

The human family has come to recognize—by experience, through rational reflection, and by the light of faith—that every human being is of transcendent importance and that each has inalienable rights. The convergence of philosophy and theology on the dignity of human life reaffirms the ancient wisdom "that faith and reason 'mutually support each other'; each influences the other" in the pursuit of deeper meaning and the truth (see Pope John Paul II, *Fides et Ratio* 100; internal quotation from the First Vatican Council, *Dei Filius* 4).

Our conviction about the dignity and sanctity of human life is confirmed in the Scriptures, the word of God. The Book of Genesis teaches us that human beings are created in the image and likeness of God (Genesis 1:26). "Thou shall not kill," says the Lord in transmitting the commandments to Moses (Exodus 20:13). "Choose life, then, that you and your descendants may live," Moses warned the chosen people (Deuteronomy 30:19). And, of course, the whole life, teaching, and ministry of Jesus confirmed the dignity of human life and showed how dear each individual person is to God.

Jesus said, "Even the hairs of your head have all been counted" (Luke 12:7). This teaching of the Scriptures, along with the clear and consistent teaching of the Church throughout the ages, reveals God's infinite love for the life he has created and therefore the love we should have for life. In view of this testimony, the primordial transgression against God, the giver of life, is the act of destroying human life itself.

God holds us responsible for upholding human dignity. Each person, created by God, is endowed with a sacred and inviolable human dignity. In the Book of Genesis, God describes the persons he creates as "very good"—not because of anything they have accomplished or produced, but by the very fact of their existence as his creatures.

Never has that responsibility for upholding human dignity been more difficult than in our day, in the third Christian millennium. At a time when many in society tend to judge a person's worth on an obscure and subjective "quality of life" scale, we are convinced that human dignity is not based on productivity or usefulness. As members of the human family and as Christians, we must ensure that every human life is protected from conception until natural death. This responsibility must be accepted on many levels. Each person has a charge; society and its leaders have a duty, and most assuredly so does the church community. Respect for every human being should be our first priority. Our words, actions, and prayers must reflect God's command that we love one another as he has loved us (John 13:34).

TODAY'S SIGNS OF GROWING DISREGARD FOR HUMAN LIFE

We have seen society's tragic acceptance of the devaluation of human life gain momentum on what has been appropriately termed the "slippery slope." A watershed in this movement was the Supreme Court decision in January 1973, when abortion on demand was legalized in this country. With one stroke, the Justices obviated the political consensus across this land that abortion needs to be controlled and created a new right, "the right to privacy," that is supposed to take precedence over even the right to life. After that the number of abortions escalated and fostered an increasing level of disrespect and violence throughout society.

Two generations after the Supreme Court legalized abortion, we are now experiencing a disheartening increase in all the social problems that abortion was supposed to fix. Teen pregnancy, promiscuous activity, sexually transmitted diseases, child abuse, and the number of children born to single-parent families are dramatically higher now than in 1973 before abortion was legalized.

Pope John Paul II rightly warned that we are abandoning a "civilization of love" for a "culture of death" (*Evangelium Vitae* 12). Since court-approved abortion on demand, we have seen a huge increase in the incidence of infanticide. The judgment that our children are disposable if we deem them inconvenient has had a tremendous impact on the way our society looks at all life. Violence has become a regular, if not accepted, phenomenon in our society. Our youth now struggle in the midst of violence within the walls of their schools, on the streets in their neighborhoods, and even in their own homes. The irrefutable connection between the abortion mentality and increasing violence, especially among our youth, can be denied only at the risk of still more upheaval. Violence breeds violence.

An important indicator of a growing indifference toward human life is the position of those who excuse themselves from the abortion debate by arguing that they are "personally opposed to abortion but publicly neutral." This display of indifference sends the message that it is acceptable to withhold protection from certain persons. The idea that a person can oppose abortion personally and defend and support it publicly is no more applicable to abortion than it is to any other critical social or moral question that challenges our nation today.

Sanctioned disregard for the unborn has broadened into a so-called "right to die" and a "duty to die" mentality. Our elderly and disabled brothers and sisters are now seen as burdensome to society. Isolated but well-publicized efforts to give legal sanction to assisting in the suicide of sick or elderly people are only thinly disguised attempts to legalize the killing of such persons. This eugenic philosophy only adds to the problems of our society, already mired in violence and death.

TODAY'S SIGNS OF HOPE FOR IMPROVING RESPECT FOR LIFE

While we must acknowledge that a culture of death is growing up around us, we can also identify emerging signs of hope. Currently we have the lowest annual rate of abortion since 1975. The number of abortion providers and abortion clinics has dropped significantly in recent years. Even some proponents of legalized abortion admit that abortion is a "bad thing," "a failure," and "killing."

More Americans than ever before are pro-life. Many believe that abortion should not be legal in any circumstance. Even more believe that abortion should only be legal in those rare cases when the pregnancy is a result of rape or incest or when the mother's life is threatened by the pregnancy. Almost three quarters of all Americans believe that killing the unborn child merely to give a woman a choice is wrong. Yet these significant statistics are not usually presented in much of the media discussion over abortion or in the laws of the land.

CAPITAL PUNISHMENT

Pope John Paul II has persistently reminded us of our duty to reverence every life, and he asks us to be faithful to this ideal in reflecting on capital punishment. The Catholic Church's moral teaching has always agreed that lawful authorities have the power to enforce law, prosecute law breakers, and imprison convicted criminals. It has also recognized the right, in extreme circumstances, to execute certain convicted criminals, especially when there seems to be no other way to guard innocent lives. Today, however, the Church is convinced that less than lethal means are available and morally appropriate to punish criminals convicted of certain crimes and still protect society from them.

Pope John Paul II has taught that "the nature and extent of the punishment must be carefully evaluated and decided upon, and ought not go to the extreme of executing the offender except in cases of absolute necessity: in other words, when it would not be possible otherwise to defend society. Today, however, as a result of steady improvements in the organization of the penal system, such cases are very rare, if not practically non-existent" (*Evangelium Vitae* 56).

In the same ways that abortion, euthanasia, and infanticide disrespect human life, so too does capital punishment. We believe that human life is sacred and deserves to be protected. While the state has the right and responsibility to punish, the Catholic Church teaches, as we see in the *Catechism,* that if other means, such as lifelong imprisonment, are sufficient to protect the safety of persons, public authority should limit itself to those means, and thereby better conform its policies to the inherent dignity of all human beings (see section 2267 of the *Catechism*).

QUESTIONS TO THINK ABOUT:

1. What do I do to work for justice in my own community?
2. How are the "right to abortion" and the "right to die" connected?
3. Why is capital punishment so popular? Is the motive for capital punishment in our society the common good, or is it anger and revenge?

CHAPTER 60

Christian Discourse: Building Up the Church and Society

WE DO NOT LIVE alone. While each of us can claim a unique identity and a personal relationship with God, we are nonetheless called to live out our lives in relationship with others.

All human community is rooted in this deep stirring of God's created plan within us that brings us into ever-widening circles of relationship: first with our parents, then our family, the Church, and finally a variety of community experiences: educational, economic, cultural, social, and, of course, political.

We are by nature social. We have a natural tendency to come together, so that in the various communities of which we are a part we can experience full human development. All of this is part of God's plan initiated in creation and reflected in the natural law that calls us to live in community.

TRUST IS THE BASIS OF COMMUNITY

No community, human or divine, political or religious, can exist without trust. At the very core of all human relations is the confidence that members speak the truth to each other. The covenant between God and his people also obliges us to a relationship of truth. It is for this reason that God explicitly protected the bonds of community by prohibiting falsehood as a grave attack on the human spirit: "You shall not bear false witness against your neighbor" (Exodus 20:16). To tamper with the truth or, worse yet, to pervert it is to undermine the foundations of human community and to begin to cut the threads that weave us into a coherent human family.

The *Catechism of the Catholic Church* reminds us that the Ten Commandments are "a privileged expression of the natural law" (section 2070). They are also an articulation of our part in the covenant with God that he would be our God and we would be his people (see section 2060). The beautiful relationship with God initiated in creation is elevated to a new level of grace in Christ. Falsehood can have no role in this family of the Lord, who himself is "the way, and the truth, and the life" (John 14:6).

Christians must not only speak the truth but must also do so in love (Ephesians 4:15). It is not enough that we know or believe something to be true. We must express that truth in charity, with respect for others, so that the bonds between us can be strengthened in building up the Church of Christ.

THE CHURCH NEEDS RESPECTFUL COMMUNICATION

In establishing his Church, Christ chose apostles and charged them to lead, to teach, and to sanctify his flock entrusted to them. The bishops, as successors to the apostles, carry on the work of protecting, caring for, nurturing, and building up God's people. In communion with them, priests as coworkers offer their lives, talents, and abilities to assist in the same task.

The hierarchical structure of the Church does not mean that the bishops and priests continue Christ's ministry all alone. In an ever-increasing appreciation of the role of the laity fostered so explicitly by the Second Vatican Council, religious and laity are invited into the work particularly of evangelizing the wider community in which we live. Lay participation in the life of the parish and the diocese, in the liturgy, and in the many programs and efforts that reflect the Church's ongoing teaching, healing, and caring ministries is a very real part of Church life today.

We should not be surprised that, with so many people with different responsibilities engaged in the life of the Church, there is a particular need for good, constant, and respectful communications. Today more than ever we recognize in the Church a wide-ranging number of meetings, discussions, and exchanges of views that should have as their focus the building up of the Church. We engage in discourse and we live out our commitment as members of the Church—as people of profound respect for the truth and as a family of faith committed to expressing our thoughts, opinions, and positions—always in love.

Even though there may be disagreements within the ecclesial community on policies and procedures, there is a presupposition that we are all one in our faith. One of the reasons why we should find it easy as a Church to arrive at consensus is because it is Christ who calls us together in the first place. We are already one in what we believe, in our loyalty to the Church and in our commitment to live by God's commandments.

Effective and respectful communication is essential to community life and must be rooted in truth. Lying contradicts what one believes to be truthful and, therefore, is a sin. It destroys human bonds built on trust. "Put on the new self, created in God's way in righteousness and holiness of truth," Saint Paul writes in his letter to the Ephesians. He continues: "Therefore, putting away falsehood, speak the truth, each one to his neighbor, for we are members one of another" (Ephesians 4:24–25).

TRUTH IS A RESPONSIBILITY

The *Catechism* reminds us that the seriousness of a lie is "measured against the nature of the truth it deforms, the circumstances, the intentions of the one who lies, and the harm suffered by its victims." If a lie in itself is only a venial sin, it can become mortal or deadly to human relationships and the community it affects when it seriously violates the virtues of justice and love (see section 2484).

The call to truthfulness is far from being a denial of freedom of speech. Rather it is a God-given obligation to respect the very function of human speech. We are not free to say whatever we want about another, but only what is true and what can be said with a charitable heart. To the extent that freedom is improperly used to sever the bonds of trust that bind us together as a people, to that extent it is irresponsible. The eighth commandment obliges us not only to avoid false witness but also to tell the truth. We have an obligation to ascertain that what we say is really the truth.

In the gospel of John, we read that Jesus will send us the Spirit of truth and that he expects his disciples to abide with that Spirit (John 14:16–17). Every generation of disciples stands to be judged in light of that directive of Christ. Even more important, every individual Christian is called to live in fidelity to that truth.

To speak the truth requires personal self-discipline and conscious effort. We must search out the facts and avail ourselves of the information necessary to make a judgment based on truth. It is a disservice to the truth when our opinions, positions, or proposals are based on unverified gossip, unsupported rumor, or partial information when all the facts are readily available to us. Serious research and study are demanded in serious matters.

Christian discourse should help a person move beyond an emotional response to some issue or occurrence to a more reasoned understanding. As a people of faith, we need to direct our energy to recognizing the truth that should be the basis of our response, and that will help move us beyond those powerful feelings or high emotions that might affect our good judgment.

Because we live in a society that sometimes treats lightly the importance of truth, those who engage in Christian discourse need to be keenly aware that simply because something is said on the radio or television or printed in a newspaper or magazine does not necessarily make it true and reliable. To base one's judgment on such sources alone is to enter into the realm of rash judgment and its ruinous effects not only to individuals but also to society itself. If we choose to speak, we ourselves must accept the responsibility to discover the truth.

TRUTH MUST BE SPOKEN IN LOVE

We are called to a higher level of respect for the truth and for each other than is often witnessed on some radio and television talk shows. The intensity of one's opinion is not the same as the truth. Speaking out of anger does not justify falsehood. Frustration or disappointment does not condone a lack of charity. The *Catechism* reminds us, "Respect for the reputation of persons forbids every attitude and word likely to cause them unjust injury" and calls "rash judgment," "detraction," and "calumny" offenses against truth (see section 2477).

At the heart of who we are as the Church is Christ's call to love one another. Whatever diminishes love diminishes the Church. A measure of our love for God and for each other is how well we deal with frustration and disappointment. Both are a normal and frequent part of life. They need not lead to anger, rash judgment, or their public expression, but rather to tolerance, trust, and patience after the example of Christ. Love calls us to a higher standard as a part of God's family.

QUESTIONS TO THINK ABOUT:

1. What are some of the significant relationships in my life and why are they important to me?
2. Why are trust and truth an important part of those relationships and in the proper functioning of society?
3. What does it mean to speak the truth in love?
4. What kind of harm can telling lies cause?

CHAPTER 61

Fashioning a Moral Compass

"IT WAS THE BEST of times, it was the worst of times." How many times have people used these words from *A Tale of Two Cities* to describe our own age? The quotation certainly seems applicable today. How often we encounter, on the one hand, the quiet struggle to live a virtuous life, and, on the other hand, the arrogant ease of "anything goes."

Recently I visited a number of our Catholic elementary schools and colleges as they began another academic year. There was something refreshing and good about those energetic and wholesome young people who recognize the need for basic Christian morality as a part of their education. Education includes the mind, the heart, and the soul. It encompasses academic excellence that forms the mind; an appreciation of values that motivates the heart; and a knowledge and love of God that sustain the soul. As I left those schools, I felt it really can be the "best of times."

In direct and stark contrast to this message is another one summed up in so many of the television and radio talk shows, and also on what passes for prime-time television entertainment. On one evening, surfing the TV channels, I saw a program ridiculing religious conviction in God, whose host performed a comic routine that had his audience rolling in laughter at the suggestion that there could be such a thing as "adultery." On another program, the clear message was: Truth is only what you are clever enough to convince people to believe; morality is every person's opinion of what they can get away with; and decency, while not a four-letter word, ought to be. As I clicked off the TV, I thought this really is "the worst of times."

HOW SHALL I LIVE?

Saint Augustine used another equally well-known description for this dichotomy. Side by side in our world we find the City of God and the City of Man. Both have their own values. Each offers a vision of life. Both provide an answer to the fundamental human question: "How shall I live?"

There seems to be a general acceptance of sex as not much more than a form of personal recreation. This is reflected not only in the ease with which so many people apparently view infidelity, adultery, fornication—even the extremes expressed in some forms of pornography—but also in the general malaise in editorials, television commentaries, and radio talk programs that say much of this is perfectly all right.

When I read the story of John the Baptist in the New Testament, I often wonder how it was possible for King Herod to get away with what he did. He committed the sin and John the Baptist had to die. Herodias was apparently a clever, cunning, ambitious, and powerful woman. She was able to point the accusing finger at John the Baptist. We all know the story. How did it happen? I wonder if polls taken at that time would have shown a large number of people complacent with immorality, comfortable with recreational sex, and oblivious to the fact that they had lost their moral compass altogether.

Not too long ago, in my hometown, we lamented the death of a baby left in an alley behind a church. The baby died of exposure because no one found him in time. We are horrified when another newly born baby is thrown into a trash can by its parents and dies smothered in other people's garbage. We are shocked when an infant is beaten to death by drug-addicted parents. And yet, too many people sit back silently and unconcerned while partial-birth abortion is paraded as a triumph of choice.

We organize all types of efforts to deal with children who, in effect, have become wards of this community because after generating them their parents abandon them. And yet, we do not seem to have the moral resolve to say to these same young parents that recreational sex is more than inappropriate. It is immoral and destructive. It is not a private personal activity that affects only two people; it is one that impacts all of us because it is the God-created means by which the family and society come into being and are sustained.

WHY WE HAVE LOST OUR MORAL COMPASS

All of us can and do fail. The Lord reminds us that only the one without sin should cast the first stone. What is wrong today—why we have lost our moral compass—is not that we sin but that we refuse to call it sin. What is disturbing is not that there is failure but that so many try so hard to call it by other names: "freedom of expression," "privacy," "liberty," "personal privilege." The real worry is that so many are prepared to call the darkness light, falsehood truth, and moral evil perfectly acceptable human behavior—because it is done by consenting adults. "If no one is being harmed, what could possibly be wrong?"

In addressing the issue of the human community, the person and society, the *Catechism* prefaces the discussion with a reference to sin and God's mercy and the realization that sin can be destructive not only of the person but also of society itself. "Sins give rise to social situations and institutions that are contrary to the divine goodness" (section 1869). Here the *Catechism* quotes from Pope John Paul II's apostolic exhortation *Reconciliatio et Paenitentia* (*On Reconciliation and Penance*). "Structures of sin are expressions and effects of personal sins. They lead their victims to do evil in their turn. In an analogous sense, they constitute a social sin" (16).

The *Catechism* continually holds up for us a vision of a world in which there *is* right and wrong—an absolute moral norm against which we can judge our personal behavior, and an expectation that collectively we should be held to moral accountability just as we are individually. In applying the teaching of the *Catechism* to the circumstances of our day, we find a challenging context.

In the past, many spoke often about virtue, obligation, responsibility, the common good, our trust in God, and our recognition of moral principles. Today the emphasis is on self-satisfaction. The increasing response of many people to the concept of a cross in our lives is to flee from it or to blame others for it, even to sue everyone and everything in sight for some real or imagined harm.

In contrast, faith offers us a vision of another world—a world at peace because there is goodwill among people who recognize that life is difficult, that there is a common good we must all struggle to attain and maintain, that we have a responsibility beyond ourselves, and that into each life there come burdens that we sum up in the simple word "cross."

In addressing social justice, the *Catechism* reminds us that respect for the human person and the recognition of basic human solidarity are foundational for a good and just society. It also reminds us that "the virtue of solidarity goes beyond material goods. In spreading the spiritual goods of the faith, the Church has promoted, and often opened new paths for, the development of temporal goods as well" (section 1942).

THE NEW SECULAR IDEAL

Our roots, civic and religious, remind us that we are a people who see our lives guided by the sure hand of a loving and provident God. Yet little by little the First Amendment to our nation's Constitution has been interpreted to mean God and religious sentiment, conviction, and religion-based morality have no place in our public life and policy. What was once a constitutional protection of religion and the rights of religious people to be free from the interference and impositions of the state has come to mean the removal from our lives, our world, our public institutions, and our social convention any reference to God—as if we were totally self-sufficient.

In this new secular vision, the concept of morality has given way to a convolution of legal loopholes, ethics has been replaced with a "don't get caught" mentality, and moral obligation has been emptied of any significance. One opinion, whether informed or not, is as good as any other—or, for that matter, as good as the teaching of the Church.

If we look for peace in our families, on our streets, and in our schools, do we really think we will find it by carefully instructing our youngsters that any mention of God in a public facility is a violation of the American Constitution? Someone once remarked that by the time a child is in the third grade in our public school system, he or she knows that God is "illegal."

Do we really think that we will build goodwill among all people by fostering a society that admits of no spiritual principle of integrity or no moral bond of cohesion other than "don't get caught" or "if I think it's right, it is?"

As the *Catechism* reflects on the meaning of Life in Christ, it challenges us to recognize that religious faith has social consequences, and that Christian discipleship carries with it obligations when we address the social order and public policy.

QUESTIONS TO THINK ABOUT:

1. What evidence do I see around me to make me think this is the best of times? What evidence do I see to make me think this is the worst of times?
2. How would I support the claim that there is an absolute standard of morality?
3. Do modern secular ideals make it difficult to profess belief in Christ publicly? How much is my public practice of Christianity influenced or suppressed by secularism?

CHAPTER 62

The Natural Moral Law

AT THE END OF World War II a number of Nazi leaders were put on trial. These trials held at Nuremberg would clearly lack jurisdiction were it not for the common-sense basic understanding, as articulated by Pope Pius XII, that there are "crimes against humanity." Such crimes do not need to be written down in a code of civil law because they are already engraved in the hearts of human beings. Those who violate such laws should be held accountable.

WRITTEN IN OUR HEARTS

The *Catechism of the Catholic Church* tells us that "The moral law is the work of divine Wisdom . . . It prescribes for man the ways, the rules of conduct that lead to the promised beatitude" (section 1950). Saint Paul in writing to the Romans points out that "when the Gentiles who do not have the law by nature observe the prescriptions of the law, they are a law for themselves even though they do not have the law. They show that the demands of the law are written in their hearts, while their conscience also bears witness and their conflicting thoughts accuse or even defend them . . ." (Romans 2:14–15). Goodness comes from within, as does evil.

Some things seem so clear that they defy questioning. One of these realities is the universal moral law, or the natural law as it is sometimes called. The foundation for this self-evident manifestation of human experience is our common human nature. While humans vary according to a variety of superficial distinctions, such as skin color, weight, height, and language, there is a common reality we all share—human nature. Since we all are one in something as basic as our human nature, it is not surprising that we share the same aspirations, nurture the same dreams, and harbor the same fears.

THE DANGERS OF REJECTING NATURAL LAW

Nonetheless, there is a surprising number of people today who would reply "no" to the question, "Is there a universal moral law binding on all people?" To them there is only what we call "positive" or civil law. In this theory, law does not develop out of the very nature of creation, human life, and the interrelation of human beings according to God's plan, but rather from the will of the lawgiver. This approach to law has brought us today to a crossroads.

If we choose to set aside the millennia-long tradition of understanding law in light of our human nature, we are left only with political expedience—or, as it is more commonly seen today, political correctness—as the norm for human living. More and more detailed legislation is needed, since common sense is no longer normative, and the result is the wide-ranging appeal to more law and more court intervention to regulate human activity.

We should also note here that if a society claims there is no intrinsic right and wrong, and therefore no common moral obligation incumbent upon all of us, then the logical conclusion soon follows that any type of civil direction must be imposed from outside. If there is no moral imperative—no absolute right and wrong—then everything is a matter of opinion. To enforce opinion, one needs more and more external force. Perhaps that explains why we as a society have in recent decades witnessed an explosion of our prison population and a level of commonplace violence in our day that convulses most of our major metropolitan areas.

NATURAL LAW IS PART OF CREATION

In the beginning when God created, he placed within the works of his hand a law that would govern creation. The natural physical law expressed in something as simple as the law of gravity or the law of physics is built into creation. So it is with the natural moral law. We as human beings are rational and capable of understanding God's plan for us and how we ought to act.

The Church speaks of "those principles of the moral order which have their origin in human nature itself" (*Dignitatis Humanae* 14). The Second

Vatican Council, for example, in a section on international hostilities, states, "Contemplating this melancholy state of humanity, the Council wishes to recall first of all the permanent binding force of the universal natural law and all its embracing principals" (*Gaudium et Spes* 79).

As many documents of the Church indicate, however, the language of "natural law" is not used by the Church in the same sense in which it was used by Greek philosophers or the Roman lawyers of old; nor is it used in the sense of "laws of nature" in the physical or biological sciences. The Church uses "natural law" in a classical Christian sense. For us, "natural law" signifies the plan of God in relation to human life and action, insofar as the human mind in this life can grasp that plan and share with God the role of directing human life according to it (see *Dignitatis Humanae* 3).

In explaining natural law, Saint Thomas Aquinas starts with God's wisdom as it creates. This he calls God's eternal law. He goes on to describe our limited human understanding of that plan as the natural law. The Angelic Doctor defines the natural law as "nothing other than the light of understanding placed in us by God; through it we know what we must do and what we must avoid. God has given this light or law at the creation" (see section 1955 of the *Catechism*).

Since we are able with our intelligence to understand something of our own human nature and the laws of God's created world, we are obliged to follow them. There is nothing mysterious about the natural law; it is as evident as common sense.

In exploring the definition of natural law, the *Catechism* tells us that it is "present in the heart of each man and established by reason" and "is universal in its precepts and its authority" (section 1956). Since the natural moral law exists within our human nature, and since all of us share that nature, the moral law applies to everyone. Since our human nature is unchangeable, even though its manifestation takes on many forms, so the law remains immutable.

THE CHURCH'S DUTY TO TEACH ON MORAL ISSUES

In an encyclical letter on moral truth entitled *Veritatis Splendor,* Pope John Paul II reaffirmed the Church's obligation and authority to teach on moral issues so that there is never confusion among the faithful about what is right and wrong in specific, sometimes complex, matters.

In this document, we find a concise and authoritative presentation of the understanding of the Church's authority to teach on matters that are clearly rooted in our human nature, manifest in the natural moral law and confirmed in a general way in God's revelation. To what we could know from our human reason, if we had the time, the ability, and the inclination to do so, the Church now adds its authority as the voice of Christ speaking to us today as we face contemporary moral dilemmas.

Ours is an age that is uncomfortable with moral absolutes and the claim of the Church to be able to speak for Christ and his gospel—particularly when such teaching runs counter to the prevalent secular mores. While we live in a secular society that increasingly finds little place for God, or for an understanding of God's creation and our moral obligation in the light of that reality, we are not absolved from recognizing the truth and obligation of the moral law. Its precepts take precedence over any positive civil law. It is out of this understanding that we are called to work in our society to see that all public policy is consonant with the natural moral order.

Deep within us is the voice of God's natural moral law that finds expression in our conscience. Even when that voice has been silenced by so many alternative views of life in our highly secular and materialistic world, it continues to echo in our hearts. Some things we know are right and others wrong. Only human beings have the gift of knowing what we "ought to do." The awareness of this distinction so critical to a civilization of love is rooted in the moral law etched into our very being by God at our creation.

QUESTIONS TO THINK ABOUT:

1. What do I know about right and wrong from what is written in my heart or from common sense?
2. Why shouldn't political expedience or political correctness be accepted as the norm for human living? What are some examples where it has?
3. Why does the natural moral law apply to everyone and not to any one group of people?
4. Where does the Church receive her authority to speak out on the complex issues that we face today?

CHAPTER 63

Justification

IT IS GOD'S WILL that all people be saved. It is for this reason that God created us. However, the simple fact is that man introduced sin into a world that was otherwise in harmony with God. There followed in each successive generation our own personal sin as a consequence of the original sin that we inherited from our first parents.

As we read in the *Catechism:* "Called to beatitude but wounded by sin, man stands in need of salvation from God. Divine help comes to him in Christ through the law that guides him and the grace that sustains him" (section 1949). We are called to glory; we have been wounded by sin; we need salvation; and that wonderful gift comes to us from God by way of the grace that elevates us to be able to live God's law and to reach union with Christ.

JUSTIFICATION COMES THROUGH CHRIST

In the *Catechism of the Catholic Church,* justification is treated together with grace, since it is in itself a manifestation of the grace of the Holy Spirit. That grace has the power "to justify us, that is, to cleanse us from our sins and to communicate to us 'the righteousness of God through faith in Jesus Christ' and through Baptism" (see section 1987).

All justification takes place in and through Jesus Christ. With the coming of Christ, God's only Son, into our world to become one of us, God has taken on our fallen human nature. Through grace and by the outpouring of the Holy Spirit, he has elevated it to a level where now we can claim to be adopted children of God. This is why we speak of a new law, the law of Christ. The commandments remain in force, but now we willingly accept their obligations, because we are motivated by the grace of the Holy Spirit, which touches our heart and mind, urging us to walk in God's path and to become one with the Lord.

The order of grace, initiated in the incarnation and birth of God's Son Jesus, was established through the death and resurrection of Christ and by him alone. The grace of the Holy Spirit is at work in us through Christ to heal what was broken, to restore what was destroyed or damaged, and to make it possible for us to have original sin washed way and our own failures forgiven.

GRACE MAKES US WANT TO DO RIGHT

This is the healing power of Christ's new law. It does not just *tell* us what we are to do. Rather, by God's grace freely given, it touches and changes our hearts to make us *want* to do what we ought to do. We speak of the old heart being replaced by a new heart (see Ezekiel 36:26). This new heart would beat with the power of the Holy Spirit in rhythm with Christ's plan and God's will for us. This is the difference between the old and the new law. The old law, given as a teacher, always remained to some extent outside us. The new law is planted deep within the recesses of our heart. "The New Law is the grace of the Holy Spirit received by faith in Christ, operating through charity. It finds expression above all in the Lord's Sermon on the Mount and uses the sacraments to communicate grace to us" (see section 1983 of the *Catechism*).

Justification is God's grace freely given to us, by which we are restored and made holy. The *Catechism* describes the power of God's grace within us: "Justification *detaches man from sin* which contradicts the love of God, and purifies his heart of sin. Justification follows upon God's merciful initiative of offering forgiveness. It reconciles man with God. It frees from the enslavement to sin, and it heals" (section 1990).

We are justified by faith in Christ. There is no other source of our sanctification. Christ alone is the mediator between God and man. It is through his death on the cross that we are saved. Access to this wondrous world of grace is through faith in Jesus Christ.

JUSTIFICATION AND THE REFORMATION

The doctrine of justification was of central importance at the time of the Lutheran reformation in the sixteenth century. It was the occasion of considerable theological digression over the centuries as the Lutheran community and the Catholic Church struggled more clearly to define what each meant by justification in relation to the teaching of the other.

Much of the long history of division over the doctrine of justification focused on the role of good works. As Saint James tells us, faith is evident in its works. "What good is it, my brothers, if someone says he has faith but does not have works? Can that faith save him? If a brother or sister has nothing to wear and has no food for the day, and one of you says to them, 'Go in peace, keep warm, and eat well,' but you do not give them the necessities of the body, what good is it? So also faith of itself, if it does not have works, is dead. Indeed someone may say, 'You have faith and I have works.' Demonstrate your faith to me without works, and I will demonstrate my faith to you from my works" (James 2:14–18).

The joint declaration on justification between the Catholic Church and the Lutheran World Federation (1999) was a moment of joy because it heralded a closer understanding of Lutherans and Catholics about this central issue of the faith. Cardinal Edward Cassidy, president of the Pontifical Council for Promoting Christian Unity, said at the presentation of the joint declaration: "To put this achievement in perspective, it is necessary to recall that the doctrine of justification was a central issue in the dispute between Martin Luther and the Church authorities in the 16th century. . . . The consensus now achieved will be of importance . . . also for progress in the search for unity between Catholics and other communities coming out of the Reformation controversies."

The joint declaration confirms that good works, made possible by grace and the working of the Holy Spirit, contribute to growth in grace, so that the righteousness that comes from God is preserved and communion with Christ is deepened. The document attributes this understanding to both Catholics and Lutherans and declares that "the understanding . . . shows that a consensus in basic truths on the doctrine of justification exists" (38–40).

It is not difficult to see how important the doctrine of justification is. Put simply, it means that we are saved through the merits of Christ, and that through our faith in Christ and our baptism into new life in Christ we are made holy. Our actions, our works, flow from our redemption in Christ and manifest the presence of the Holy Spirit within us.

To see a closer understanding theologically among the Lutherans and Catholics is to witness another step in the ecumenical effort that, God willing, one day will bring us all once again together as God's family should be—one and undivided. As we seek to share in this effort, we can commit ourselves in prayer to ask God to open the hearts and minds of all involved so that the will of God for our unity may be truly accepted, understood, and lived.

QUESTIONS TO THINK ABOUT:

1. How would I explain original sin to a non-Christian? Could I cite any evidence from common human experience?
2. Do I always willingly accept the commandments? How can I overcome my own moments of unwillingness?
3. How are good works related to grace? How would I explain the Catholic understanding to a non-Catholic Christian?

CHAPTER 64

The Church, Mother and Teacher

THE APOSTOLIC LETTER *Ad Tuendam Fidem* (*To Defend the Faith*), issued by Pope John Paul II, makes a clear and self-evident statement: "The faith of the Church is found in its Creed and in its ordinary teaching as articulated by its shepherds, the Pope and the bishops in communion with him."

Some Catholics, however, have found difficulty with both the document and its teaching. The displeasure with the Pope articulated in some of the media seems rooted in an almost obsessive discomfort some people have with limits. This is particularly true when it comes to religious faith. For some people any attempt to call members of the Church to accept its creed and its definitive teaching is viewed as an unacceptable limitation to their personal freedom.

FREEDOM IS LIMITED

In addressing the topic "man's freedom," the *Catechism of the Catholic Church* reminds us that it "is limited and fallible. In fact man failed. He freely sinned . . . From its outset, human history attests the wretchedness and oppression born of the human heart in consequence of the abuse of freedom" (section 1739).

We seem willing to accept limits in most areas of our life. My HMO, for instance, tells me where I can go for medical attention and even when. It seems that just about every airline flight now announces, "This is a nonsmoking flight." On nearly every corner of the street are signs telling us if and when we can park. Then, of course, there is the Internal Revenue Service, which tells us how much of our income we can keep.

Despite some grumbling, we all seem to live well within limits, particularly when we recognize that it is to our advantage. A tow-away sign may be ominous, but it is necessary if the road is going to stay open for the use of all of us. While I may not like driving around looking for an open place to park, I do not think of these restrictions as an attempt to stamp out driving or parking.

THE TRUTH OF THE CHURCH DOES NOT BOW TO "PRESSURE"

As members of the Catholic Church, we belong to something larger and more significant than each of us individually. We are members of the Body of Christ. The Church is a community of faith. We are bound together on a spiritual and sacramental level that transcends any other bonds that we share with any other group. We are a faith community. We do not claim to be a cultural, political, social, or economic community, even though each of these also has very clear limits. We profess that we are a people made one in our common faith. And this faith is a gift from God.

In speaking about the Church as our mother and teacher, the *Catechism* reminds us that "It is in the Church, in communion with all the baptized that the Christian receives his vocation. From the Church he receives the word of God containing the teachings of 'the law of Christ' " (section 2030). We receive our identity as members of the Church from the spiritual reality that is the Body of Christ with which we are united in baptism, in the sacramental life of the Church, and in the living out of the Church's proclamation of the gospel.

The faith, worship, and discipline of the Church are not changed because an individual or a group does not agree with them. Nor does a headcount or an appeal to the "pressure" of the secular media determine what the Church should believe or how its communal life should be expressed. The assertion, made by some, that just as many Catholics as non-Catholics have abortions does not justify abortion any more than it makes the Church's teaching of the inviolable nature of innocent human life less true. The sad fact that many Catholic marriages end in divorce is not "proof" that the Church's teaching is "outmoded" and "out of touch." Rather, it only proves that the teachers in the Church need to do a better job.

CATHOLICS HAVE A DUTY TO ACCEPT THE TEACHING OF THE CHURCH

What the Pope is addressing is the obligation that Catholics have to accept Church teaching. *To Defend the Faith* teaches that Catholics must believe all that is contained in the written word of God and all that has been proclaimed as divinely revealed. The Pope then goes on to assert that "Each and every thing definitively proposed by the Magisterium of the Church regarding faith and morals, that is those which are required in order to piously safeguard and faithfully expound the deposit of faith, also must be firmly accepted and held; one who denies the propositions which are to be held definitively, therefore, opposes the doctrine of the Catholic Church."

When specific, practical judgments have to be made about what the Church actually believes or what is the best practice for the Church, the decision rests with the shepherds of the Church, its pastors—the Pope and the bishops, successors to Peter and the apostles.

THE CHURCH'S RIGHT TO TEACH

In the *Catechism,* we are reminded that the Church has the right to pronounce on moral issues "always and everywhere," and also to make judgments on human affairs "to the extent that they are required by the fundamental rights of the human person or the salvation of souls" (section 2032; see also *Code of Canon Law,* canon 747.2).

This nearly two-thousand-year-old understanding does not mean that there can be no discussion or differences of opinion within the Church. If anything, the twenty centuries of the life of the Church indicate a Body of Christ alive with a variety of opinions and views. What it does mean, however, is that when a definitive decision has been reached by legitimate authority in the Church, it is precisely that: a final decision.

Limits are a part of life. Athletic competition needs officials. However much we dislike it when a call goes against our team, it is foolhardy to suggest that we play the game without an umpire or referee. A football official has to throw a flag when a play is offside. There are limits. It is not an unjust infringement on "athletic freedom" to point out that the player stepped over the line. It is not a move to "stamp out" athletic prowess when a baseball umpire calls a runner out!

Who would take seriously the position of a judge who announced that he or she dissents from the rulings of the Supreme Court and thus is free to fashion his or her own decisions that run counter to the law of the land?

This is all the more applicable to one who claims to teach constitutional law. How seriously would we take the claims of a school of law that bragged that its professors dissented from the decisions of the Supreme Court and thus taught their students "liberated jurisprudence"? Perhaps more significantly, how many law firms would hire its graduates?

Definitive magisterial judgments are a lot like Supreme Court decisions. They settle an issue. They are the last word. One major difference is, of course, that the Church's teaching office can claim the guidance of the Holy Spirit in a way no one else can. "The Advocate, the Holy Spirit that the Father will send in my name—he will teach you everything and remind you of all that I told you" (John 14:26).

One may decide to reject the Catholic faith. But we are not free to do so and then insist that we are still "Catholic."

Jesus taught: " 'I am the living bread that came down from heaven; whoever eats this bread will live forever; and the bread that I will give is my flesh for the life of the world. . . .' " As a result of this, many of his disciples returned to their former way of life and no longer accompanied him. "Jesus then said to the twelve, 'Do you also want to leave?' Simon Peter answered him, 'Master, to whom shall we go? You have the words of eternal life' " (John 6:51, 66–68).

What is at issue today is the question of who speaks for the Church. Who determines what is the faith of the Catholic Church? In every rational process we reach the point where a judgment must be made. In the Church, when we deal with matters of faith and morals, legitimate judgment is made by the Pope and the bishops. If we reject the teaching authority, we reject a part of the very essence of the Church. To reject a judgment described as "final" or "definitive" is to set our personal wisdom above that of the Church, which believes that the Holy Spirit guides and protects the deposit of faith entrusted to the legitimate pastors of the flock.

QUESTIONS TO THINK ABOUT:

1. Which limits on my own freedom do I find most difficult to accept? Which ones do I accept without question?
2. On what issues do people most frequently bring "pressure" against the Church in my community? What can I do to help those people understand the position of the Church?
3. Do I know any people who call themselves "Catholic" but refuse to accept the important teachings of the Church? Why do those people still try to maintain an attachment to the Church? Is there something in that attachment that I could use to help them?

CHAPTER 65

The Ten Commandments

AS WE MAKE OUR way through the *Catechism of the Catholic Church,* we come to the Ten Commandments. Most of us learned them as children and from our youth understood them as God's law—the rules for right living. Beginning with our parents as the first teachers of the faith on through the lessons we learned in Catholic school or in the parish religious education program, we came to understand the importance of these guidelines for living. As we grow older and face increasingly more complex life situations, we recognize that the commandments continue to serve us as a sure norm. They remain direction signs along the road of life. If we pay attention to them and heed the guidance they provide, we are guaranteed a safe outcome to our journey.

The Decalogue or Ten Commandments are recorded twice in the pages of the Old Testament. In the Book of Exodus (20:2–17) we find the first and longest version of God's law. A second and shorter form in the Book of Deuteronomy (5:6–21) corresponds most closely to the traditional catechetical formulation of the commandments. In the *Catechism* after section 2051 and before section 2052 the Ten Commandments are listed in three formulations. Following the formulations, the *Catechism* speaks of each commandment and its meaning and application to our lives today.

HOW SHALL I LIVE?

One of the most persistent questions in life, and in fact the most significant one that we need to ask—one that occurs over and over again as we seek to define our lives and our relationship with one another and with God—is: "How shall I live?" In response to this perennial human inquiry, a host of answers have been proposed. It is not unusual today to find advertised in the media responses ranging from personalized psychics to catalogs of advice on every aspect of human experience. At the root of all of the many voices responding to the question, "How shall I live?" is the assumption that somehow we can find this answer on our own, apart from God and without reference to our ultimate goal—life eternal. In a secular age we should not be surprised by the plethora of alternatives to the simple words of the Decalogue.

In Matthew's gospel (19:16–22) we read the story of the rich young man who came up to Jesus and asked our question, Everyman's question: "Teacher, what good must I do to gain eternal life?" Jesus' response is clear, concise, and direct: "If you wish to enter into life, keep the commandments" (Matthew 19:17).

There is no great mystery to how we should live. True, life many times unfolds in a manner beyond our comprehension. God's providential plan for us is not evident with that clarity we would all desire. Nonetheless in life's journey, which we all make, the guideposts are clearly marked: "If you would to enter life, keep the commandments."

YOU ALREADY KNOW THE WAY

In the gospel narrative, Jesus assumes that the young man—all of us—already knows the commandments. He, like us, must have heard the Decalogue in various forms and expressions throughout his young life, since he was old enough to hear of God and God's way. The same is true also for us.

Perhaps the most important lesson of this gospel narrative is the reminder that the commandments continue to be applicable to us. In the world in which we live, the difficulty is not so much in knowing the Ten Commandments but in opting to choose them. What Jesus tells us is that "you already know the way!" Have you made up your mind to follow it? Have you chosen to make God's law your rule of life? This is the way, the path that leads us through all of the complications and vicissitudes of life with all of its crosses. This is the path that leads us in union with Christ to life everlasting.

At the same time Jesus also confirms the validity of the commandments for the new covenant. The revelation of the commandments takes place in the Old Testament, God speaking to Moses and Moses speaking to the people. In the New Testament, Jesus assures us of the continued validity of the commandments and reaffirms their value.

A study of the Decalogue reveals that it is really a confirmation of the natural moral order, that order we find through our understanding of God's plan rooted in creation and in our human nature. The *Catechism* teaches us that "The Decalogue contains a privileged expression of the natural law" (section 2070). The Ten Commandments belong to God's revelation. At the same time, they teach us the true humanity of man. There is nothing arbitrary about these rules of life. They grow directly out of our human nature. The Author of creation is the Author of revelation. God's choice to make explicit what is already a part of our human nature and experience is the result of God's gracious care and desire that we would have before us a clear expression of how we are to relate to each other and to God.

We have a human nature and that nature calls forth responses, actions, choices, and decisions on our part. Just as birds fly through the natural physical laws and through their instincts, so human beings through the natural moral order respond to the human condition. The Ten Commandments merely make explicit that which we are capable of learning about ourselves if we were to reflect with sufficient care, time, and attention on our human condition.

A BRIEF LOOK AT THE TEN COMMANDMENTS

The Ten Commandments are basically divided into two sections. The first three commandments speak about our relationship to God, and the last seven about our relationship to each other. We have an orientation to God who made us and a relationship to those around us who share in God's creation. In outline form, let us briefly look at the Ten Commandments, each of which will have its own chapter later.

The first commandment is the call to recognize God. God is our creator; God made us; we should acknowledge that God is and that there is only one God.

The second precept of the Decalogue calls upon us to reverence God. Since God is our creator, we should have a respect for God's name, since it identifies God.

The last of the three commandments devoted to our relationship with God tells us that we must find time to honor God. We need to recognize the holiness of God and worship him at an appropriate time and in a proper way.

The rest of the commandments relate us among ourselves. It is evident that we owe respect to those who have given us life and helped us to grow, to learn, to be nurtured, and eventually to reach a status where we can stand on our own. Hence the fourth commandment to honor our parents.

The next commandment, "You shall not kill," speaks of the most basic human law, the law of life. Every one of us has a right to the life that is ours and just as we would not want someone to take our life, so too we have no right to take the life of another.

If we are going to come together in community, if we are going to nurture the family as the building block of society, we have to be able, in fidelity, to live with our partner and raise that family. "You shall not commit adultery," the sixth commandment, follows on the basic understanding that the communal tie of man and woman and the raising of their family are essential to human society.

The next commandment has to do with our property—the means to sustain life. "You shall not steal." The seventh commandment tells us we cannot take what belongs to another if we intend to have a well-ordered society. You cannot take what belongs to someone else and expect society to flourish.

No human community can exist unless it rests on truth and the confidence it generates. The eighth commandment simply confirms, "You shall not bear false witness against your neighbor." You shall not lie; you shall reverence the truth.

Finally the ninth and tenth commandments call upon us to recognize that our attitudes are every bit as important as our actions. "You shall not covet your neighbor's wife or goods."

As we make our way through life, all of these guideposts serve as God's revelation to us of something absolutely essential to our human development. These "privileged expressions of the natural law" remain always with us. It is up to us to accept the challenge and live them.

QUESTIONS TO THINK ABOUT:

1. What are the Ten Commandments? Why did God give them to us?
2. How can each of the commandments be applied to how we live our lives today?
3. Why do some people reject the Ten Commandments? How would I convince them that the commandments are important?
4. Why are the commandments important not only to us as individuals but also to society?

CHAPTER 66

The First Commandment: Have No Strange Gods

GOD IS. THERE IS only one God. All other "gods" are false. We who benefit from living in a Christian culture can take for granted this declaration, but it has not always been so.

When God chose a people and began to form and mold them into his own, they were not so readily disposed to accept the existence of the only one, true God. While today we may be tempted to substitute in our hearts other created goods—such as wealth, power, or fame—in place of God, rarely does such neglect of God rise to the level of the idolatry of ancient times. In order to understand the first commandment and its meaning for us today, we need to begin with the simple realization that God is.

RECOGNIZING GOD

At the very beginning of the Decalogue is the clear declaration that God *is* and that we should have no false God before him. In this first commandment, God calls us to recognize him. God reveals himself more clearly and directly than do his works which speak of him. He himself speaks. He personally seeks out the creatures he has made to give them saving knowledge of himself. "For thus says the Lord God: I myself will look after and tend my sheep. . . . The lost I will seek out, the strayed I will bring back, the injured I will bind up, the sick I will heal . . . shepherding them rightly" (Ezekiel 34:11, 16).

To seek God is nothing more than to respond to one's maker, the Creator who keeps us in being, who cares for us and pursues us. To seek God is really to allow oneself to be found, and to say yes in the light of wisdom that is clearly greater than all human thought.

THE FIRST COMMANDMENT IN A SECULAR SOCIETY

The first commandment has a lot to say to our society. Our American culture is aggressively secular, to such an extent that the environment is actually hostile to religious faith. To begin with, the social mores, particularly in large urban centers, have so changed in past years as to produce a climate that is not only secular but almost entirely focused on the material world. Often today commentators speak of a generation that has lost its moral compass. Priests often tell us that they deal with a portion of the population that pays only lip service to the concept of a living God.

Along with the change in focus comes the disintegration of the community and the social structures that once supported religious faith and encouraged family life. In fact, the heavy emphasis on the individual and his or her own rights has greatly eroded the concept of the common good and its ability to call people to something beyond themselves. This impacts strongly on our capacity to call people to accept revealed teaching and the recognition of a God who can make demands on them that will not be changed by the democratic process.

Sometimes the damage to faith is done more by undermining than by direct assault. Too often the case is made that every opinion is as good as any other—that what really counts is freedom of choice rather than what is chosen—and that religious faith is so personal as to admit of no ecclesial guidance, let alone the expectation that faith could have an impact on society. In a word, religion and religious conviction are marginalized by the reduction to personal preference—much as one chooses a long-distance phone service or credit card without any serious consequence.

By far the most pervasive challenge to the concept of a living God is the powerful voice of secularism and its arrogant claim to the sole possession of the public forum. In the United States, this is expressed through the "privatization" of religion and morality. Against this background, religion becomes a sentimental experience or a comforting emotion. But the thought that at the center of all religious faith stands God, who can make claims on our love and loyalty, is a disquieting one for many who would rather not have to face the question, "Is there truly a God?"

In the version of the first commandment in the Book of Exodus, as well as in the Book of Deuteronomy, we are reminded who God is: the one "who brought you out of the land of Egypt, out of the house of bondage" (see Exodus 20:2, Deuteronomy 5:6). Later in salvation history,

Jesus will reveal to us that God is our Father. "This is how you are to pray: Our Father in heaven . . ." (Matthew 6:9). This is the God who promises us eternal life. "Amen, amen, I say to you, whoever hears my word and believes in the one who sent me has eternal life and will not come to condemnation, but has passed from death to life" (John 5:24).

MODERN IDOLATRY

How does one offend against the first commandment today? One way would be the outright denial of the existence of God, or the decision to worship another reality as God. I am not sure that this happens in the same manner that it did at the time of Exodus, when there were identifiable false gods. We know the account of how the Hebrew people fashioned the golden calf so that they might have a visible god to worship. Their response was to make an idol and worship it. To them God says very clearly this is a false god. All other gods are false. "I alone am the true God and I alone you should worship" (see Exodus 20:1–6, Deuteronomy 5:6–10).

Today we may not fashion statues and models of a god to worship as the pagans of earlier centuries did, but I suspect there is a more subtle and pernicious way of ignoring the first commandment. The story of the golden calf in the Book of Exodus is as much a parable for our time as it is a historical memorial. We are not to put other gods—that is, money, possessions, career, and other created realities—before the true and living God.

In an age that considers itself highly sophisticated and capable of solving most problems, there is the temptation to resolve the perennial human question "How shall I live?" without reference to the transcendent, all-powerful, and ever-present God. Our mentality is so deeply rooted in scientific method that we have convinced ourselves that if something cannot be quantified, measured, physically probed, and accounted for, it is at best a personal preference and at most a possibility. Against this background, faith in an objective, verifiable, living God is presented as naive or quaint.

One of the offenses against the first commandment today is the way our society simply chooses to ignore God. In our world, which is so very secular and so comfortable with its reasoned approach to all problems, the recognition is simply disregarded. In a sense, "secular" is a euphemism for exclusion of God. Perhaps the modern comfort with what is "politically correct" instead of what is "morally right" derives from the more fundamental rejection of the first commandment, and of the claim that God is, God speaks to us, God places a claim on our lives, in our conscience, and in our hearts. Rather than face this reality and the obligations that follow upon it, for some it is easier just to ignore the possibility of a living God.

FAITH IS A GIFT

Faith is essentially an obedience to the word of God, yet it calls us to bear witness to that word. The life of faith is built on God. It is his gift. The gift of faith is the beginning of a new life that God freely gives, a gift that only God can give. "For by grace you have been saved through faith, and this is not from you; it is the gift of God" (Ephesians 2:8).

It was not merely words and visible signs that led Christ's disciples to the fullness of faith. When the apostles began to realize who Christ really was, they cried out in longing to the God they were aware of only obscurely: "Increase our faith!" (Luke 17:5). For faith is the living fruit of two freedoms, that of God, who freely speaks to us, and that of a person who personally uses free will to respond to God with the power that God's grace gives.

Faith is a wonderful gift from God. We should never take it for granted. We are responsible for seeing that, like the seed that is sown in the gospel parable, it falls on good, fertile ground, so that it grows and flourishes.

The "Act of Faith" is a beautiful prayer that calls us to renew our faith in one God and three divine persons, the Father, the Son, and the Holy Spirit. It asks God to strengthen our belief because it is God who has revealed, "who can neither deceive nor be deceived." This prayer should be a part of our regular devotional life as each day the seed of faith takes deeper root in our heart.

QUESTIONS TO THINK ABOUT:

1. What are some of the ways that we can break the first commandment? What are some of the false gods that can be substituted for the one, true God?
2. Where have I discovered God's presence in my own life? What do I know about God from my own experience?
3. What is secularism? What are some of the ways in which our culture is hostile toward religious faith?
4. How can a weakened faith affect both the society in which we live and the family?

CHAPTER 67

Nurturing a Lively Faith

IN THE PARABLE OF the sower and the seeds, Jesus likens the word of God to the seed and our human hearts to the ground on which it falls. Unfortunately, the seed can wither because it does not take deep root, or because it is entangled in weeds, or because it is trampled underfoot. Only the seed that falls on good ground grows and flourishes.

REASON CAN LEAD TO SIN AGAINST THE FIRST COMMANDMENT

We live in an age that prides itself on the power of human reason. We develop technology to advance the human condition far beyond what our predecessors experienced. But in the enthusiasm for science and in the exultation of human reason, there is the danger that we lose the perspective that faith brings, and that we may even be tempted to see faith and reason in contradiction to each other.

In dealing with faith under the heading of the "First Commandment," the *Catechism of the Catholic Church* touches on the tension that can be introduced between faith and reason. When exalted disproportionately, reason can lead to atheism, which the *Catechism* points out "is often based on a false conception of human autonomy, exaggerated to the point of refusing any dependence on God" (section 2126). At the same time, we are reminded in the teaching of the Second Vatican Council that "The Church knows full well that her message is in full harmony with the most secret desires of the human heart" (*Gaudium et Spes* 21:7).

IT IS IMPORTANT TO USE REASON

The most extensive treatment of the relationship of faith and reason that the Church has presented in recent years is the encyclical letter *Fides et Ratio,* published by Pope John Paul II on September 14, 1998. Here the Pope goes into great detail on the rooting of both faith and reason in God's wisdom. We approach wisdom, knowledge, our understanding of reality through the use of our intellect, but also through the free gift of God's revelation. Since the truth is one, how we arrive at it does not change the truth. Both roads—reason and faith—lead us to the same God, who is all truth. Human reason, however, has limits that are intrinsic to its very nature. It is finite and easily swayed by prejudice, emotion, and misunderstanding. Its conclusions are often wrong.

Revelation, on the other hand, is God's word breaking into our world to help us see directly and immediately the truth. Not that revelation is free from misuse or abuse—it often happens that some will quote the Scriptures for their own purposes. But when the meaning of God's revelation is presented and authenticated by the teaching Church under the guidance of the Holy Spirit, we know we have a sure guide to the truth.

It is from this perspective that Pope John Paul II speaks of the relationship between faith and reason and how important it is that we use our human intellect and its capabilities to try to penetrate more deeply the mystery of God's revelation. Ultimately, this brings us to the relationship of philosophy (the wisdom of reason) and theology (the wisdom of revelation) and how they are so deeply related. Any student of Catholic theology knows and recognizes with gratitude the contribution of philosophy to the Church's ongoing effort to understand more deeply God's word given to us in the Scriptures.

FAITH IS PRIMARY

At the heart of John Paul's message is the recognition that, while faith and reason are related, the primacy of faith is clearly understood because it is ultimately God's word that we receive in faith. It is in that faith that we are saved. "Faith is the beginning of human salvation, the foundation and root of all justification, 'without which it is impossible to please God' (Hebrews 11:6)." Because faith is so important, the *Catechism* reminds us of the sins against faith—those things that could empty our faith of meaning.

The *Catechism* teaches us that the sins against faith include voluntary doubt about the faith or a refusal to assent to it. A difficulty in understanding an article of the faith is not the same as a voluntary doubt. Even the question that can arise, "How is this possible?" is not the same as a doubt or a refusal to assent to the faith.

DISSENT IS A SERIOUS MATTER

The apostolic letter *Ad Tuendam Fidem* reminds us that at the heart of the faith is our assent. We offer our assent of mind and will to all that God reveals, all that his Church defines, and all that is presented by the Church in her ordinary and universal magisterium as Christ's way to salvation.

One of the concerns in recent decades has been the ease with which dissent has been accepted in the Church and its proliferation especially among the teachers of the faith. To dissent from the ordinary magisterium of the Church is to place one's own judgment against that of the whole Church. There was a period of time following the Second Vatican Council when a number of theologians publicly chose to do this. In effect they said that, regardless of the teaching of the Church and the promise of the Holy Spirit to guide the bishops in their presentation of the faith, they, the theologians, had arrived at another teaching. This becomes all the more serious when such dissent is presented as a "second magisterium."

It is one thing to discuss theologically the underpinnings or presuppositions of an article of faith. It is altogether another thing to present one's own teaching as the correct and true way to salvation, even when such teaching runs contrary to that of the Church with whom Christ promised to remain until the end of time.

The *Catechism* goes on to list a number of sins against the faith. *"Heresy* is the obstinate post-baptismal denial of some truth which must be believed with divine and catholic faith, or it is likewise an obstinate doubt concerning the same; *apostasy* is the total repudiation of the Christian faith; *schism* is the refusal of submission to the Roman Pontiff or of communion with the members of the Church subject to him" (section 2089).

SINS AGAINST HOPE

The virtue of hope is the expectation of what we believe. It is an attitude of anticipation of what God reveals and a general orientation that accepts what we believe in faith as true. In a sense, the virtue of hope gives us the confidence to proclaim and live what we accept in faith.

Personally, I am convinced that this is a period in the life of the Church of greater hope. I find that many of our people and clergy are more comfortable with the Church's teaching, even some of her "hard sayings." For a time, it appeared that there was a strong tendency toward apologizing for much of what the Church proclaimed, especially in the area of human sexuality and life issues. Today so prophetic has the voice of the Church been in these very issues that I detect a sense of renewed confidence and less timidity in the face of opposition.

High on the list of sins against hope are despair, when we cease to hope for personal salvation, and presumption, which refers either to our total reliance on our own capabilities or to the idea that God could not possibly punish us.

SINS AGAINST CHARITY

Finally, we come to the virtue of charity. We often use the word "charity" as if it meant solely alms or some kindly gift to those in need. The word, however, is a synonym for love. Hence the primacy of charity.

We are to love God above all things simply because God is. Our posture before God is always that of creature to creator, child to father, seeker to the one who satisfies all our most profound needs. Given the great love God has shown us, it is easy to see how the sins against the first commandment include indifference to God, ingratitude, being lukewarm in our relationship to God, sloth, or—worst of all—hatred of God.

The commandment to recognize God and to have no other God is the starting point for our faith life. Secure in the realization that God is and that God loves us, we can proceed with our life's journey hopefully anticipating the promises of our faith that some day we shall live forever in the love of God.

QUESTIONS TO THINK ABOUT:

1. What is the relationship between faith and reason? What is the role of each in discovering truth? Why is faith primary?
2. Why should we be faithful to the teaching of the Church?
3. What is the virtue of hope? How can we sin against hope?
4. What is the virtue of charity? How can we sin against charity?

CHAPTER 68

The Second Commandment: You Shall Not Take God's Name in Vain

NAMES ARE IMPORTANT. THEY have a personal significance to each of us because they speak of who we are and relate us to others. If we are tempted to minimize the significance of the second commandment, all we need to think of is how much energy and resource goes into creating name recognition.

Brand names, for example, are the object of intense advertisement. Companies struggle and spend a fortune just to have the names of their products out before the public. The ultimate mark of success is when the consumer identifies the generic product with the name of a specific one. When you call any gelatin dessert "Jell-O," or when you call any facial tissue a "Kleenex," you're paying the highest tribute you can pay to a brand in a consumer society. During some sporting events, for example the Super Bowl, a small fortune—in fact a large fortune—is paid to have just a small bit of time to proclaim the name of a product to a vast audience.

NAMES DEFINE RELATIONSHIPS

That tells us how important a name is. We are aware of the importance of our own name. It expresses our identity. It lays hold to us. If you walk down the street in the midst of the noise and traffic of a busy city thoroughfare and you hear your name, what is your first response? It breaks through everything else, through your concentration, your thought, the noise around you, and claims your attention. Our name is identified with us and to use it touches us. When someone uses our name, it relates us in some way, even if only in passing, to the person using it.

When we use our full name, our Christian name and our family name, we are all the more conscious of its relational nature. Our Christian name identifies each of us individually. Our family name fits us into the whole picture—our relationship to other human beings, our family.

Names also identify a wider relationship. Sometimes the name is linked to an office, which we substitute for the person. People speak of the President. We often hear him introduced in this way: "Ladies and gentlemen, the President of the United States." The office substitutes in a way for the name of the person, because it is the office and the responsibilities attached to it that take precedence over the individual and his or her particular personality. In the courtroom we address the judge as "Your Honor." The same is true within the Church. The Pope takes a new name upon election to signify his new relationship with all of the faithful through the office he holds.

So it is with God. God has a name, and his name expresses both who God is and our relationship to God. This is why in the Decalogue we are told that "you shall not take the name of the Lord your God in vain." The name of the Lord is holy.

"I AM WHO AM"

As we turn to the pages of Sacred Scripture, we find the revelation of God's name. In fact, God has many names, because of his numerous aspects and attributes. Each name tells us something of the glory of God.

In the Book of Exodus, Moses asks God a direct question: "If they ask me, 'What is his name?' what am I to tell them?" The book tells us that "God replied, 'I am who am.' Then he added, 'This is what you shall tell the Israelites: I AM sent me to you' " (Exodus 3:13–14).

This most revered name of God proclaims the simple reality that God is. In his reflection on this scriptural text, Saint Thomas Aquinas speaks of the total independence, transcendence, and everlasting quality of God who is in himself very existence. In John's gospel Jesus uses the very name I AM in reference to himself. "Amen, amen, I say to you, before Abraham came to be, I AM" (John 8:58). Those who heard him knew exactly what he was saying. "They picked up stones to throw at him . . ." (John 8:59).

THE NAMES OF JESUS

God himself gave Jesus his name. Speaking to Joseph in a dream God told him, "For it is through the Holy Spirit that this child has been conceived in her. She will bear a son and you are to name him Jesus, because he will save his people from their sins" (Matthew 1:20–21).

Throughout his ministry Jesus came to be referred to by a number of names. The Church continues to use the many designations of Jesus as if they were his own name: Son of Man, Lamb of God, Prince of Peace, Risen Lord.

The ultimate revelation of God is found on the lips of Jesus, who announces that God is our Father. While it is true that we are adopted children, we are nonetheless children of God because God has poured forth the Spirit into our hearts elevating us to a level of a whole new relationship with God. "As proof that you are children, God sent the spirit of his Son into our hearts, crying out, 'Abba, Father!' So you are no longer a slave but a child, and if a child then also an heir, through God" (Galatians 4:6–7).

LOSING THE SENSE OF THE SACRED

Listening to the level of conversation today on so much of television, it is hard to believe that we are obliged out of love to respect God's name and that we are called in an explicit commandment of the Lord to avoid defiling it. There is hardly a movie—or a stand-up comedian or some Hollywood-type personality—that does not blithely profane God's name, ridicule our faith, and insult every believer—all to great applause and considerable income.

Loss of the sense of the sacred is one more characteristic of the secular society in which we live. Our society's excessive preoccupation with vulgarity has created a climate in which the roughshod treatment of the sentiments of so many who hold the name of God and his Son sacred is not only permitted, but even roundly applauded. Each of us needs to look at our own use of the language to see if we contribute to this malaise.

The *Catechism of the Catholic Church* teaches us that the second commandment "forbids the abuse of God's name" (section 2146). While the failure to observe this precept may be rather commonplace, it does not diminish the seriousness of the sin. It would be a wonderful testimony to the reverence in which we hold God's name if more people would feel free to correct others who blaspheme in their presence. If it is socially acceptable to call to people's attention their use of a vulgarity in reference to any one group, surely it should be equally acceptable to point out our own offended sensitivities when the most holy name of the Lord is used in a situation that can hardly be called worship.

We are reminded in the *Catechism* that "promises made to others in God's name . . . must be respected in justice" (section 2147). It is no light matter to call upon God to witness what we say. The gravity of the situation is increased when the words spoken are not true.

Blasphemy is an offense in a category all by itself. The *Catechism* notes that blasphemy consists "in uttering against God—inwardly or outwardly—words of hatred, reproach, or defiance" (section 2148). This in itself is a grave sin. The step from taking God's name in vain to outright blasphemy is not a large one. The habit of using God's name with disrespect builds up an attitude that easily allows God's name to be the object of reproach.

As part of an effort to restore respect to the Lord's name, the Holy Name Society was founded many years ago. One of its activities was to organize regular opportunities for prayer in reparation for the sins against the second commandment. Perhaps this is a time to revisit the effectiveness of that form of reparation. Given the way we use the prayer of the faithful today in so many parishes, it seems that a petition calling for respect of the name of the Lord would serve both as a means of education and as a source of reparation.

Everyone's name is significant. It demands respect as a sign of the dignity of the one who bears it. Perhaps as we come more fully to recognize and respect the name of God, we shall do the same for ourselves. Our respect for God's name is a starting point for treating each other with that dignity and reverence that is due each person as an image of God.

QUESTIONS TO THINK ABOUT:

1. Why are names important? Why is my own full family name important?
2. Why is it wrong to take the name of God in vain? What are some of the ways in which this is done?
3. When was the last time I examined my own language?
4. What can we do to restore respect for God's name?

CHAPTER 69

The Third Commandment: Keep Holy the Lord's Day

IT IS INCREASINGLY DIFFICULT to recognize any difference between Sunday and the other days of the week. Our secular society has nearly erased the special quality of Sunday in favor of a continuous commercial calendar that would have all days the same. The only concession most malls make to the Lord's day is to close a few hours earlier than every other day.

Aside from the theological and spiritual dimension of the third commandment, there is a common-sense and practical aspect. All of us need some time at regular intervals set apart from the routine of our daily lives. The commandment to "remember to keep holy the sabbath day" goes on to remind us: "Six days you may labor and do all your work; but the seventh day is the sabbath of the Lord, your God. No work may be done then. . . . In six days the Lord made the heavens and the earth, the sea, and all that is in them; but on the seventh day he rested; therefore the Lord blessed the sabbath day and hallowed it" (Exodus 20:8–11).

THE DAY OF REST

Deep within us is the need to find time for ourselves. We cannot make every day a tribute to our physical and temporal needs. Some time needs to be given as a gift to God. As a part of an ancient Judeo-Christian tradition, the day set aside to rest from our labors is the day made holy to the Lord and given over to him—the sabbath, the Lord's day. The *Catechism of the Catholic Church* reminds us: "The sabbath brings everyday work to a halt and provides a respite. It is a day of protest against the servitude of work and the worship of money" (section 2172).

The Christian tradition has always recognized Sunday as the Lord's day. Jesus rose from the dead on "the first day of the week" (Matthew 28:1). Because it is the "first day," the day of Christ's resurrection recalls the first creation. But it is also the "eighth day" following the sabbath. Here it symbolizes the new creation ushered in by Christ's resurrection. As the *Catechism* teaches: "For Christians it has become the first of all days, the first of all feasts, the Lord's Day . . . Sunday" (section 2174). Sunday is our time of prayer and rest, the day given over to the Lord.

THE LITURGY IS AT THE HEART OF THE SABBATH

At the heart of our celebration of the third commandment is the Eucharistic liturgy. The excellence of liturgical prayer comes not only from the devotion of the persons united in it, but especially from the fact that this is the prayer and action of Christ and of his mystical body, the Church. The Second Vatican Council, in its *Constitution on the Sacred Liturgy,* reminds us that it is "the outstanding means by which the faithful can express in their lives, and manifest to others, the mystery of Christ and the real nature of the true Church" (*Sacrosanctum Concilium* 2).

The Church precept to assist at the celebration of the Eucharist on Sundays grows out of our recognition that Christ is with us in a particular way when we gather as Church to celebrate the Eucharist. The council reminds us that "Christ is always present in his Church, especially in her liturgical celebrations" (*Sacrosanctum Concilium* 7). When God's people gather, they do so in a way that manifests the presence of Christ. The Lord is also present as the word is read in the course of the Mass. In a most unique and heightened manner the Lord is present in the bread and wine consecrated to become his Body and Blood. For all these reasons, the uniqueness of the celebration of the Eucharist is clear, and the need for a gathering of the faithful one day a week—the Lord's day—to enter this mystery and thank God for it should be equally evident.

On the night before he died, Jesus took bread and wine and made it his Body and Blood. "Do this in remembrance of me," he proclaimed (compare Matthew 26–29). Obedient to her Master the Church does what Christ did, in remembrance of him. The worship of the Church and its whole inner life have always centered on the Eucharistic sacrifice, the Mass. It is for this reason that every Christian is called to the Eucharistic banquet, the public celebration of our faith in the resurrection of the Lord, and our share in that mystery through the Eucharist.

The commandment to make holy the sabbath has been defined in the new covenant. "The precept of the Church specifies the law of the Lord more precisely: 'On Sundays and other holy days of obligation the faithful are bound to participate in the Mass' (*Code of Canon Law,* Canon 1247). The precept of participating in the Mass is satisfied by assistance at a Mass which is celebrated anywhere in a Catholic rite either on the holy day or on the evening of the preceding day" (*Code of Canon Law,* canon 1248; see section 2180 of the *Catechism*).

WHY COME TO MASS?

The obligation to attend Sunday Mass is not an arbitrary exercise of authority. It grows out of our recognition that we are members of Christ's Body, a family of faith that strengthens each other through our public witness. Coupled with the divine sanction that we turn over to the Lord one day and make it holy, the Church's designation of Sunday as a day of worship calls each of us to recognize who we are and how we relate to God.

In the Acts of the Apostles, we find a description of an early Christian faith community. This book of the New Testament traces the life of the Church from the ascension of Jesus on through the earliest decades. Here at the beginning of this book we find that the Christians "devoted themselves to the teaching of the apostles and to the communal life, to the breaking of the bread and to prayers" (Acts 2:42). It is easy to envision this as a prototype of our own parish where we too gather to do the very things that brought together the ancient Christian community.

We come together to pray. The church, the house of God, is a place of prayer. When we enter a church, we do so conscious that those who are there have come not so much to talk to us but to speak to God. When we gather for public prayer or liturgical worship, we recognize that this is a time and place for speaking to God. Even as we enter a church when there is no public celebration of liturgy, we are usually intent on finding a moment of calm and quiet in which to open our hearts to God or to seek the intercessions of his saints. The church is a house of prayer and continues to demonstrate today the same function it did when the first community of Christians came together.

The Acts of the Apostles tells us that they also gathered to listen to the teaching of the apostles. An important piece of furnishing in every sanctuary is the pulpit or ambo. In some churches the pulpit is a beautifully carved marble or wooden sanctuary of the word. Whatever the decorative quality of the pulpit, it is from that place that, at every Mass and certainly on Sunday with the whole Christian assembly gathered, the teaching of the apostles—the word of God—is proclaimed. It is here as well that the priest offers his instruction and application in the form of a homily that is meant to be nourishment for the Christian community.

One of the reasons the ancient Christian community came together was to celebrate their communal life. That remains true as well today. We join at Mass so that we can confirm each other in the faith, strengthen our own communal bonds, and offer each other that support that is so necessary as we try to live out our spiritual life in a secular and material world.

At the heart of the Christian community described in the Acts of the Apostles is the Eucharist. It continues to be the very core of our worship today—our Sunday celebration. The central piece of furnishing in every Catholic Church is the altar—the Lord's table. Here the bread and wine become the Body and Blood of our Lord, and it is to this table that we come to be nourished by the bread of angels.

It is no wonder that Sunday is set aside with the obligation that we "refrain from engaging in work or activities that hinder the worship owed to God, the joy proper to the Lord's Day, the performance of the works of mercy, and the appropriate relaxation of mind and body" (see section 2185 of the *Catechism*).

There is something natural in our need to stop and be replenished, be refreshed, be renewed. We cannot continue day in and day out without "stopping to smell the flowers," without pausing to refocus on why we are engaged in such frenetic activity on the other six days of the week. If the sabbath had never been established for spiritual reasons, there would still have been need to set aside this day for our re-creation. Yet the day is meant to signify so much more. It recalls the covenant of the first creation, the covenant of the resurrection, the covenant of the new creation in a way that we can participate individually and collectively, as a Church—God's people.

Perhaps the next time we are tempted to reduce Sunday to just one more day, when we are urged to use it as a regular shopping day, to crowd into it that extra bit of work left over from the rest of the week, we might wish to recall the third commandment, a commandment for our good—our rest—and God's glory.

QUESTIONS TO THINK ABOUT:

1. Why should Sunday be different from the other days of the week? Has Sunday lost its special character?

2. What is special about the celebration of the Eucharist on Sundays? Why do we need to attend Sunday Mass?
3. What does it mean to gather as a community at Mass and not just as individuals?
4. What opportunities do I take in my schedule for spiritual renewal? Where could I find more opportunities?

CHAPTER 70

The Fourth Commandment: Honor Your Father and Mother

EVEN THOUGH IT HAS a commercial overtone, the recognition of Mother's Day and Father's Day in recent years is a good thing. While it has been suggested that these two holidays have their roots in a highly successful plan to sell greeting cards, there is in the celebration of these days a basic and profound intuition. We need to honor our parents. Honor your father and your mother.

THE DEFINING RELATIONSHIP

The relationship with our parents is the most universal of all. It is the primary, fundamental, defining relationship. We would not exist without our parents, and so much of what we have become is the result of the care, the guidance, the direction, and the love of our parents.

With our study of the fourth commandment, we begin the second section of the Decalogue. The first three commandments are devoted to our relationship with God. From the fourth commandment on, we turn our attention to our relationship with others. The *Catechism of the Catholic Church* points out that this commandment constitutes one of the foundations of the social doctrine of the Church (section 2198). In fact it is under this commandment that the *Catechism* directs our attention to the Church's teaching on the family and the relationship of family to society. It is also important to note that this is the only commandment to carry with it an explicit promise. Honor your father and your mother, that your days may be long in the land which the Lord your God gives you (Exodus 20:12).

The first and most immediate human relationship we experience is with our parents. Through their cooperation with God, they give us life. In an ongoing commitment that creates the family and provides a context for our life, our parents devote their time, energy, resources, and love so we can grow, develop, mature, and eventually become capable of forming our own family.

Gratitude, while not always as commonplace as it should be, is a truly noble virtue. We all need to say thank you for the gifts we have received—and from none have we received more than from our parents. The fourth commandment sets forth the need to honor those who have done so much for us. In a sense, Mother's Day and Father's Day are two secular, public affirmations of the fourth commandment.

Perhaps the fourth commandment has a singular significance for our age. Locked as we are in such a strong concentration on individuals, individual rights, individual prerogatives, and individual privileges, we may be less prone to see all the ties that bind us together and make us more than just individuals but rather members of a family, a community, a society.

MARRIAGE AND THE FOURTH COMMANDMENT

In God's plan, humans are created male and female. He created them to come together so that they might express their love and produce the next generation. Following this natural created order, children come to be. But we are the only species where the child cannot fend for itself for years. It has to be nurtured, cared for; it has to be formed and educated over a period of time. We were created in this way precisely so that parents could lavish on their child the love, affection, and education that each child needs. In return the child recognizes not only its relationship to its parents but the depth and meaning of that relationship.

Out of this first experience of relating to others comes a whole series of human ties. From the family we move into an ever-widening range of social contacts and communities. These can be educational, cultural, social, economic, and, of course, political. There can be no human society without the family. At the heart of the family is the permanent commitment of the spouses in a manner that allows them to beget and raise children. Out of this first building block of society—out of the first cell of human society—comes a number of relationships. First is that of the spouses themselves, followed by the mutual relationship of parents to children and children to parents. Necessarily, then, we have to understand correctly what marriage is.

Marriage is meant to be permanent, exclusive, and fruitful. It would be impossible to sustain a family if the covenant of partnership between a husband and wife were not recognized as a permanent and exclusive one binding the two together as one. The fruitfulness of marriage is evident in the children. (For a fuller treatment of marriage, see Chapters 44 and 45.)

FILIAL PIETY

Children have an obligation first to *filial* piety—respect for their parents. This increasingly takes the form of care for elderly parents. For some, this can become at times an almost overwhelming burden. We speak of people being sandwiched in between their need to care for their children and their need to care for their aging parents. Some parishes respond to this situation with an apostolic activity to provide personal support and assistance, usually in the form of visits to households where an individual couple's attention is spread very thinly among all who look to the couple for care and attention.

One of the blessings of our age is the advance in medical technology that makes possible a longer life span. However length of days does not always mean continuing vigor. The fourth commandment calls children to the awareness of the reversal of roles that can take place as the child becomes more capable of providing for the parents than before.

THE DUTY OF EDUCATION

Parents also have duties to their children, including providing for their education and formation in the faith. Since the family is described as the domestic Church, parents should take care that from the earliest days they instruct their children in the faith and raise them as members of Christ's body the Church. This responsibility is carried out in a number of ways, including teaching children in rudimentary form the basic articles of the faith, a belief in God, love of Jesus, and an awareness of the place of prayer. Surely each child by the time he or she is ready to go off to kindergarten should be capable of such basic Christian responses as the sign of the cross, age-appropriate morning and evening prayers, and, of course, grace before and after meals. Participation in the liturgical life of the Church should also be a natural part of the raising of a child. God's house should not be a strange abode that a young person becomes familiar with only later in life.

In an increasingly secular age, where schools have become centers and fonts of values inimical to the Christian faith, parents have a particular obligation to oversee the education of their children. The obvious partner with parents in the education of their child is a Catholic school. Part of our tradition in the United States has been the strong presence of parochial schools, which have fostered the faith and Christian life of generations of students.

Where Catholic schools are not an option for parents, their involvement in the direction of the public school to which their children go should be a matter of supreme importance. The assumption that the values parents work so hard to instill in their children are continued once they leave the home and enter school is contradicted by the facts of today's secular educational system. For this reason, parents need to be particularly attentive, so that they can have a remedial and corrective influence when values hostile to the faith—and in some instances to basic human decency—are a part of the educational environment of their children.

The needs of many families today are urgent and great. As Pope John Paul II pointed out in his apostolic exhortation *Familiaris Consortio,* "The modern Christian family is often tempted to be discouraged and is distressed at the growth of its difficulties; it is an eminent form of love to give it back its reasons for confidence in itself, in the riches that it possesses by nature and grace, and the mission that God has entrusted to it" (86).

The family is an essential part of our civilization. Whatever we do to build up the family, in whatever way we honor parents, we not only meet our obligations to the fourth commandment but also provide for ourselves and our children a wholesome, positive, and enriching future.

QUESTIONS TO THINK ABOUT:

1. What are some of the ways in which I honor my parents? Why are they special to me?
2. Why is the family so important? Why is this commandment especially important for our age?
3. What is meant by the obligation of filial piety? What obligations do parents and children have toward one another?
4. What can we do to strengthen our families?

CHAPTER 71

The Fifth Commandment: You Shall Not Kill

YOU WOULD THINK THAT something as basic as human life would not need to be so forcefully protected by a special commandment. Human life is the foundation of everything we are and have. Without it there is nothing. Yet mankind is often so caught up in human selfishness and disregard for others that it is necessary for God to clearly decree, "You shall not kill."

If you lose your life, you have nothing left. The sense of self-preservation is instinctive. You do not have to teach people to try to defend themselves, to preserve their lives, to enhance or enrich their lives. Yet along with that comes the deeply rooted human temptation to look at one's own life as if it were the only reality and as if other lives might be expendable.

HUMAN LIFE IS SACRED

What God is saying to us is that all human life must be treated with respect because all life comes from God. None of us have the power to create life, nor to bring it back once it is gone. In the long-standing Judeo-Christian tradition, we speak of the sacredness of human life because we recognize that it is totally beyond us. We do not bring life into the world. We can cooperate with God in generating human life, but we do not create life. Once life is ended, we cannot restore it. Even the best of medical technology and expertise can only prolong a human life—it can never bring it back from death.

We do not hesitate to use the word "sacred" when speaking of human life. It comes from God and only God is the true author, judge, and Lord of life. In the fourth chapter of the Book of Genesis, soon after God has created human life as the very pinnacle of all of his wondrous and generous creative action, we learn of Cain killing Abel. As if to say how profoundly pervasive is human violence one against another, the sacred writers confront the taking of human life early on in the story of God's love for us. The guilt of Cain is evident, and the judgment of God equally clear. What has happened is evil.

After the flood, when God reestablished a covenant with the human race, the prohibition against taking human life was reaffirmed. In the ninth chapter of the Book of Genesis, we read that "from man in regard to his fellow man I will demand an accounting for human life. If anyone sheds the blood of man, by man shall his blood be shed; for in the image of God has man been made" (Genesis 9:5).

THE ATTITUDE OF RESPECT FOR LIFE

In the New Testament, Jesus raises this principle to an even higher level. In Matthew's gospel we read: "You have heard that it was said to your ancestors, 'You shall not kill; and whoever kills will be liable to judgment.' But I say to you, whoever is angry with his brother will be liable to judgment . . ." (Matthew 5:21). Jesus is telling us that not only must we avoid the impulse or urge to be disrespectful to the life of another, but that we should not even have an attitude that diminishes or downplays the life, value, and dignity of another person.

Perhaps more than anything else, at the root of the continuing violence in our community is the reduction of human life to a commodity, a property, something we feel we own as a possession. That attitude is exactly what comes across so often when we hear the argument that "my life belongs to me," "what I do with my life is my business," "when life is inconvenient either before it is born or at the end of its cycle it can be terminated."

Some years ago, Pope John Paul II published a magisterial encyclical letter *Evangelium Vitae* (*The Gospel of Life*). It says something of the state of our society when it became necessary for the Pope to devote an entire encyclical to a defense of the simple injunction of the fifth commandment, "You shall not kill."

Why is there such a need to hold up the fifth commandment today? To begin with, we live in a society that is radically changing the internal attitude that Jesus spoke about—how we look at human life. Increasingly public policy reflects a disregard for God's dominion over life and attempts to substitute our own power. This is the most significant single attitudinal change in modern history. Our culture and civilization are based on the principle that God alone has dominion over human life, and neither individually nor collectively are we free to destroy innocent human life. Opposing this truth is the contention that we are the lords of life and that, if we decide we have good reason, we can make legal the taking of innocent human life.

THE CULTURE OF DEATH

Nothing has more advanced this vision—this *false* vision—of life than the case for legalized abortion. At the heart of the abortion argument is the belief that we have dominion over human life and can take that life if it becomes inconvenient to us. Scrape away all of the rhetoric, and at the core of the abortionist movement is the rejection of the injunction, "You shall not kill."

The effect of the culture of death on our society is increasingly evident. Violence stalks our communities, our streets, our schools and homes. For the first time in our land we have a generation raised and nurtured in the conviction that if life is inconvenient to you, you may freely destroy it. Where one generation has drawn the line at nine months, another generation is choosing its own marker. The fact that partial birth abortion is considered by any aspect of this community to be a less than barbarous action speaks of how far we have fallen as a nation.

The careful reader may have noted throughout this text a number of references to legalized abortion and its destructive effect on our society. This repetition is not accidental. No other action legalized by our public policy so undermines our values as a people and knocks out of kilter the moral compass by which we steer our course. Personally, I remain convinced that future generations will look back on this era and ask how it was possible for a whole nation to engage in such horrific activity. Perhaps they will ask, much as we do of World War II Germany, "How could such a thing happen?"

At the other end of the spectrum is euthanasia—the termination of our life prior to natural death. Here we find, as well, increasing activity in the area of public policy to recognize the "legality" of the actions of those who would bring what they consider useless life to an end. This too is a sin against the fifth commandment.

It should be noted that the *Catechism of the Catholic Church* recognizes the right to legitimate defense. Citing Saint Thomas Aquinas, the *Catechism* points out, "The act of self-defense can have a double effect: the preservation of one's own life; and the killing of the aggressor . . . The one is intended, the other is not" (section 2263).

The encyclical letter *Evangelium Vitae* addresses more fully the question of capital punishment. While such an action on the part of the state to defend itself from a violent person is morally defensible, Pope John Paul II stressed the increasing possibility of dealing with such a violent person in a way that obviates the need for capital punishment. In our highly developed society, where one can be incarcerated for life and therefore removed from society and the possibility of bringing grave physical harm to others, imprisonment is clearly a preferable alternative to execution.

As we conclude our reflection on the fifth commandment, we must also consider that in addition to what we must avoid, there are actions we must also take. We are obliged to respect our health. "Life and physical health are precious gifts entrusted to us by God. We must take reasonable care of them, taking into account the needs of others and the common good" (see section 2288 of the *Catechism*). We are also challenged on the societal level to do our best to sustain and maintain peace and to avoid war. "All citizens and all governments are obliged to work for the avoidance of war" (section 2308).

Perhaps the larger issues of war and peace would be more easily dealt with today if on the level of each person we witnessed that profound respect for human life, and the avoidance of anything that would do it harm, which we are taught in the fifth commandment.

QUESTIONS TO THINK ABOUT:

1. What is sacred about human life?
2. What are some of the biblical stories that illustrate the fifth commandment?
3. Why is there so much violence in the world today? Why is there such a lack of respect for human life?
4. What can we do to overcome the attitude that you can freely destroy life if it is inconvenient to you?

CHAPTER 72

Challenges to Human Life in Our Time

A RELATIVE OF ONE of the young people killed in 1998 at Columbine High School in Denver remarked during an interview on an anniversary of that tragedy that "We need a whole change of mentality in America." He was referring to the casual disregard for the value of human life that has permeated our whole culture. It finds expression routinely in our language, sports, entertainment, and media—and sometimes tragically in mass killings of young people by young people.

The *Catechism* quotes the Second Vatican Council's document the *Pastoral Constitution on the Church in the Modern World* when it reminds us that "Everyone should look upon his neighbor (without any exception) as another self . . ." (27; see section 1931 of the *Catechism*). Respect for the human person proceeds from respect for that principle.

ASSISTED SUICIDE AND EUTHANASIA

The effects of the culture of death are not confined to the unborn. The elderly and disabled of our society are more and more considered as burdens. The disrespect for human life that began with the very first legal abortion has now grown into a culture where people will have to meet a "quality of life" standard in order to justify their continued existence.

The assumption that to be old, disabled, or dying renders you worthless has fostered a terrible premise that seeks to eliminate the "imperfect" from our society. Masked by a false mercy, euthanasia is often promoted as the right and good thing for society to do. Many are actively working to legalize euthanasia, already a reality in one state.

The word "euthanasia" means a "happy" or "easy death." Today in our culture the word is translated as "mercy killing." Most of the media emphasis is now on *mercy,* but we must never forget that the action is *killing.* Advocates of assisted suicide, carried out either by a physician or by a family member, challenge the Church's teaching. They say, in effect, "I can end life if I have the intention of doing it with mercy." Yet suicide and euthanasia are "false mercy." We do not respect human life by destroying it, whether in the womb or near the end of life. Our faith challenges us to care for those who are dying with our presence, our prayers, and the sacraments of the Church.

There is a long-standing Catholic tradition of praying for a blessed and peaceful death. To Saint Joseph, who is the patron of a happy death, we offer prayers that when the time for our death arrives we might be provided the sacraments—the anointing of the sick, an opportunity for confession, and viaticum—as we conclude our pilgrimage to the Father.

CARING FOR THE TERMINALLY ILL

Our faith provides the context not only for our own death but also for the way in which we approach the death of others. For those who believe "life is changed, not ended"; and when, as the liturgy teaches us, "the body of our earthly dwelling lies in death, we gain an everlasting dwelling place in heaven" (Preface for Masses for the dead, "Christian Death 1"). It is this lively faith that instructs us in how we are present to and stand with someone who is dying.

The caring presence of family, friends, chaplains, and parish priests cannot be underestimated. Prayer brings comfort, and the ritual invites participation of the family members. In conformity with an ancient practice referred to in the Letter of Saint James, the priest celebrates the rite of anointing of the sick. For the dying, the priest (or other pastoral care worker) brings viaticum, which is the Eucharist for the journey through death to eternal life.

Death is the natural conclusion to our earthly life. Rather than deny it, we need to be able to embrace its reality and assist one another in our encounter with death. As Pope John Paul II teaches: "We never celebrate and exalt life as much as we do in the nearness of death and in death itself. Life must be fully respected, protected and assisted in those who are experiencing its natural conclusion as well" (Address to Pontifical Academy for Life, February 27, 1999).

END-OF-LIFE DECISIONS

The call for uninterrupted respect for all human life requires that people of faith act responsibly in end-of-life situations. When we deal with the last stages of human life, we need to be particularly sensitive to both our capabilities and our limitations. Eventually all physical remedies fail. All life begins, grows, matures, declines, and ends in death. As responsible Christians, we are called to provide medical treatment for the body while there is still hope of healing and restoration of health. But even when healing is no longer possible, treatment is futile, and death is inevitable, we are still obliged to care for the dying.

The provision of nutrition and hydration is a normal part of human care. The United States Bishops' pro-life committee provides us direction in this area when it writes: "We reject any omission of nutrition and hydration intended to cause a patient's death. We hold for a presumption in favor of providing medically assisted nutrition and hydration to patients who need it, which presumption would yield in cases where such procedures have no medically reasonable hope of sustaining life or pose excessive risks or burdens" (NCCB, Pro Life Committee, *Nutrition and Hydration: Moral and Pastoral Reflections,* 1992).

The Church wisely makes a distinction between medical treatment and common care. We are obliged to utilize ordinary medical treatment in dealing with our physical condition. The Church also distinguishes between morally ordinary and extraordinary treatment. No one is obliged to use morally extraordinary treatment to sustain human life. We are, however, to use basic human care, sometimes described as comfort care, even when treatment is no longer indicated.

The Catholic Church teaches that when medical treatment becomes futile, and it is no longer possible to prevent a patient's death, or when the only result of intensive medical treatment would be to add suffering or prolong dying, we must accept the inevitability of death. At this point, respect for the dying indicates that it is no longer necessary to offer medical treatment. Yet normal comfort care must be provided.

While it is true that the means of supplying nutrition and hydration can in themselves become morally extraordinary in some circumstances, the presumption should always be in favor of sustaining human life through the provision of nutrition and hydration (see proceedings of Pontifical Academy for Life, February 1999).

Never, however, is it acceptable to take actions that deliberately take the life of a dying person. Lethal injections or any other means to assist in suicide are never condoned as acts that respect the inherent dignity of the human person. Advances in hospice care and palliative care have made it possible to control pain and suffering during the last days of a person's life.

Our Judeo-Christian heritage believes that life is the gift of a loving God and that we may never choose to cause our own deaths. As a people who believe in God and in eternal life, we must always remember that despite its human tragedy, death is the gateway to our final and eternal union with God.

HUMAN CLONING AND GENETIC TECHNOLOGY

Respect for human life is also challenged by technological advances and the desire to perfect the genetic makeup of human beings. Religion and science are not adversaries but can influence and complement one another. Pope John Paul II clearly articulated this relationship when he wrote, "The Church remains profoundly convinced that faith and reason 'mutually support each other,' each influences the other, as they offer to each other a purifying critique and a stimulus to pursue the search for deeper understanding" (*Fides et Ratio* 100).

While science seeks to find the best solution for physical human problems, the Church reminds science that there is more to a human being than just physical form—the material dimension. We welcome science that serves and enhances the human person by upholding criteria of respect, generosity, and service while resisting the slide to a new criterion of efficiency, functionality, and usefulness.

As society moves to understand genetic makeup and provide for the possibility of human intervention to alter life in future generations, we must remember that God is the author of life. We need to acknowledge the role that the Creator continues to play in the creation of life.

Human embryo research raises ethical problems because it either allows for scientific experimentation on human beings or redefines human life in a way that classifies some human beings as "subhuman." Most research of this type ignores the fact that, at the moment of conception, God creates a new, unique, individual human being, who, from that moment through all of life, is worthy of the protection and respect that every human life deserves.

Human cloning and human embryo research deny the dignity and uniqueness of the human being. Human persons should never be treated as means to an end. We have only to look at our environment to be reminded that we often do not have the necessary insight to understand all the consequences of our actions. Simply because we have the ability to do something does not mean that we should do it. A healthy religious reverence for the Providence of God, as well as a respect for the law of unintended consequences, call us to observe the moral law whenever we move forward in scientific discovery.

ETHICAL REFLECTION ON TECHNOLOGY

As Catholics, we believe that the reason some procedures are prohibited is because they are in themselves wrong and therefore undermine and hinder our very attempts to achieve human good. In this day of widespread moral relativism, if not outright confusion, it is all the more important that the Church continue her witness to moral truth. Some actions, even if technologically feasible, are still wrong.

Our society approaches ethical and moral decisions in sharply contrasted ways. One view accepts God's plan and the preservation and enrichment of human life within that plan. Another position concentrates on the autonomy of the human person, who is assumed to have virtually limitless freedom to manipulate and reorder the human body according to norms accountable only to some human convention. This divergence of views is what Pope John Paul II, in his encyclical *Evangelium Vitae,* describes as a struggle between the civilization of love and the culture of death.

QUESTIONS TO THINK ABOUT:

1. Why can we assert that legal abortion and the shootings at Columbine High School are related?
2. How do I contribute to the violence rampant in modern culture? How could I work for the "civilization of love"?
3. If we could use genetic research to create children less prone to violence, would that be wrong?

CHAPTER 73

Medical and Moral Issues

THE FIFTH COMMANDMENT DEALS with life. Nowhere are life issues engaged on a daily basis with such intensity as in health care institutions, from hospitals on through nursing homes. Catholic health care is a response to God's command that we respect life, care for and nurture it, and act as good stewards of this precious gift. Today, in addressing such weighty obligations, we need to look at our Catholic health care efforts.

CATHOLIC HEALTH CARE TODAY

All across the United States, with almost dizzying speed, the face of Catholic health care ministry is changing. This we recognize not only from the media accounts but also from our own personal experience. These changes affect everyone. The response to an illness, perhaps our own, is considerably different than even a decade ago. How the medical profession deals with us, the amount of time we spend in an acute care facility, who pays for what, and even the process of diagnosis of our illness may all be very different from the way we would have been treated a short time ago—and certainly from the way our parents were treated.

With so much change, we also hear the word "struggle" used to describe the effort to sustain Catholic health care ministry and institutions on the ever-shifting ground of the health care marketplace today. In the face of much change and "struggle," two questions arise: "Why is the Church in health care?" and "How is its presence and involvement in health care distinct from any other organized effort?"

WHY IS THE CHURCH IN HEALTH CARE?

The Catholic Church is involved in health care because it believes that care of the sick is an important part of Christ's mandate of service. Throughout all the change, the one constant in the involvement of the Church in health care is the motivation that brings the Church, in the first place, to health care ministry. Catholic health care ministry carries out the healing ministry of Jesus Christ himself. It is not just an optional good work, even though the form it takes is conditioned by historical circumstances. Catholic health care ministry responds to and follows an inner vision very different from that which can drive what is now so universally referred to as an "industry." The desire to bring the compassion and healing of Jesus to those in need is the very heart and soul of a vast network of Catholic hospitals, nursing homes, long-term-care facilities, and medical and nursing schools.

There is more to Catholic health care, however, than just compassion for someone who is ill. We are convinced that sickness, pain, suffering, and death are a part of God's providential plan. A true follower of Christ helps others to understand that plan, live it, and make suffering and death redemptive actions. For the Christian, illness and death take on a positive and distinctive meaning when placed in the context of the redemptive power of Jesus' suffering and death.

HOW IS CATHOLIC HEALTH CARE DIFFERENT?

The "how" of Catholic involvement in health care is answered in the over six hundred Catholic health systems, hospitals, and institutions sponsored and directed for the most part by religious communities, particularly of women. It is not just an institutional commitment to provide it, but also the personal and institutional commitment to do so in a specific way, within a particular context, according to a unique vision of human life ultimately grounded in the person of Jesus Christ and his revelation.

It is precisely this understanding of Catholic health care that drives so much of the concern today over the enduring Catholic identity of our health care systems in this period of transition. It also explains the concentrated efforts by those in leadership positions in health care, the sponsoring religious institutions and bishops relative to the formation of future leaders, particularly lay leaders, in the world of Catholic health care.

As a ministry, Catholic health care, in its many institutional expressions, is an integral part of the life of the Church and must, therefore, always be responsive to Church leadership. Two documents from our own

National Conference of Catholic Bishops reflect how that commitment should be expressed:

1. *The Pastoral Role of the Diocesan Bishop in Catholic Health Care Ministry,* which deals with the ecclesial dimension of Catholic health care ministry.
2. *The Ethical and Religious Directives for Catholic Care Services,* which deals with the moral dimension of the activity that is the ministry in action.

Catholic health care is built upon a natural and a divine love for the human person. As *The Ethical and Religious Directives* state at the very outset: "First, Catholic health care ministry is rooted in a commitment to promote and defend human dignity; this is the foundation of its concern to respect the sacredness of every human life from the moment of conception until death" (Introduction to Part One). Each human life is sacred because it reflects the divine life itself. As the *Directives* state in the Introduction to Part Two: "The dignity of human life flows from creation in the image of God (Genesis 1:26), from redemption by Jesus Christ (Ephesians 1:10; 1 Timothy 2:4–6), and from our common destiny to share a life with God beyond all corruption (1 Corinthians 15:42–57)."

It is this awesome reverence toward the human person, created by God and redeemed by Christ, which provides the motivation for Catholic health care and which lies at the heart of *The Ethical and Religious Directives.* The moral concerns in the *Directives* can all be seen as expressing in one way or another a repugnance to ever violating or offending human dignity.

THE MORAL DIMENSION OF HEALTH CARE

As Catholics, we believe that some procedures—such as sterilization, physician-assisted suicide, and human cloning—are prohibited because they would actually undermine our attempts to achieve human good. In this day of widespread moral relativism, if not outright confusion, it is all the more important that the Church continue her witness to moral truth. Indeed, Catholic health care, with its dispersion throughout American society, can itself serve as a tremendous witness to moral truth in a society given over to moral relativism.

Perhaps the most succinct summary of the role of moral directives in medical-moral ethics today is found in the *Catechism of the Catholic Church,* which refers to the Ten Commandments as a "privileged expression of the natural law" (section 2070). Here, we are reminded that the Ten Commandments "teach us the true humanity of man. They bring to light the essential duties, and therefore, indirectly, the fundamental rights inherent in the nature of the human person."

This ancient tradition of moral norms that guides human activity is perhaps the most challenged today in our increasingly technological world, where scientific advances often outstrip the necessary moral reflection. The real worry begins when the conclusion is reached that moral reflection is not necessary.

Even a brief review of some of the major areas of debate in medical-moral issues today tells us of the significance of these issues: euthanasia, organ donation, reproductive technology, cloning, and behavior modification through medication.

The Church has an obligation and a right to speak out in defense of the natural moral order, for the right of all to adequate health care, and on behalf of the poor. It is this duty that leads to all the statements and declarations that are the expression of Catholic moral and social justice teaching and the recommendations from the Catholic perspective for good public policy.

In our country there existed from the beginning significant Judeo-Christian moral sentiment and religious teaching to provide a basis for a communal sense of morality. Some things were right; others were wrong. Some things were accepted and other things were not. The fundamental starting point for communal morality was essentially rooted in the Ten Commandments. Personal virtue was ultimately authenticated against the verifiable norm of right and wrong.

In one way or another, we are all challenged to care for each other. This is part of the obligation of the fifth commandment. In that sense, we are all expressions of the Church's commitment to the ministry of Jesus Christ, who was and continues to be our Lord, Redeemer, and Healer. Our involvement in health care, we pray, will continue to manifest the teaching and love of Christ through the caring ministry that serves the whole person—body, mind, and soul—embracing that person with all the compassion and love that says to the sick, the infirm, and all of those in need of health care, "As Christ would reach out to touch and heal, so too do we."

QUESTIONS TO THINK ABOUT:

1. Which changes in modern health care seem like improvements? Which ones seem less helpful?
2. Why is it so important to have moral direction for medical practice?
3. Which medical procedures common today seem morally wrong or dubious? Why?

CHAPTER 74

Confronting Racism in America

THERE ARE A NUMBER of prejudices that seem to be acceptable in our land. None is more blatantly common than anti-Catholicism. But as annoying as the narrow-minded manifestation of religious bigotry can be, it has not had the effect on Catholics that racism has had on African-Americans. Perhaps it is for that reason that the Church calls our attention to the evil of racism and reminds us—as it does in both the *Catechism* and the *Pastoral Constitution on the Church in the Modern World*—that "Every form of social or cultural discrimination in fundamental personal rights on the grounds of sex, race, color, social conditions, language or religion, must be curbed and eradicated as incompatible for God's design" (29; see section 1935 of the *Catechism*).

To address racism, we need to recognize two things: that it exists in a variety of forms, some more subtle and others more obvious; and that there is something we can do about it even if we realize that what we say and the steps we take will not result in an immediate solution to a problem that spans generations. We must confront this issue with the conviction that we can help to resolve it.

RACISM IS A DENIAL OF HUMAN DIGNITY

The divisions we face today that are based on skin color or ethnic background are obviously not a part of God's plan. In the first chapter of the Book of Genesis we read at the beginning of the story of creation, "God created man in his image, in the divine image he created him; male and female he created them" (Genesis 1:27). The human race is rooted in the loving, creative act of God, who made us and called us to be a family—all God's children—made in God's image and likeness. There is no basis for asserting that some are made more in the image of God than others.

In whatever form, intolerance of other people because of their race, religion, or national origin is ultimately a denial of human dignity. None are better than others because of the color of their skin or the place of their birth. What makes us equal before God, and what should make us equal before each other, is that we are all sisters and brothers of one another, because we are all children of the same loving God who brought us into being.

Racism denies the basic equality and dignity of all people before God and one another. For this reason the United States bishops, in their November 1979 pastoral letter on racism, *Brothers and Sisters to Us,* clearly state: "Racism is a sin." It is a sin because "it divides the human family, blots out the image of God among specific members of that family and violates the fundamental human dignity of those called to be children of the same Father." The letter goes on to remind us that "Racism is the sin that says some human beings are inherently superior and others essentially inferior because of race."

UNITY, NOT UNIFORMITY

We are called to recognize that racism continues to manifest itself in many ways. It can be personal, institutional, or social. What should be a blessing—the diversity of our backgrounds, experiences, and cultures—becomes a hindrance to unity and a heavy burden for some to bear. As we struggle to remove the attitudes that nurture racism and the actions that express it, we must show how the differences we find in skin color, national origin, or cultural diversity are enriching. Equality among all men and women does not mean that they must all look, talk, and think alike and act in an identical manner. Equality does not mean uniformity. Rather, each person should be seen in his or her uniqueness as a reflection of the glory of God and a full, complete member of the human family.

Among Christians, the call to unity is greater because it is rooted in grace. Racism, therefore, merits even stronger condemnation. Everyone who is baptized into Christ Jesus is called to new life in the Lord. Baptism unites us with the Risen Lord, and through him with every person who sacramentally has died and risen to new life in Christ. This unity, sacramental and real, brings us together on a level above and beyond the purely physical. It carries that oneness we all share through the natural reality of creation to a higher level—the realm of grace.

WE ARE CALLED TO ACTION

Intolerance and racism will not go away without a concerted effort on everyone's part. Regularly we must renew the commitment to drive it out of our hearts, our lives, and our community. While we may devise all types of politically correct statements to proclaim racial equality, without a change in the basic attitude of the human heart we will never move to that level of oneness that accepts each other for who we are and the likeness we share as images of God.

In the bishops' statement on racism, *Brothers and Sisters to Us,* we read: "To the extent that racial bias affects our personal attitudes and judgments, to the extent that we allow another's race to influence our relationship and limit our openness, to the extent that we see yet close our hearts to our brothers and sisters in need—to that extent we are called to conversion and renewal in love and justice."

Responding to Christ's love calls us to action. We need to move to the level of Christian solidarity. This term often spoken of by Pope John Paul II as a virtue touches the practical implications of what it means to recognize our unity with others. There is a sense in which solidarity is our commitment to oneness at work in the practical order. The *Catechism* speaks of human solidarity, which is also articulated in terms of friendship or social charity, and notes that it is "a direct demand of human and Christian brotherhood" (see section 1939).

We need to be alert to and condemn racism wherever we meet it. In housing, citizens need to insist that the government enforce fair housing statutes, and they themselves need to welcome new neighbors regardless of race. In the workplace, recruitment, hiring, and promotion policies need to reflect true universal opportunity. In public education, we should support the teaching of tolerance and appreciation for each culture. In the public debate on the deficiencies of our age, we ought also to insist on the place of religious faith. Without God and the sense of right and wrong that religious convictions engender, we will never adequately confront racism.

PRAYER IS AN IMPORTANT TOOL

The elimination of racism may seem too great a task for any one of us or even for the whole Church. Yet we place our confidence in the Lord.

Prayer is an important tool in the struggle against racism. In Christ, we are brothers and sisters to one another. With Christ, we have received the Spirit of justice, love, and peace. Through Christ, we are called to envision the new city of God, not built by human hands, but by the love of God poured out in the Savior. On the journey to that "new heaven and new earth," we make our way with faith in God's grace, with hope in our own determination, and above all with love for each other as children of God.

QUESTIONS TO THINK ABOUT:

1. How does racism show itself in my community? In my parish? In my family?
2. What judgments do I make about people based on their race? How can I overcome the tendency to prejudge people by their skin color?
3. What evidence of racism can we see today? How can I help overcome those problems?

CHAPTER 75

The Sixth Commandment: You Shall Not Commit Adultery

IT IS SOMETIMES SAID of the Church's teaching on human sexuality that, like the sixth commandment, it is primarily a list of "do nots." Such a perception fails to take into account the profoundly human and beautiful vision of love that is the foundation for the Church's moral teaching on marriage, human sexuality, and the integrity of the human person.

THE CATHOLIC VISION OF LOVE

There is a specifically Catholic vision of love. It finds its origin in the loving communion that God intended when he created man and woman (see Genesis 1:27). Deep in the heart of each human being created in the image and likeness of God is the call to love. The model of this love is God's own life, since we are created in God's image. The Father, Son, and Spirit live a life of profound personal loving communion. Each of us is called to share somehow in that love and manifest it in our world.

In creating man in his own image—male and female—God blessed them and said, "Be fruitful and multiply" (Genesis 1:28). As partners and as complementary members of a loving communion, God created man and woman—all men and women. Human sexuality, then, is a part of that wondrous creative act of God, which he finds so very good. Human sexuality is not incidental to life. The covenant of marriage is a way to express, at a most profoundly human level, both the mutual support that love brings to a couple and the fruitfulness of that love in their children.

The *Catechism of the Catholic Church* speaks of sexuality as affecting "all aspects of the human person in the unity of his body and soul" (section 2332). It especially touches on the capacity to love and to procreate, and the aptitude for forming bonds of communion with others. Human sexuality brings with it physical, moral, and spiritual differences that are also complementary to man and woman and are "oriented toward the goods of marriage and the flourishing of family life" (section 2333).

MARRIAGE CANNOT BE DISSOLVED

When Jesus was questioned about marriage and divorce—the relationship of a man and woman in marriage and the duration of that bond—he made it very clear that the right ordering of human relations and human sexuality is immutable, because it is rooted in our human nature as God created us. "From the beginning of creation, God made them male and female. For this reason a man shall leave his father and mother and be joined to his wife, and the two shall become one flesh. So they are no longer two, but one flesh. Therefore what God has joined together, let no one separate" (Mark 10:6–9).

Since they are created as man and woman, made to come together and form a lasting partnership in the covenant of marriage that would become a family, nothing that would destroy that bond could be good. "You shall not commit adultery": you shall not weaken or harm the marriage bond upon which everything else—the communion of love, the fidelity of the couple, the fruitfulness of their marriage, and the procreation of children—is based.

CHASTITY IS THE PROPER DIRECTION OF SEXUALITY

It goes without saying that the drive which brings a man and woman together—human sexuality—is very powerful. It was created in this manner so that a man would leave his family—his father, his mother, his sisters and brothers, his home—so that with his wife, who would do the same, they would come together as one and form a new family. The sexual drive would have to be strong enough for them both to overcome the desire to remain where they find themselves—in the comfort of the family created by their parents.

God created the human sexual drive as a forceful reality, but, like all human drives or urges, it needs to be controlled and properly channeled. Hence the Church speaks of the value of chastity and human integrity. The *Catechism* states that "chastity means the successful integration of sexuality within the person and thus the inner unity of man in his bodily and spiritual being" (section 2337).

Chastity is the virtue that allows each of us to order rightly our human sexual drive. The use of that sexual drive must conform to God's plan. It must bear witness to the integrity of the marriage covenant, the mutual support of husband and wife in love, and the expression of their love in children. Chastity, like all virtues, requires what the *Catechism* calls "an apprenticeship in self-mastery which is a training in human freedom" (section 2339).

This virtue has always been won at the price of a struggle. As a consequence of original sin, this human drive is easily disordered. Every society has always recognized this frailty of self-restraint as a fact of life and thus has directed its mores, its public policy, and the instruction of its youth in a way to ensure its survival. It is perhaps a commentary on our age and how far we have digressed from the path set out by the Creator that chastity is now a "forgotten virtue."

THE FORCES ARRAYED AGAINST CHASTITY

Communal amnesia concerning the value and place of chastity carries with it painful consequences. When we reflect on the offenses against the sixth commandment, we will find them rampant, condoned, and even encouraged in our age. The "lifestyles" and "momentary commitments" that are the storyline of most television "soaps" and a great number of movies help form the attitudes and mores of our young people. In contrast, the Church holds up the image of personal integrity.

Since the powers of life and love possessed by each of us are directed according to God's plan, as manifested in his commandments and in the teaching of the Church, the struggle to sustain our personal integrity is not only worth the effort but also essential to a fully complete and properly oriented life. The *Catechism* reminds us that "this integrity ensures the unity of the person; it is opposed to any behavior that would impair it" (section 2338).

Just as there are powerful drives that bring a couple together, so there are powerful forces that would work against the good ordering of human sexuality. The sixth commandment addresses those actions that would wound the marriage bond and attack the fidelity and trust of the couple.

Faithful to Scripture, the Church insists that love of God is incompatible with every form of fornication, sexual promiscuity, licentiousness, and other sexual behavior that deviates from the proper use of this gift from

God. Christ warns that fidelity to God can be broken even by our desires (see Matthew 5:28).

The offenses against the sixth commandment are fed by lust. The *Catechism* defines this vice as "a disordered desire for or inordinate enjoyment of sexual pleasure" (section 2351). Sexual satisfaction is morally disordered when sought for itself, disassociated from its procreative and unitive purposes.

First among the offenses against the marriage bond and family community is adultery, which grievously wounds a marriage, hurts the unity of the family, and disrupts the proper relationship of parent and child. The distrust and doubt introduced into a family is evidence enough of why this action is considered wrong.

THE DIFFERENCE BETWEEN DIVORCE AND ANNULMENT

Divorce is an attack against the marriage bond. What God has joined together we are not permitted to undo. For this reason, the Church cannot recognize the right of the state through the civil action of divorce to dissolve the covenant made before God.

Sometimes it happens that a marriage is irretrievably lost. At this point a separation between the two partners may not only be advised but encouraged. Separation is a fact of the human condition. Not everything turns out the way we hope. But divorce and remarriage take us beyond God's plan. Divorce, for civil purposes, may be necessary after a marriage has collapsed, but remarriage after a separation and divorce cannot be reconciled with Christ's words (see Matthew 5:32).

The Catholic Church does not recognize the power of a civil divorce to end a sacramental marriage. Catholics who remarry in civil ceremonies are still sacramentally married to their first partner. A Catholic who has entered a sacramental marriage can remarry after divorce only through a proper Church ruling that the right conditions never existed from the beginning for the original marriage to be valid.

This is perhaps a good place to speak of a marriage annulment, or—the more exact term—"declaration of nullity," even though we have already made some reference to this subject in Chapter 44. When an ecclesiastical tribunal—that is, a Church court—issues a declaration of nullity, it does not mean that there was no sexual or emotional marriage relationship, nor does it mean that the children of such a union are illegitimate. The declaration means that no sacramental bond exists because at the time of the wedding at least one partner was unwilling or unable to meet the standards for a sacramental marriage.

Some usual grounds for nullity include "lack of due discretion," which concerns the maturity of judgment of either party; marrying due to force or fear; an intent to be unfaithful, or not to have children, or not to remain married; or the placement of unacceptable conditions on the marriage.

THE SIXTH COMMANDMENT ALSO APPLIES TO THE UNMARRIED

Offenses against the sixth commandment are not limited to those who are married. Saint Paul in his first letter to the Corinthians points out a number of attacks on the virtue of chastity. Fornication ignores the permanency of the commitment and partnership that human sexuality is designed to create. Pornography attacks the dignity of human sexuality by rendering it a product and by reducing the person to nothing more than an object. While there may be temporary physical satisfaction, the attitude that it generates and what it says about another person is so degrading as to make it an offense against God's law and the human community.

All sexual activity outside of marriage is wrong. The Church does not invent laws. It passes on and interprets what God has revealed through the ages. No one has the right to change what Jesus has taught. To do so would be to deprive people of saving truths that were meant for all time. Our Christian faith teaches that a sexual relationship belongs only in marriage. Sex outside of marriage shows disrespect for the sacrament of marriage, the sacredness of sex, and human dignity.

"Cohabitation" or "living together" describes the relationship of a man and woman who are sexually active and share a household, though they are not married. Such a relationship cannot be reconciled with God's plan for human sexuality and marriage. A pamphlet called *Living Together,* published by the Pennsylvania Catholic Conference, explains how "cohabitation" falls short of God's plan. A sexual relationship involves a "total self-giving between a man and a woman" that can be fulfilled only in marriage. Marriage "is the only 'place' where children can be raised with the secure, committed love of a mother and a father. So sexual intimacy belongs only in marriage. Outside of marriage, sex is a lie. The action says: 'I give you my whole self'—but the man and woman are really holding back their commitment, their fertility, and their relationship with God. Before giving your body to another person, you need to give your whole life, and you need to receive your spouse's whole life in return—and that can happen only in marriage."

The *Catechism* reminds us that homosexuality "refers to relations between men or between women who experience an exclusive or predominant sexual attraction toward persons of the same sex" (section 2357). Such activity is contrary to the natural law. Both homosexual and heterosexual persons are called to chastity.

While there are many "lifestyles" and opinions on the meaning of life and sex, they fall short of the beauty of Christ's plan for each of us. The Catholic vision of love holds out for us the promise that we can find in this life a communion of body and spirit, a level of happiness and joy, and the satisfaction and commitment that are signs of that ultimate completeness we will experience in heaven.

QUESTIONS TO THINK ABOUT:

1. If it is between "consenting adults," why is sex before marriage wrong? How would I explain my answer to someone who insists that sex before marriage is perfectly all right?
2. What effects does a divorce have on a family? How can we help children of divorced parents develop a proper idea of the sanctity of marriage?
3. What are some sins against chastity? How does one overcome those sins?

CHAPTER 76

The Seventh Commandment: You Shall Not Steal

WHY DOES THE SEVENTH commandment seem self-evident? Like so many of the commandments, this one seems very clear. You should not take what belongs to another. Why is it so apparent? The answer to that question reminds us that all of the commandments, but particularly the fourth through the tenth, are divinely revealed statements about something that we as human beings already know in our hearts.

The *Catechism of the Catholic Church* makes this point in a very direct way. It tells us that the commandments belong to God's revelation and, at the same time, are inherent within our human nature. It is for this reason that the *Catechism* declares "the Decalogue contains a privileged expression of the natural law" (section 2070). In the beginning, God implanted in our hearts the precepts of the natural law. Then he chose to manifest them clearly in his revealed word. This is the Decalogue.

THE MEANING OF "YOU SHALL NOT STEAL"

We need created goods in order to live. We work so that we may produce what we need or earn the means to purchase what is essential to human life. Therefore, it is wrong for another to take what is ours. The commandment "You shall not steal" reinforces with the authority of God what we already know—"to each his own."

For a more explicit definition of what we find in the Book of Exodus (20:15), Deuteronomy (5:19), and Matthew's gospel (19:18), we can look to the *Catechism,* where we find this comprehensive statement: "The seventh commandment forbids unjustly taking or keeping the goods of one's neighbor and wronging him in any way with respect to his goods" (section 2401).

The context for this commandment is the recognition that God created all things and that these resources are entrusted to all people. There is a common ownership as well as a stewardship of the goods of the earth. They are created so that human beings might flourish. All of us are entitled to goods sufficient enough to support our well-being. No one can claim exclusive possession of the goods of the earth while excluding others in need of them. What God has created is for all. How we come to possess them brings us face to face with an aspect of justice.

SOCIAL JUSTICE

A variety of social systems over recorded human history have demonstrated that people can achieve ownership of property in different ways. Work, however, is the fundamental means by which we accumulate the goods of the earth necessary for our needs and those of our family. In other words, personal work is the normal, natural way by which one accesses a share of the goods of the earth. History has also witnessed excesses that have severely compromised the right of individuals to obtain and maintain a sufficient share of the goods of the earth.

Recently, we have witnessed the collapse of the economic system called communism. In this centrally managed economy, which denied many basic human rights including the right to own and keep property, the thesis was put forward that everything would be owned in common, that there would be a division of labor to produce what was needed by all, and that all would have free access to these goods. This philosophy may sound good, but it failed in practice. Extensive and pervasive government control of the lives of citizens and the regulation of property to the extent that individuals had little or no real access to what was needed to sustain life contributed to a dehumanizing structure that collapsed under the weight of its own falsehood.

Closer to home, in our own country we experienced an economic system that minimized and almost eliminated any form of government intervention. So-called *laissez-faire* capitalism was predicated on the principle that there should be almost no state or government regulation of the marketplace. This gave rise to a few incredibly wealthy people, many of whom made their fortunes at the expense of the integrity, dignity, and even lives of countless workers.

The gradual but important recognition that social justice obliges an equitable distribution of the goods of the earth has led to a significant modification in our capitalistic system. We have incorporated many of the more moderate principles of socialism, allowing for both respect of the individual and his or her right to private property and the need for the state to regulate to some extent the actions that take place in the marketplace.

The social doctrine of the Church is presented in the *Catechism* under the seventh commandment. A foundation block of that teaching includes the universal destination and the private ownership of goods. This means that while each of us may acquire and own privately a certain portion of the goods of the earth, we need also to recognize our obligation to those who have little or nothing. The universal destination of goods, that is the intention that they be available to all, remains "primordial, even if the promotion of the common good requires respect for the right to private property and its exercise" (section 2403).

Clearly there is a need to find the proper balance between our accumulation and use of the goods of the earth and the needs of those around us who are poor. At the same time, all are called to respect the property and possessions of others.

OTHER OBLIGATIONS THAT COME FROM THIS COMMANDMENT

We also have an obligation to keep agreements. Promises must be kept and contracts honored insofar as the commitments made in them are morally just. It would be impossible to sustain communal life, a society, or any type of collectivity if one could not count on agreements being respected and contracts followed. It is a part of our human nature to want to work with others in order to accomplish what is beneficial to all but perhaps beyond the capability of any one of us. Agreements that allow for division of labor and a just exchange of the fruits of such an agreement are part of a foundation of society. To violate them is to undermine community life.

We need also to respect the world in which we live. The environment that provides our home was created and given into our care. It is not to be pillaged. The responsible use of the resources of the earth requires us to be concerned about future generations, who will also need to derive their sustenance from the goods of the earth. The careful husbanding of natural resources and their prudent consumption is a challenge we face in a way far more demanding than earlier generations. Perhaps this is a time for each of us to review how well we care for or waste the products of our consumer society.

In a world where so many people, clearly more than one-half, survive day to day on what they can find to eat that day, it is wrong to casually waste enormous amounts of food. A visit to almost any restaurant in this country provides numerous examples of well-fed people—some overfed—throwing away enormous amounts of perfectly good food that they cannot consume. We need also to raise questions about the laws we make that oblige restaurants to discard great quantities of unused food simply because it has been placed on the table. Have you ever witnessed baskets of bread being thrown away for no other reason than that it has been on a table even though it remained untouched? We do this while numerous "soup kitchens" and "food pantries" for the needy go begging.

The *Catechism* calls us to reflect that there is more to the seventh commandment than simply not stealing. In concluding its teaching on this commandment, the *Catechism* closes with a section entitled "Love for the Poor." Here we are reminded of another fact of life. While the goods of the earth were created for all, it happens that some are more successful in accumulating wealth than others. We must always recognize that whatever we have is through the goodness of God, his mercy and his love. God's poor, however, have a special claim on us.

True generosity calls us to be prepared to share with those in need without passing judgment on the reason for their need or their failure to meet their own needs. A "generous giver" is praised in Scripture. The *Catechism* reminds us that God rewards those who come to the aid of the needy and rebukes those who turn away from them (see section 2443). "Give to him who begs from you, do not refuse him who would borrow from you; you received without pay, give without pay" (Matthew 5:42, 10:8).

The corporal works of mercy provide us a wide range of ways to express our generosity in the same way that God graciously and generously shares with us. The corporal works of mercy include feeding the hungry, sheltering the homeless, clothing the naked, visiting the sick and imprisoned, and burying the dead. In exercising these works, we are reminded of the final judgment so vividly depicted in the twenty-fifth chapter of Matthew, where those who exercise these works were told that when they did them to one of the least of their brothers and sisters they did them to Christ.

As we reflect on the obligations of the seventh commandment to respect what belongs to others and to recognize the obligations of social justice, we do well to conclude with the reminder that those who have the least in terms of material goods are described by Jesus as having the most in their unity with him.

QUESTIONS TO THINK ABOUT:

1. In what other ways do we "steal" from people besides direct theft? Are there legal ways of stealing?
2. What aspects of our economic system are still unjust? What can we do to address that injustice?
3. How could I show better respect for the environment?
4. In light of what we believe about corporal works of mercy, how should we respond to street beggars? Is it always best to give them what they ask for?

CHAPTER 77

The Eighth Commandment: You Shall Not Bear False Witness

WE HEAR A LOT about some of the commandments. About others we hear practically nothing. Yet all the commandments are God's word speaking to us about how we should live and associate with each other and how we are to relate to God.

Somehow the eighth commandment, "You shall not bear false witness against your neighbor," while of equal standing with the others, seems to be easily brushed aside by just about everyone. It is one of the least respected and most ignored commandments. All we have to do is look at the way words and communications are used today to realize that many people are not concerned about telling the truth.

THE LOSS OF RESPECT FOR TRUTH

Did you ever stand in a checkout line at a supermarket and read the covers of the tabloids and magazines lined up for sale? Less and less distinguishable from these supermarket tabloids are some radio and television talk shows. Serious news journals and the evening news roundup are increasingly perceived as running neck and neck with these fonts of sensationalism. There is little or no concern for truth. One gets the impression that the importance of truth is no longer generally recognized because its relationship to a well-functioning and responsible human community is no longer understood.

There can be no true human society without trust. Trust is based upon how people communicate with one another and their adherence to and respect for the truth. Trust begins at the basic level of all human society—the family. How would it be possible for two people to come together to form a family in trust, in confidence, in openness, in willingness to commit themselves to each other, if they were not truthful with each other? Truth is an absolutely essential part of the relationships among the growing family membership. As we move beyond the circle of family into the wider community, it is not possible to sustain societal life at any level if the relationships are not founded on truth.

Jesus Christ came into this world "to bear witness to the truth" (John 18:37). His revelation is, according to the Second Vatican Council, of "the deepest truth about God and the salvation of man" (*Dei Verbum* 2). It is an aspect of God's invitation to us to enter into a fellowship so complete that it amounts to sharing in the divine nature.

SELF-DECEPTION IS A SIN AGAINST TRUTH

Understanding the truth and living it are basic aspects of the full human freedom that Christ came to restore to us. Indeed, understanding is possible only because the created person, as the council continues, "shares in the light of the divine mind" (*Gaudium et Spes* 15). The ultimate value of intelligence is that, through "wisdom's gentle attraction of the human mind to a quest and a love for what is true and good, man passes through visible realities to those which are unseen" (*Gaudium et Spes* 15) and so comes to understand the truth about God, created reality, and ourselves.

Truth is attained primarily in an interior judgment of the mind. Hence, one way of dishonoring truth is by an inward, willful blindness or a determination to think only what is convenient, a willingness to rationalize and accept one's prejudices. Too often great damage can be done to people's lives and even to institutions because of prejudices that rise to the level of jury decisions or court actions.

HALF-TRUTHS ARE ALSO SINS AGAINST TRUTH

The truth is, of course, dishonored by a lie. A lie is an assertion, in a context in which genuine communication is reasonably expected, of something that one considers to be false. Lying is wrong. It is forbidden by the eighth commandment.

Many times, however, another level of falsehood touches our lives. Someone once described a gossip as a person who will never tell a lie if a half-truth will do as much damage. Gossip, innuendo, false inferences, all, like a cancer, eat away at the fabric of truth, trust, and ultimately the human community. Since we are obliged to bear witness to the truth, we must also be attentive to the source of what we claim to be true.

One of the casualties of our modern age—particularly in recent years—is the confidence that we used to place in the media, whether radio, print, or television. Perhaps it is for that reason the Second Vatican Council devoted an entire document to these instruments and why Pope John Paul II has often addressed those responsible for them and called to our attention the importance of the means of social communication and their impact on society, calling them "gifts from God."

Part of the problem is the very nature of "stories." When the media cover a "story," they usually have time to deal with only one aspect of a very large picture. So they focus on one piece of the picture, which they depict as "the story." The rest of the picture gets left out. While this may not be deliberately falsifying the news, the fact is that sometimes 90 percent of the picture is undeveloped. We are given only 10 percent of the picture and after a while we begin to realize what is happening. Cynicism develops that begins to eat away at the very fabric of our community life. How many times have we heard people say, "You can't believe what you read in the papers"; "You can't believe what you see on television"?

The *Catechism of the Catholic Church* tells us that "within modern society the communications media play a major role in information, cultural promotion, and formation" (section 2493). As technology continues to grow at a staggering pace, the role of the media will expand—together with the amount and diversity of the news transmitted, and especially the influence exercised on public opinion. Therefore, it is all the more important for these channels of information to be both truthful and reliable.

The offenses against truth include false witness and perjury, as well as outright lies, and the misuse of the truth that causes harm to individuals and to society. It is a small step in terms of a person's attitude to move from gossip, to white lies, to bearing false witness in serious matters, to perjury. At the heart of these steps is the same disregard for the truth.

SPEAKING THE TRUTH IN CHARITY

We have a duty to seek the truth and to speak the truth. We must be honest with ourselves and with others. But even when we do speak the truth, we are obliged to do so with respect. Saint Paul challenges us to speak the truth in love (see Ephesians 4:15). One sign of God's presence is the truth, but another is the fruits of the Holy Spirit—love, joy, peace, patience, kindness, goodness, faithfulness, gentleness, and self-control (see Galatians 5:22–23).

The *Catechism* reminds us that regard for the reputation of persons "forbids every attitude and word likely to cause them unjust injury" (section 2477). Among such actions are rash judgment, detraction, and calumny. Offenses against truth and justice demand reparation. We are obliged by the eighth commandment to do our best to repair the damage done to another's name or reputation, even if this involves considerable personal effort.

Why is there so much emphasis on this often ignored and little respected commandment today? The Church's call and God's commandment to reverence the truth teach us that without truth there can be no trust, and without trust there can be no true community—human or ecclesial. It should be not just our obligation but also our privilege and joy to do all in our power to strengthen our civic community, as well as the life of the Church. Speaking and respecting the truth will go a long way in helping us accomplish that goal.

QUESTIONS TO THINK ABOUT:

1. How do I sin against the eighth commandment? What tempts me to commit those sins?
2. What are ways in which we can support and encourage accurate journalism in the media?
3. Does respect for the truth oblige me to tell people exactly what I think of them?

CHAPTER 78

The Ninth and Tenth Commandments: You Shall Not Covet

ACTIONS OFTEN SPEAK LOUDER than words. Even as youngsters, we knew that we would often be judged by what we actually did rather than on what we said we would do. In the New Testament, Jesus raises the question about who really did the will of the father, the son who said he would and didn't or the son who said he wouldn't and did (see Matthew 21:28–31).

INTERIOR DISPOSITION IS AS IMPORTANT AS EXTERIOR ACTION

Just as there is a connection between what we say and what we do, so too there is a connection between what we think and what we do. In his Sermon on the Mount, Jesus made it very clear that our attitudes and innermost thoughts can be every bit as compromising of our spiritual life as what we do. This should not be surprising, since, as Christians, we are convinced that the real transformation taking place is within us through the power of the Holy Spirit, and not just external to us in what we do.

By the grace of God we have been freed from sin and have become a dwelling of the Holy Spirit. It is that Spirit within that urges us to take the actions we do. This is all the more reason why there should be a conformity between our innermost dispositions and what we actually do. It was Jesus who pointed out to the disciples that it is not what goes into a man—the following of the ritual rules for eating—but what comes out of a man, out of his heart, that defiles him.

The ninth and tenth commandments are linked together because they both deal with interior disposition as opposed to exterior action. The other commandments present us with some directive concerning how we should act, whether in relation to God or to our neighbor. We are called to know God, reverence God's name, and worship the Lord. We are commanded not to kill or commit adultery, not to steal or lie. All these commandments have to do with our actions.

The last two commandments of the Decalogue speak about our interior attitude: "You shall not covet your neighbor's wife" and "You shall not covet your neighbor's goods." These two commandments go to the very heart of Christian conversion. When we turn to God, we turn from everything that would hold us back from him. The word "conversion" comes from a word that means "to turn." In the context of living a Christian life, "conversion" means "turning to God." Such a turning does not involve just our external actions but especially a true conversion of the heart and mind.

When we commit ourselves to Christ, we give our heart to Christ, we place it in his hands and ask the Lord to mold it—our desires, our attitudes, and our mentality—to be like his. Our prayer is that we put on Christ—that we have the attitude of Christ (see Philippians 2:5).

THE DIFFERENCE BETWEEN TEMPTATION AND COVETING

"Covet." What does "covet" mean? You shall not covet what belongs to another. It is not the same as temptation. Each of us can be tempted without giving in to it. Covet implies an interior surrender of our commitment and virtue in everything except its exterior manifestation.

How can this covetousness be so wrong if we never act upon it? There is a sense in which the real struggle for virtue and true morality takes place and is manifest in the interior chamber of our heart. The *Catechism of the Catholic Church* points out "The heart is the seat of moral personality" (section 2517). "For from the heart come evil thoughts, murder, adultery, unchastity . . ." (Matthew 15:19). The struggle against carnal covetousness requires a cleansing of the heart and the development of the virtue of temperance.

In Matthew's gospel, Jesus teaches us: "Blessed are the clean of heart, for they shall see God" (Matthew 5:8). What does "clean of heart" mean? Here the *Catechism* tells us that the beatitudes are all about our interior attitude—our interior disposition. It is not just a question of chastity but rather of all our legitimate human drives and desires. All of these must correspond with God's law. Our interior thought is every bit as important as our action—and, in a sense, even more so, because our actions flow from what is contained in our heart.

There is in the heart of each of us an ongoing struggle. It is part of a great cosmic battle. Saint John describes the ultimate struggle between good and evil, light and darkness: "The light shines in the darkness, and the darkness has not overcome it" (John 1:5). Each one of us has been baptized into the light, and we walk in God's truth. Yet the raging struggle within us is the old person, the "unredeemed" part of our being that struggles against the Spirit, God's grace, and our own desire to draw every day closer to Christ. Saint Paul described this struggle as the contest between the "old man" and the "new man."

Even though we personally have made our commitment to Christ, the powers of darkness struggle to turn us back. The disobedience of the first sin of Adam has left us a legacy of concupiscence, and hence we find ourselves regularly tempted.

THE SPECIAL TEMPTATIONS OF MODERN LIFE

The moral climate in which we live presents a particular challenge as we attempt to avoid the pitfalls of concupiscence. Our culture is characterized by moral laziness or lassitude. We see this not only in the demise of any meaningful standard in the entertainment industry when treating matters of sex and violence but also in the extreme vulgarity and crudity that is the hallmark of so many comedians, talk-show hosts, and television personalities. It is increasingly difficult to speak to young people of developing wholesome attitudes and perspectives on life when they are inundated daily by wave after wave of culturally acceptable invitations to sexual promiscuity, self-centered and self-satisfying behavior, and what might be best described as moral bankruptcy.

The *Catechism* reminds us that the "so-called *moral permissiveness* [the emphasis is in the original] rests on an erroneous conception of human freedom" (section 2526). The starting point and presupposition for the development of true freedom is a willingness and openness to be educated in the moral law.

Certainly it is one of the goals of Catholic education to assure that young people receive instruction and formation that is respectful of the truth, the qualities of the human heart, and the moral and spiritual dignity of human beings. Faith formation is as important as academic excellence in a Catholic education. A Catholic education must help a young person develop an outlook and attitude on life that resonates with God's commandment: we not only must not act out in ways contrary to his law, but we also must not foster in our hearts all of the evil that we restrain from our actions.

WITH GOD'S GRACE, WE CAN WIN THE STRUGGLE

The wise follower of Christ distinguishes clearly between a temptation to which we do not give in and coveting, which carries with it already a designation of our moral collapse. Temptation we will have always with us. But we need not give in, and we need not allow it to develop into what the ninth and tenth commandments prohibit.

How do we win this continuous ongoing struggle? How do we keep our hearts pure, our attitudes correct, and our interior disposition of soul directed to Christ? Only with prayer. Only by a reliance completely and totally on God's grace.

As the *Catechism* concludes Part Three, there is a brief reflection that brings our own study of how we live our life in Christ and how we observe the Ten Commandments to a conclusion. This part of the *Catechism* is entitled *I want to see God.* Everything we have reflected on in this portion of the *Catechism* that speaks of how we live out our Christian life and how we attempt faithfully to observe the commandments of God is in response to a cry deep within the heart of each of us: "I want to see God." The *Catechism* gives us these words of encouragement: "It remains for the holy people to struggle, with grace from on high, to obtain the good things God promises" (section 2549).

We are never alone. Christ is with us. God's Holy Spirit enlivens us, and, at the end of the pilgrimage we make through life together with all of our sisters and brothers who are a part of the Church, the glory of God awaits us.

In our struggle, we take great consolation in knowing that "on this way of perfection, the Spirit and the Bride call whoever hears them to perfect communion with God . . ." (section 2550). In reviewing with you these many chapters of the *Catechism,* it has been my hope that these reflections have been of some help as you and I together make our journey through this life while sharing the same basic goal: "We want to see God."

QUESTIONS TO THINK ABOUT:

1. How am I most often tempted to covetousness? What about those particular temptations is so strongly attractive?
2. How well do my legitimate human needs and desires correspond with God's law? Do I expect too much?
3. How can I teach my children or other young people that the standards of behavior they see on television are not really acceptable?

CHAPTER 79

What Is Prayer?

PART ONE OF THE *Catechism,* the Profession of Faith, centered on the creed; Part Two, the Celebration of the Christian Mystery, directed our attention to the sacraments; Part Three, Life in Christ, focused on the Ten Commandments. Now we come to the final portion: Christian Prayer.

CHRIST IS THE MODEL

This section begins with a reproduction of a miniature from the monastery of Dionysius on Mount Athos, which was painted in Constantinople some time around the year 1059. It pictures Christ turned in prayer toward the Father as he prays alone in a deserted place. The *Catechism* tells us that his disciples looked on from a respectful distance. Saint Peter, the head of the apostles, turns toward the others and points to him who is the Master and the Way of Christian prayer. The art miniature is reminiscent of the request the apostles made to Jesus: "Lord, teach us to pray" (Luke 11:1).

Christ is the model and the teacher of prayer. A person who faithfully accepts Jesus will necessarily devote careful attention to the Master's pattern of living as well as to his teaching. Both the lifestyle and the words of Jesus show that prayer should have an important place in the life of every Christian. The gospels, especially Saint Luke, often describe Christ at prayer, publicly as well as privately, before the most important acts and decisions of his ministry and as a source of nurture and strength as he carried out his mission.

Saint Mark, after describing a day of intense activity by Christ, notes:

"Rising very early before dawn, he left and went off to a deserted place, where he prayed. Simon and those who were with him pursued him and on finding him said, 'Everyone is looking for you.' He told them, 'Let us go on to the nearby villages that I may preach there also. For this purpose have I come' " (Mark 1:35–38). This one vignette perhaps describes for us the rhythm of Christ's life, which should also be applicable in our own. A certain amount of time is set aside for prayer, so that we can then carry on the work to which we have been called. In this way whatever we do is consecrated to God. At the same time, setting aside time for prayer more clearly expresses for ourselves how all of our daily activity should respond to our vocation and our attempt to follow it.

WHAT IS PRAYER?

The first question the *Catechism* raises is "What is prayer?" Among the answers is the definition of Saint John Damascene: "Prayer is the raising of one's mind and heart to God or the requesting of good things from God" (see section 2559 of the *Catechism*). This traditional definition has endured so long because it sums up what is an otherwise complex and multifaceted activity. The verb "to pray" means literally to ask for something—and yet prayer is much more than just asking God for a specific response. A definition of prayer needs to include that it is more than an activity of the intellect. A person's will, affections, and activities are all to be lifted up to God, bringing about an intimate personal relationship with him.

While each of us longs for a sense of fulfillment and that satisfaction that comes from knowing that things are right, we are not able to initiate a conversation with God. God speaks to us first. In the section on prayer, the *Catechism* invites us to look at the experience of prayer both in the Old Testament and in the New Testament.

In the Old Testament, we find that prayer is about our relationship with God—an enduring, compelling relationship that directs the believer's activities and calls him or her regularly to speak with God. The most dramatic figure in the patriarchal period is Abraham. When God calls him he goes forth, "as the Lord directed him" (Genesis 12:4). What emerges from the description of Abraham is the picture of a man who has heard God's voice, struggled with the implications of the call, responded to it, and attempted to live in fidelity to God's word. While the conversations between Abraham and God are directed to specific purposes, it is also clear that they rest upon a profound relationship rooted in God's call and Abraham's response.

Our own prayer begins with a sense of humility before God. We recognize that, in any conversation, it is God who calls us and it is only with the grace of God that we are capable of responding. From Abraham we learn that prayer is an act of faith, and at the same time calls for a strengthening of faith.

THE PRAYER OF THE MEDIATOR

Another example that the *Catechism* holds up to us is Moses and the prayer of the mediator. As the promise made to God's people begins to be fulfilled in events such as the Passover, the exodus, the gift of the law, and the ratification of the covenant, the prayer of Moses is directed more and more toward intercession on behalf of God's people. The *Catechism* reminds us that this prayer will reach its preeminent fulfillment in "the one mediator between God and men, the man Christ Jesus" (compare 1 Timothy 2:5; see section 2574 of the *Catechism*).

In the fullness of time, God sent his only Son, so that the final and most perfect mediation could take place between us and our Father. It is Jesus who is God's Son, "God with us," who teaches us how to pray. In his prayer life, Jesus demonstrated that he was quite familiar with the traditions of the Hebrews concerning prayer. He prayed the psalms (Matthew 27:46), especially the Hallel, the great hymn of praise formed by psalms 113–18 (see Matthew 26:30). He was well versed in the Shema, the ritual prayer said by the Jews twice a day: "Hear O Israel! the Lord is our God, the Lord alone!" (Deuteronomy 6:4; compare Matthew 22:37).

The Scriptures tell us that Jesus addressed God the Father as "Abba," which is the simple, familiar address used by children to their father. Jesus uses that title at Gethsemane. Saint Paul refers to it twice (Romans 8:15 and Galatians 4:6), as if by this time it had gained usage in liturgical prayer. As Jesus used this distinctive form of addressing God in prayer, so too the earliest Aramaic-speaking community formally adopted it.

The gospel of John portrays Christ (John 17), as he comes to the hour of his passion, offering to the Father his solemn "priestly prayer." This prayer reveals how free and intensely penetrated with love for the Father and for us is his coming death. This, the longest and most moving of the prayers of Christ found in the gospels, is particularly close to the heart of the faithful today.

IN CHRIST'S NAME

In many ways he showed his disciples how to pray from their daily experience of his own prayer life. The Sermon on the Mount includes his instructions to pray in private and with simple and direct words.

The *Catechism* reminds us of another important element of our prayer. We are to pray in Christ's name. When Jesus offered his disciples the instruction on prayer to the Father, he revealed to them the generosity of his love. "Whatever you ask in my name, I will do, so that the Father may be glorified in the Son. If you ask anything of me in my name, I will do it" (John 14:13–14). Faith in the Son introduces the disciples, the *Catechism* points out, into the knowledge of the Father, because Jesus is "the way and the truth and the life." "In this new covenant the certitude that our petitions will be heard is founded on the prayer of Jesus" (section 2614).

From the example and teaching of Christ, it is clear that his follower should be a person of prayer. All who know that their existence and life of grace come from God can recognize the need to remain in communication with God. This brings us to the realization that prayer, therefore, is neither useless nor selfish. It flows from one's filial relationship with God. It is the loving, obedient response of a child to a father's love. Any life lived in faith, hope, and love will have to express itself at some point in prayer.

QUESTIONS TO THINK ABOUT:

1. How do I follow the example of Jesus in praying? How could I learn from his example?
2. How does prayer prepare me for my daily life?
3. Why do we pray in Jesus' name?
4. Do I make some room each day for prayer, conversation, with God?

CHAPTER 80

Kinds of Prayer

TRADITIONALLY THE CHURCH HAS referred to four general types of prayer, according to the reasons or purposes for which one prays: adoration, thanksgiving, petition, and contrition. The *Catechism of the Catholic Church* uses a slightly expanded list as it treats this subject. Included as the forms of prayer are adoration, thanksgiving, petition, intercession, and praise.

VARIOUS EXPRESSIONS OF PRAYER

We should expect prayer to take multiple forms. Our relationship with God finds expression according to our particular need at any given time. We find ourselves in moments of joy and contentment. There are also times of sorrow and need. At other occasions we may be caught up in the wonder of God and find ourselves praising the goodness of God or kneeling in simple adoration before the mystery of a God who loves us so much.

These various expressions of prayer find articulation in the liturgy as well as in the public and private devotions of the faithful. Benediction of the Blessed Sacrament provides us a time of adoration and praise. Novenas are usually an occasion of petition and intercession. The public or private recitation of the rosary may include all of the elements, perhaps even mingled together, as we move from decade to decade recognizing our love of God, our sorrow for sin, prayers for our loved ones, and praise and adoration for the God who makes all of this possible.

In the Church's great public prayer, her liturgy, we find moments of adoration, petition, intercession, contrition, thanksgiving, and praise reflected in the preface, the prayers of the faithful, the liturgical prayers of the day, the Eucharistic Prayer itself, and the hymns and responsorial psalms.

One of the reasons the Church uses the psalter so extensively is because its many forms of prayer "take shape both in the liturgy of the Temple and in the human heart" (see section 2588 of the *Catechism*). The range of human emotions from exhilaration and joy to depression and sorrow is magnificently expressed in the Book of Psalms. Whether we pray psalm 51 in humble recognition of our sinfulness, or psalm 23 for the consolation of God's presence in difficulty, or psalm 150 in a spirit of exultant praise, we find a reflection of our own multifaceted relationship with God—and inspired words in which to express that communion.

PUBLIC PRAYER AND PRIVATE PRAYER

Before we review the forms of prayer, we need to remind ourselves that the great distinction in the prayer life of the Church is between her public prayer—the liturgy—and all forms of private prayer. Liturgical prayer is the prayer of the whole Church, of the family of God, united with Christ. The sacred liturgy is the public worship that our Savior as head of the Church renders to our heavenly Father. The Second Vatican Council reminds us in its *Constitution on the Sacred Liturgy* that in the liturgy full public worship is performed by the mystical Body of Jesus Christ, that is, by the head and his members. No other action of the Church can equal its efficacy to the same degree (see *Sacrosanctum Concilium* 7:2–3).

The Mass, the other sacraments, the divine office, and public ritual are all part of the Church's liturgy. Here, regardless of how many are present, it is the Church that prays. At Mass, for example, whether celebrated in a cathedral overflowing with people or in a small mission outpost with perhaps just the priest and a few faithful, it is the whole Church at worship. The stations of the cross, the rosary, prayer services, and many other forms of prayer, even when said together by a group of people, are private devotions distinct from the liturgical or public prayer of the Church.

ADORATION

The *Catechism* tells us that adoration is our first attitude before God, acknowledging that he is our Creator and we are his creatures (see section

2628 of the *Catechism*). Psalm 95 reads: "Enter, let us bow down in worship; let us kneel before the Lord who made us. For this is our God, whose people we are, God's well-tended flock" (Psalm 95:6–7). In prayers of adoration we express God's excellence and our absolute dependence upon our Creator, Redeemer, and Sanctifier. The obvious posture of one who makes this prayer is with profound humility and yet deep joy and confidence.

PETITION

Possibly the most frequent form of prayer is that of petition. There is a tendency to turn to God only when we want something, and to pray only prayers of petition, and then to be displeased with God if we do not promptly get what we have asked for. This is clearly not the Christian attitude. Prayer is not a bargaining process with God whereby we offer so much in return for something. Approaching prayer in this way can lead to great disappointment. Our prayer will be answered, but not always in a way we have determined.

On the other hand, Christ himself told us to ask God for things: "Amen, amen, I say to you, whatever you ask the Father in my name he will give to you. . . . ask and you will receive, so that your joy may be complete" (John 16:23–24); compare Matthew 7:7). This promise is fulfilled for every Christian who truly prays in Christ's name with a proper disposition and for something that will be helpful to eternal salvation.

We must be confident in our prayer. God always hears our prayers. He knows how to give good things to his children (see Matthew 7:11). Sometimes, however, we ask for the wrong things. For what should we pray?

In response to this question, the *Catechism* tells us that "Christian petition is centered on the desire and search for the Kingdom to come" (section 2632). Such prayer is in keeping with the teaching of Christ. Our prayer needs to be situated in the context of God's plan for us and his call directed to each of us. There is, therefore, a certain order of priorities in what is worth praying for.

For some things we *must* pray. In keeping with the Our Father, we should ask for God's glory, the coming of his kingdom, the fulfillment of his will on earth, the forgiveness of our sins, freedom from temptation, protection against evil, and the graces necessary and useful for salvation.

For other things we are *free* to pray. The Christian must be careful in praying for specific material goods and possessions. These can be asked for, if they are helpful toward salvation. The poverty of Christ and his warnings about riches should make us cautious about prayer for superfluous material goods. Surely no Christian would expect God to give something to us that might be detrimental to our salvation.

The prayer of contrition is located in the *Catechism* under the prayer of petition. "The first movement of the prayer of petition is asking forgiveness like the tax collector in the parable" (section 2631). "O God, be merciful to me a sinner!" (Luke 18:13). At Mass this prayer takes the form of the Confiteor or other expressions in the Penitential Rite.

INTERCESSION

In explaining what is meant by a prayer of intercession, the *Catechism* tells us that it is a prayer of petition that guides us to pray as Jesus did. "He is the one intercessor with the Father on behalf of all men, especially sinners" (section 2634). Perhaps one of the most regularly experienced forms of intercession is found in the prayer of the faithful at Mass. Even here there is some structure to the prayer, since we are urged first to pray for the Church and then the needs of the whole community before we turn our attention to our own concerns and those of loved ones.

THANKSGIVING

The prayer of thanksgiving is the basic prayer of the Church. "Thanksgiving, characterizes the prayer of the Church which, in celebrating the Eucharist, reveals and becomes more fully what she is" (see section 2637 of the *Catechism*). God calls us to be a people who thank him for the great gift that is Jesus Christ our Redeemer and Savior. Every prayer in some way participates in this great cry of thanksgiving as God's people come together collectively or individually to render gratitude to God for all that we are and someday will be.

PRAISE

Finally, we come to the prayer of praise. The gospels often express wonder and praise at the marvels of Christ. In presenting the reflection on the prayer of praise, the *Catechism* tells us that it is "the form of prayer which recognizes most immediately that God is God" (section 2639). Prayers of praise or adulation glorify God simply because he is God. In this form of lifting our hearts to God, we do so to give him glory, not because of what he does, but simply because he is.

Whatever form our prayer takes, it is essential that we pray and pray often. The language of the Church is prayer. As a member of God's family, we should be proficient and comfortable speaking in our spiritual native tongue.

QUESTIONS TO THINK ABOUT:

1. What form do my private prayers most often take?
2. What do I ask for in my prayers? Am I asking for the right things? How is what I ask for conducive to my salvation?
3. Do I leave enough time in my private prayers for adoration, praise, and thanksgiving?

CHAPTER 81

Ways of Praying

PRAYER, WHEN IT FOLLOWS the pattern of Christ's prayer, has a transforming effect on one's life. Genuine prayer is a part of the whole rhythm of life and thus affects the way we live. We cannot pray well unless we are prepared to change in our lives those things that separate us from God. We do not set our lives in order first and then pray. We pray—and are prepared to discover that as we go on praying there are things in our lives that need to be changed.

WE NEED TO CONVERSE WITH GOD

We sometimes hear that "My work is my prayer." While there is a sense in which this is true—what we do should be a living expression of our relationship with God—our daily activity cannot be the only conversation we have with God. We cannot sustain any loving relationship solely by all of the activity that is a part of communal human life. At some point, the breadth and depth of the relationship need to find expression in words. Some time must be set apart so that the relationship can truly grow. Prayer is that time for the Christian to grow in communion with the Father through the Son in the gift of the Holy Spirit.

JESUS GAVE US THE MODEL OF PRAYER

The *Catechism* offers us a reminder that "Jesus' filial prayer is the perfect model of prayer in the New Testament. Often done in solitude and in secret, the prayer of Jesus involves a loving adherence to the will of the Father even to the Cross and an absolute confidence in being heard" (section 2620).

We cannot ask for a better model as we approach our own personal prayer life. Whatever the format, and whether we use a specific formula or just open our heart to God, some time must be set aside each day if our relationship with our loving God is to grow, prosper, and flourish.

Whatever form of prayer we choose, Christian prayer should have certain qualities—attention, devotion, confidence, and perseverance. Christ requires that we pray with an absolute inner sincerity, not with the hypocritical externalism of the Pharisees (see Matthew 6:5–8). The devout Christian consequently will pray thoughtfully. "I will pray with the spirit, but I will also pray with the mind. I will sing praise with the spirit, but I will also sing praise with the mind" (1 Corinthians 14:15). Involuntary distractions may come and go, because of human weakness, but they do not destroy the value of prayer.

PRAYER IS NOT JUST FEELING GOOD

Prayer is more than an exercise of the mind. It is also a genuflection of the will to God. Genuine devotion should not be confused with feeling satisfaction or with emotion. Sometimes we hear people say that they do not pray or attend Mass because they do not feel uplifted or experience an emotional "high." Effective prayer is not measured by the rapidity or intensity of our personal satisfaction. True devotion is properly directed to God. At times our prayers may result in personal peace and joy, but such a response is not the gauge of their effectiveness. The more devoted to God one is, the closer is one's friendship with him, and the more likely that prayer will be heard—but not necessarily in the manner we determine. After all, it is God who answers. It is God who makes up the other side of the conversation.

The Lord told us to pray with an unshakable confidence born of faith (see Matthew 17:20; Luke 17:6; James 1:6). We do this by praying in the name of Jesus our mediator, with full confidence in his redemptive love and the power of his merits to obtain from the Father what is asked. For this reason, the official prayers of the Church that are addressed to the Father end the petition with the words "through Christ our Lord."

We learn from the gospels to pray with perseverance. "Will not God then secure the rights of his chosen ones who call out to him day and night?" (Luke 18:7; compare Matthew 7:7–11; Luke 11:1–13). The Christian should never be discouraged in prayer, should never give up, should never lose heart.

THREE KINDS OF PRAYER

There are a variety of expressions of prayer. The *Catechism* calls our attention to vocal prayer, meditation, and contemplative prayer.

Vocal prayer is one expressed in words, or occasionally in gestures. It may be a fixed formula or an expression of one's own words; it may be said aloud or quietly. In any case, the words should express the thoughts of the one praying. Jesus warned against the sheer multiplication of words while praying (see Matthew 6:7), and he quoted Isaiah to rebuke the Pharisees: "This people honors me with their lips, but their hearts are far from me . . ." (Matthew 15:8; see Isaiah 29:13).

The type of prayer we call vocal may be personal, a spontaneous cry that springs from the heart of a person in joy or in danger. But most regularly vocal prayer is the recitation of a fixed formula—such as the Our Father, the Hail Mary, the Glory Be, or a psalm or a hymn, or a repetitious prayer such as a litany, the angelus, or the rosary. Jesus quoted the great prayers of the Old Testament. When asked by the disciples for instruction in prayer, Jesus gave them the Our Father as a model and as the greatest vocal prayer of the Church.

Meditation or mental prayer is usually characterized by the absence of external words or gestures. The intellect and will, however, are focused on God. In both vocal and mental prayer, the most characteristic actions are praise, adoration, and thanksgiving. Mental prayer in the form of meditation is described by the *Catechism* as "a quest." The text goes on to tell us that "the mind seeks to understand the why and how of the Christian life, in order to adhere and respond to what the Lord is asking" (section 2705).

Meditation may be described as either formal or informal. Sometimes we devote a specific period of time so that we can make these internal acts of prayer and concentrate solely on that activity. At other times, in a more informal manner, we can pray internally while also doing something else. Waiting as we often do in lines at the supermarket, behind the wheel of a car, or just about anywhere else provide an opportunity for informal meditation.

The *Catechism* concludes this section with a discussion of *contemplative prayer.* Here we find the quotation from Saint Teresa of Jesus' *The Book of Her Life:* "Contemplative prayer [*oración mental*] in my opinion is nothing else than a close sharing between friends; it means taking time frequently to be alone with him who we know loves us" (see section 2709 of the *Catechism*).

For some, the highest stage of mental prayer is contemplation, which itself has many steps. Contemplation is God's gift in this life to those who have loved him with exceptional faithfulness. In its most developed form, this prayer draws one as near to God as is possible in this life. It anticipates now some of the intensity of the beatific vision. It gives a taste of the divine presence. This form of prayer bears its own unique joy and peace. The *Catechism* characterizes contemplative prayer as an intense time of prayer, a gaze of faith fixed on Jesus, a hearing of the word of God, done in silence and resulting in "a union with the prayer of Christ insofar as it makes us participate in his mystery" (section 2718).

Whatever the forms and expression of prayer, one thing is certain: followers of Christ are expected to turn their minds and hearts to God with regularity. How else can we sustain and build our relationship with the Lord? Thus the Church urges us to find time, perhaps at the beginning and end of each day and some time in the course of it, to set aside time for the Lord—time for our conversation with God.

QUESTIONS TO THINK ABOUT:

1. Do I have any favorite prayers? What appeals to me about those prayers? Why do they seem to express best what I want to say to God?
2. When do I usually pray? Do I set aside specific times for prayer? How could I find more time?
3. What about prayer do I find most difficult? What do I find most rewarding?
4. Have I ever tried to pray without formulating words—with just my heart?

CHAPTER 82

The Lord's Prayer

JESUS HIMSELF GAVE US a special prayer, the "Our Father" (see Matthew 6:9–13). The Church celebrates this as her most cherished prayer. She gives it a central place at Mass and in all her liturgical worship, and commends it to all. For in this prayer, which has been called a "summary of the whole gospel," Christ teaches us two things: the spirit in which we should pray, and the things for which we must ask.

There are few prayers that should be so regularly on our lips and in our heart. The Lord's Prayer is the chief of prayers. We can imagine the excitement of the apostles when, in response to their request for guidance in how they were to pray, their Divine Master gave them, not words of encouragement to pray, but the actual prayer itself. The slow and careful praying of the Our Father places us in direct continuity with the apostles and through them with Jesus as he gathers his Church and instructs us on how we are to turn our hearts and minds to God.

THE EXTRAORDINARY REVELATION: GOD IS OUR FATHER

The opening words from which the prayer takes its name, "Our Father," bring us face to face with the extraordinary revelation of Jesus. He alone is the true natural Son of God. Jesus is God from God, light from light, true God from true God—only begotten Son of the Father. Yet he came among us so that he could make us heirs to his inheritance. Through his death and resurrection, which we share through our baptism and participation in the Eucharist, we become adopted children of God. Saint Paul in writing to the Galatians makes this very clear: "But when the fullness of time had come, God sent his Son, born of woman, born under the law, to ransom those under the law, so that we might receive adoption. As proof that you are children, God sent the Spirit of his Son into our hearts, crying out, 'Abba, Father!' So you are no longer a slave but a child, and if a child then also an heir, through God" (Galatians 4:4–7).

We have been called to this unique relationship with God out of our former and sinful state. Each person is born in original sin, and into a world damaged by sin. But God "delivered us from the power of darkness and transferred us to the kingdom of his beloved Son, in whom we have redemption, the forgiveness of sins" (Colossians 1:13–14). Saint Paul speaks of this justifying mercy of God often, especially in his letter to the Romans.

The opening of the Lord's Prayer reminds us that we can call God our Father because of the generous outpouring of God's Holy Spirit on everyone who proclaims Jesus as Lord. The first of all God's gifts is the gift of himself. He desires to give himself to us perfectly in eternal life. But that giving begins now.

The presence of God with us as our Father is far more significant than the presence of God as Creator and Lord of all that is. To those who love and believe him, he is present in a rich new way. He is present as friend, with personal affection; he is present transforming and making us children by adoption and sharers in his nature. He is present to unite us to himself (see John 17:22–23). He is present that he may be known. He wishes all to grow in holiness and the life of prayer that we may more and more taste his presence as saints and mystics of every age have done.

Though he remains God and we remain creatures, somehow we are closely joined to him. We share his life. We remain always finite and distinct from him who is the infinite Lord of all. But the mystery that transcends our understanding is that somehow God becomes so close to us that we can call him Father.

WE ARE BROTHERS AND SISTERS

If God is our Father, then somehow we must be brothers and sisters. Just as we can call God our Father, we must be prepared to see in each other a level of identification that makes it possible for us to be brothers and sisters of each other. This is at the heart of the Christian community—the Church. We are one with each other because we are one with Jesus the Lord. While there are many ways in which we might identify with other groups—our blood ties, ethnic origins, cultural relationships—there is one reality that brings us together in a way that supersedes all these other bonds: union with each other in Christ.

To pray to God as our Father is to recognize that we have responsibilities to each other as members of the same family. We are not a cultural, political, economic, or social entity. We are a faith community. If our faith is strong enough to recognize how deep our spiritual bonds are we can accomplish that communion, that community life, that manifestation of the kingdom of God that Jesus calls for when he urges each of us to name God as "our Father."

One of the great sorrows of the human experience, and one of the great afflictions of the Church, is how reluctant we have been to accept this teaching and how slow we as Christians have been to implement it. The divisions and violence, the wars and animosities that characterize so much of history are part also of the Christian experience. Too often we have been prepared to place our personal, cultural, economic, and ethnic interests above the claims of the gospel. In the Lord's Prayer, Jesus challenges us to recognize that God is our Father and that we are his children—members of the same family.

THE HOLINESS OF GOD

In saluting God our Father, we recognize his utter transcendence. We pray, "Our Father, who art in heaven." As close as God is to us through his Holy Spirit and in Jesus Christ, he is still utterly beyond us, transcendent, all-holy and infinite. God's power and majesty are limitless. In the creeds of the Church, we profess our belief in God the Father Almighty. The Church proclaims the glory of God. "There is one true and living God, Creator and Lord of heaven and earth, almighty, eternal, immeasurable, incomprehensible, infinite in intellect, in will and in every perfection" (First Vatican Council).

While God is ever with us and always present to the world he made, he is utterly distinct from the world. Every kind of pantheism, every tendency to identify God with the world or to see him as some dimension or aspect of the visible creation, utterly fails to grasp the greatness of God. God is transcendent; he is exalted far above the universe, for it exists only at his bidding. His changeless and eternal reality is in its perfection entirely distinct from the dependent reality of infinite things. "Behold, heaven, even highest heaven cannot contain him" (2 Chronicles 2:6).

Scripture frequently expresses God's otherness by proclaiming that he is perfectly holy. He is "the Holy One" (Isaiah 5:24). His holiness transcends mere freedom from any touch of moral evil. God cannot sin. References to his holiness express more than his hostility to moral evil that harms creation and calls for punishment. God's holiness refers to his complete otherness from us. He is "our Father who art in heaven."

Because God is so far exalted above all things, the creature cannot be worthy even to look on or to speak to God. This same perfection is also the foundation of the divine mercy, which heals sinners and brings them to communion with God. When we pray to our Father who is in heaven, we recognize that it is the holiness of God that attracts the human heart because of the goodness it implies, a goodness of such intensity that it touches the sinful heart with awe. The splendor and majesty of God cannot be ignored. He who is holy and requires holiness is the Lord and judge of all. For this reason, we recognize that the fear of the Lord is the beginning of wisdom (see Proverbs 1:7).

In revealing God as our Father, Jesus also highlights that our God is a personal god. He relates to us not just as Creator to creature, not just as maker to artifact, but as Father to children. Prayerfully, reverently, conscientiously, we reflect on "Our Father who art in heaven."

QUESTIONS TO THINK ABOUT:

1. How often do I pray the Lord's Prayer?
2. Do the members of my parish act like brothers and sisters? Do we seem like a family to the outside world?
3. How do we reconcile the transcendent holiness of God with the idea that he is our Father?

CHAPTER 83

The Seven Petitions

THE STRUCTURE OF THE Lord's Prayer is simple. We recognize God as our Father in heaven as we address our petitions to him. The seven petitions of the Lord's Prayer are part of what Tertullian some 1,600 years ago referred to as "truly the summary of the whole gospel" (see section 2761 of the *Catechism*).

HALLOWED BE THY NAME

Among the many attractive posters and banners I see decorating classrooms and religious education centers is one that lists the names of God. I have always found this poster intriguing because there are so many expressions of God found in the pages of Sacred Scripture. Each one attempts to identify some particular characteristic of an all-perfect and all-transcending God.

One of the names reflects God's self-designation: "I AM" (Exodus 3:14). Some speak of an aspect of God's greatness. Others reflect our reverence before so great a God. All recognize God's holiness—his otherness—that quality of God that puts him beyond us. Whatever name we apply to God, we must realize that it refers to the All-Holy One whose name, because it reflects his identity, is itself holy.

The first of the petitions, "hallowed be thy name," calls upon us to keep holy the name of the Lord. Where the Lord is recognized and his name is held in veneration, there will be his people. The pledge of God found so often in the pages of the Old Testament was "I shall be your God and you shall be my people."

Since the name is a manifestation of the person, reverence, not disrespect, is the order of the day when it comes to God's name. The petition should be made with the fervent conviction that in our own lives and in our communities we would strive to see that the name of God is truly respected. The Holy Name Society has long stood in each parish as a testimony to the fact that God's name is not always hallowed and that all of us have an obligation to see that it is.

In a world that so casually takes the name of the Lord in vain, we need to ask ourselves how consistent we are when with the same lips we proclaim "hallowed be thy name" and then use the holy name of the Lord in a way that disrespects it and diminishes our own Christian identity.

As faithful followers of the Lord, we have been gifted with a unique and enduring relationship with God, who is totally beyond us, worthy of all reverence and awe, and at the same time allows himself to be called and to be our Father. This we affirm every time we pray "Our Father, who art in heaven, hallowed be thy name."

THY KINGDOM COME

The second great petition of the Lord's Prayer is "thy kingdom come." This is the cry of every believer. It manifests the longing of the whole Church and each one of us individually for Jesus. The New Testament closes with this same longing, "Marana tha"—"Come, Lord Jesus!" (Revelation 22:20).

Each bishop by tradition chooses a motto to reflect the work of his episcopal ministry. When I was appointed a bishop in 1985, I selected these words from the Lord's Prayer, because they seem, to me, to sum up the motivation for everything we do and our longing to see it completed. "Lord, let thy kingdom come" in all that we are and all that we do.

In God's plan, the fulfillment of the work of Jesus and the completion of his kingdom have been turned over to us—the faithful—his Church. Saint Paul speaks of completing "what is lacking in the afflictions of Christ" (Colossians 1:24), "building up the Body of Christ" (Ephesians 4:12). These texts refer to the potential each of us has to manifest and participate in establishing God's kingdom of peace, justice, truth, and love. Nothing we do, insofar as it builds up this kingdom, is ever lost or without value.

When we pray "thy kingdom come," we ask primarily for the total fulfillment of God's kingdom, when Christ comes again. But we also pray that his kingdom may be made present now as richly as possible in righteousness, peace, and joy.

THY WILL BE DONE

As we continue through the Lord's Prayer, we ask that "thy will be done on earth as it is in heaven." What is God's will? In creating us, God established a plan for human living. In revealing himself to us in Jesus, God taught us how we are to live so that we may become more closely identified with him. In the outpouring of the Holy Spirit, God gives us the wisdom to know the mystery of God at work in our lives.

When we pray "thy will be done on earth as it is in heaven," we ask that God's plan be fulfilled here in the hearts of humans, with our gift of free will and free choice, as it is in heaven, where all willingly and lovingly genuflect before the will of God.

The Second Vatican Council reminds us that "The disciple is bound by a grave obligation toward Christ his master even more adequately to understand the truth received from him, faithfully to proclaim it and vigorously to defend it" (*Dignitatis Humanae* 14). Our Lord asks us to shape our life by our faith. He also demands that we be prepared to profess and acknowledge our faith when it is called into question seriously or whenever silence on our part would give a bad example to others. "Everyone who acknowledges me before others I will acknowledge before my heavenly Father. But whoever denies me before others, I will deny before my heavenly Father" (Matthew 10:32–33).

When we pray "thy will be done on earth as it is in heaven," we ask for the grace to live out our own Christian commitment to manifest that will in our own daily response to Christ. This petition is not just to know God's will but to help us live it now.

GIVE US THIS DAY OUR DAILY BREAD

In asking "give us this day our daily bread" we pray for ourselves and for all—and in a special way for the poor—that the daily, necessary bread may be granted. But we pray also for that deeply needed bread that is the Word of God, and even more that we be nourished by Christ, our Eucharistic bread.

How often we have seen in the words of Jesus multiple meanings and levels to the references he makes. In this petition, we are urged to pray for our daily sustenance, but at the same time to recognize that this sustenance is not just material. Not by bread alone does man live (see Luke 4:4).

FORGIVE US OUR TRESPASSES

"Forgive us our trespasses as we forgive those who trespass against us." In this petition we beg God's forgiveness, but we do so aware that we will be forgiven only as we are willing to forgive our brothers and sisters from our hearts. This is one of the most daunting petitions of the whole prayer. Here you and I condition how we expect to be forgiven on how we are prepared to forgive. In making this petition, we need seriously to examine our conscience.

LEAD US NOT INTO TEMPTATION

The final two petitions are "lead us not into temptation, but deliver us from evil." In the first we ask God not to let us experience any temptation that would lead us to sin and ultimate death. This we do aware that we will not be tested beyond our strength (see 1 Corinthians 10:13).

It is the wise disciple of the Lord who does not recklessly place himself in an occasion of sin. The prudent Christian also realizes that in the highly secular, materialistic, not to say hedonistic, culture in which we live, those occasions are many and sometimes seemingly unavoidable. It is for this reason that we pray that God give us grace sufficient to help us tread our way through life conscious of its many temptations to sin and strong enough to avoid them.

DELIVER US FROM EVIL

The last petition urges that we be set free from the evil one, Satan, who seeks our ruin. Here we find echoes of Jesus' farewell discourse to the apostles. "I do not ask that you take them out of the world but that you keep them from the evil one" (John 17:15).

We live in the world. This is the world we are to change through our works of love. There is no way to avoid being involved in this world. At the same time, we recognize that the unredeemed part of this world is in fact the realm of the evil one. It is for that reason that Jesus urges us to pray that we continually be delivered from evil—individually, personally, and collectively as his holy Church.

The *Catechism* at this point reminds us that we are not dealing with evil as an abstraction. Rather this petition "refers to a person, Satan, the Evil One, the angel who opposes God. The devil (*dia-bolos*) is the one who 'throws himself across' God's plan and his work of salvation accomplished in Christ" (section 2851). Just as Christ was victorious over the prince of this world (see John 14:30), so too do we hope, with God's grace and our persistent prayers, to emerge victorious in our pilgrimage through life on our way to the Father in glory.

QUESTIONS TO THINK ABOUT:

1. Why do we have to pray that God's name should be holy?
2. When we pray "thy kingdom come," what do we really hope for?
3. Am I prepared to do my part when I pray "thy will be done on earth as it is in heaven?"
4. What kind of "daily bread" do I need most? Is that the daily bread I pray for?
5. Am I really prepared for God to apply the same standard of forgiveness to me that I apply to other people?
6. From what temptations do I most need to be spared?
7. Does the devil seem like an outdated idea in the modern world? What evidence do we see that there really is a devil?

Conclusion

WHEN I WAS THINKING of a title for this book, a number of possibilities came to me.

Clearly, this book is a reflection on the content of the *Catechism of the Catholic Church*. As I point out in the Preface, I have relied extensively on the *Catechism* as well as on *The Teaching of Christ: A Catholic Catechism for Adults*. I have also not hesitated to use material from the television program *The Teaching of Christ*. But when all is said and done, this volume is a review of the *Catechism of the Catholic Church*.

I hope it has provided some insight into the *Catechism*, and perhaps even some access to its compendium-like completeness. More important, I hope it will inspire (or at least encourage) you to turn to that extraordinary summary of the Catholic faith to use it as a reliable and complete sourcebook for the future. How truly blessed we are to have such a rich resource of guidance and inspiration as we make our way on that pilgrimage through life that we hope will bring us to the glory of God.

About the Author

BISHOP DONALD W. WUERL of Pittsburgh, who is recognized as the "teaching bishop" is the author of numerous books and articles and the host of over 450 television programs on every aspect of Catholic life and teaching.